HIGH FLYERS

HIGH FLYERS

DEVELOPING THE NEXT GENERATION OF LEADERS

MORGAN W. MCCALL, JR.

HARVARD BUSINESS SCHOOL PRESS

BOSTON, MASSACHUSETTS

Printed in the United States of America

02 01 00 99 98   5 4

Acknowledgments

Selections from *The Wall Street Journal* used in Chapter 2 reprinted by permission of the *Wall Street Journal*, © 1989, 1990, 1992, 1993, and 1994 Dow Jones & Company, Inc. All Rights Reserved Worldwide.

Excerpts from *The Right Stuff* by Tom Wolfe. Copyright © 1979 by Tom Wolfe. Reprinted by permission of Farrar, Straus & Giroux, Inc.

Library of Congress Cataloging-in-Publication Data

McCall, Morgan W.
      High flyers : developing the next generation of leaders / Morgan
   W. McCall, Jr.
          p.   cm.
      Includes bibliographical references and index.
      ISBN 0-87584-336-0 (alk. paper)
      1. Executives—Training of.   2. Executive ability.   I. Title.
   HD30.4.M424   1997
   658.4'07'24—dc21   97-11699
                                                                CIP

The paper used in this publication meets the requirements of the American National Standard for Permanence of Paper for Printed Library Materials Z39.49-1984.

CONTENTS

PREFACE

HOW CAN WE IDENTIFY AND DEVELOP THE EXECUTIVE TALENT needed to get through the turbulent years ahead? It was in the early 1980s that organizations were in the beginning stages of what was variously predicted to be "permanent white water" and the "white knuckle decade," and as people are wont to do in times of perceived crisis, the search for heroes had begun. Corporations wanted more leaders, better leaders, and they wanted them as soon as possible. My colleagues and I picked up the gauntlet and began a research project on how successful executives got to be that way.

What we learned contained both good news and bad news. The good news was that we were able to find quite a few highly skilled, effective executives who were capable of leading organizations through the turbulence. The bad news was that such leaders could not be produced overnight. Even knights on white horses, it turned out, had to learn to ride, master the skills required to take on dragons, and suffer a few defeats. The results of that research, published in 1988 as *The Lessons of Experience,* documented that effective executives learn how to do what they do primarily by doing it, by watching others try to do it, and by messing up.[1]

These first studies were well received, even though they offered no quick fix. It was helpful to know what experiences were important for developing executives, what could be learned from those experiences, and which flaws were fatal to talented executives. But as intriguing as the findings were, they did not go far enough. Although they called into question many current practices for selecting and developing executives, what should be done instead was less clear. There seemed to be many implications, but neither the conceptual framework nor the action steps were explicit enough to put the results to work.

The ensuing decade saw researchers and practitioners, myself included, pursuing the implications. Research results were affirmed and extended, instruments were developed to assess both the lessons learned from experience and the developmental potential of jobs, computer programs were written to generate development plans, and a cottage industry of consultants specializing in on-the-job development emerged. But even though confidence in the research grew and tools were refined, the lack of a comprehensive conceptual framework left the individual applications, like so many human resource programs, only loosely integrated with the larger organizations in which they were embedded. As a result, some organizations used the new tools without questioning their basic assumptions about development and its strategic role in the organization. Development applications sometimes were only vaguely related to the business strategy, if at all; efforts at development often were contradicted by other human resource systems and philosophies, especially selection, compensation, and succession planning; and the lack of conceptual clarity made it possible to hold on to old assumptions about talent and its development.

My path—culminating in this book—led me to explore the organizational context in which development through experience takes place and to construct a framework that would integrate executive development with the strategic intent of the organization and with other human resource systems. Along the way, I continually ran into ingrained and often implicit assumptions about talent and its development that seemed inconsistent with what we had learned about how executives develop. For example, there is apparently a widespread and fundamental need to believe that a single (and usually short) list of generic qualities can be used to describe all effective leaders and that these qualities are relatively stable over the course of a person's career. It is much more manageable, after all, to search for only one set of attributes than to contend with the possibility that people with quite different attributes might be equally effective or that people might change over time for the better *or* for the worse as a result of their experiences.

Another misleading assumption encountered frequently was that people who have the "right stuff" will, through the process of survival of the fittest, eventually rise to the top. On the basis of this belief, one might conclude that effective leaders are what remain after tough challenges weed out the frail and the flawed. And because only the best survive, polishing and refinement is all that remains to be done, requiring only modest investment in the kinds of training and program interventions that are common in organizations today.

Assumptions like these encourage organizations and their leaders to neglect without guilt their investment in executive development. The cream rises just often enough to mask the deleterious effects of such neglect, the first sign of which can be overly simplistic and fatally flawed beliefs about what constitutes "the best" and "fittest." A track record of results, regardless of how those results are achieved, frequently becomes the primary marker, creating the tautology that the best survive, therefore the survivors are the best. Believing that the fittest will survive without much nurturing, organizations not only overlook people with the potential to develop but also frequently and unintentionally derail the talented people they have identified as high flyers by rewarding them for their flaws, teaching them to behave in ineffective ways, reinforcing narrow perspectives and skills, and inflating their egos.

In 1992 Pope John Paul II acknowledged that Galileo was

right in 1610 when he supported Copernicus's assertion that the earth circled the sun rather than the other way around. In October 1996 the Pope acknowledged that Darwin's 1859 theory of evolution was "more than a hypothesis."[2] It sometimes takes a while to accept reality, but sooner or later we have to deal with its implications. So, too, with developing executive talent. However appealing the simpler assumptions may be, they can keep organizations from doing a better job of developing their leadership talent, and they can keep individuals from actively cultivating their leadership potential.

The message of *High Flyers* is that leadership ability can be learned, that creating a context that supports the development of talent can become a source of competitive advantage, and that the development of leaders is itself a leadership responsibility. Human resources specialists, who are the ones usually charged with development, know a lot about designing systems and programs but are rarely in a position to enforce strategic imperatives. Further, the primary classroom for the development of leadership skills is on-the-job experience, and that critical resource is understood and controlled by line managers, not by staff specialists.

If talent is developed through varied experiences, we need to understand how to get the people who need them into the experiences they need. If experience is the classroom of leadership, then we need to know a lot more about the curriculum and pedagogy of life's challenges. If learning from experience is the goal, we need to find better ways to develop a context that supports learning and not just short-term performance. If organizations are doing a second-rate job of developing talent, we need not only to improve their practices but also to discover better ways to help people develop themselves under less-than-ideal circumstances. Underlying it all is the belief that development involves learning and growing, not stasis and knowing —no matter how spectacular one's natural gifts or current achievements.

Those are the topics of this book, and they are presented

within an integrated framework that emphasizes how the pieces fit together and what an organization can do to improve. As for survival of the fittest as a strategy for developing organizational leadership, would that it were so. Unfortunately, we have all experienced the imperfections of organizational selection processes and know that those who reach the top of the corporate food chain are not always the most highly evolved. We also know from painful experience that training and human resource programs don't have much impact on Attila at the top.

In many respects, *High Flyers* is about human development, not just about high-potential executives, leadership, and the world of corporations. After all, don't we all grow through experiences, and aren't the experiences that help us grow, like those in the organizational world, the ones that stretch and challenge us? Can't we, too, use some help in identifying and getting the experiences we need, in converting those experiences into lessons learned, and in understanding how our strengths and weaknesses form a tapestry that determines our effectiveness? Addressing these kinds of issues in *High Flyers* will take us from fighter pilots to musicians, from physician managers to corporate executives, from Darwin's theories to the mythical hero's journey. It is an interesting trip.

Dian Fossey, whose personal adventure was the study of the great apes, begins her famous book, *Gorillas in the Mist*, with the following observation: "I spent many years longing to go to Africa, because of what the continent offered in its wilderness and great diversity of free-living animals. Finally I realized that dreams seldom materialize on their own."[3] The great adventure—in Africa, or in the business world, or in life in general—still requires someone to engage it.

It would be comforting to think that talented people who aspire to executive careers would see the long-term self-interest in their own development and perhaps even rebel against an organizational context that makes it difficult. Unfortunately, people often *like* the things that work against their growth and that the organization is inclined to do:

- People like to use their strengths, to be successful, to be the best—so they relish a competitive environment that pushes them to achieve quick, dramatic results, even if by using existing skills they aren't developing the new skills they will need later on.

- People like to believe they are as good as everyone says, so they are inclined to believe their own press and not take their weaknesses as seriously as they might.

- People don't like to hear bad news or get criticism, any more than bosses like to give it. It isn't pleasant to be reminded of flaws, so it's not always a natural act actively to seek out negative information, especially in a system that makes it difficult to do so.

- People like being rewarded for their achievements and like to believe that those achievements are in large part due to their own initiative. The idea of being held accountable for an amorphous activity like "development," which may seem far removed from concrete business results, is not always greeted with enthusiasm.

- There is tremendous risk—both psychologically and to job security—in leaving what one does well to attempt to master something new.

It is here that the streams of research on how successful executives learn their trade and on why talented people sometimes derail finally merge. There is no steady state, so success and mastery, at least for executives, are not enough. "What have you done for me lately?" may be the corporate mantra reflecting the exigencies of cutthroat competition, but "what are you learning to do that will take us into the future?" is the better question. And what we know about learning suggests that there is no easy pathway to change. If *The Lessons of Experience* did nothing else, it demonstrated that adversity, challenge, frustration, and struggle lead to change. In reality, there is a fine line between successful and derailed executives; most have been both and will be both again. Continual growth, transition, and transformation are the heart of it, and the ultimately successful leaders find the courage to resist the seduction of past success. The need to move on, of course, is not a new idea. Nor is the observation that personal growth can be painful, difficult, and risky. So timeless are such themes that they've been captured in ancient myths, such as that of the phoenix.

The mythical phoenix was a strikingly beautiful bird. Its extraordinarily long life (variously described as hundreds to tens of thousands of years), larger-than-life size, and bright red and gold feathers set it apart from more commonplace birds. Despite its remarkable qualities, the phoenix burned itself to death (or was burned, depending on the version of the myth), and only after being totally consumed did it rise from the ashes in a new and youthful form. Whereas the message of the phoenix myth is profoundly spiritual, the need for continual transformation has important corporeal implications.

At least until the final passage, the transitions of human development are not as dramatic as that of the phoenix. Nonetheless, we all experience significant personal transformations, discarding the empty shells of things left behind as we move on to the next stage of our development. Ahead lie more metamorphoses, if we are lucky, as we continue to grow in the face of new challenges and changing circumstances.

The bright plumage of the successful executive is, at least on the surface, consistent with the phoenix myth. The high flyer's accomplishments and rapid promotions seem to feed on themselves, each success opening the way to another opportunity, another challenge. Each success leads to ever-higher expectations. But no matter how pretty the emergent incarnation, it can't last. As soon as the successful executive becomes transfixed by the current plumage, expectation and reality diverge, resulting in the corporate version of the phoenix's funeral pyre. Some executives emerge from the metaphorical ashes phoenix-like, having learned and grown, while others seem unable to cull the lessons of their experience. For the mythical bird, death was integral to renewal, and destruction produced a new way of being. The derailed executive, however, has only the possibility of growth, not the assurance of it. For that reason, understanding what goes wrong is of considerable interest to the talented person whose career lurches off track, to the organization that absorbs the costs of the mistakes, and to those of us who might learn something invaluable from the misfortunes of others.

Dealing with adversity punctuates most careers. Few historical figures were without setback, and the ability to bounce back is a much-admired characteristic of many of our heroes. Winston Churchill's tumultuous career enthralls historians searching for generalizations about the nature of leadership. One of the most outstanding orators, writers, and statesmen of the twentieth century began as a poor student (the bottom of his class) with a lisp. He twice failed the college entrance exam. He lost the parliamentary election of 1899; was held responsible for a failed strategy during World War I and resigned his admiralty post in 1915; lost another election in 1922; resigned from office in 1929 when his party was defeated and was then out of the cabinet for ten years; and finally, after heroic efforts in leading Britain through the devastation and near-defeat of World War II, suffered an overwhelming political defeat in 1945. So checkered with setbacks was Churchill's career that it inspired a book entitled *Churchill: A Study in Failure*.[4]

But when things are going well, it's easy to be fooled by the plumage. The lesson of the phoenix myth notwithstanding, we nonmythical creatures often have difficulty with the changes we need to make. It is harder yet if the corporate context does not support the effort. It is my contention that organizations do not exist to develop people, but that developing people is critical to their existence. In that respect, much can be done to improve the context so that development is more likely, more appropriate, and more effective. Similarly, individuals with or aspiring to leadership roles must take responsibility for their growth, whether or not their organizations support them.

By providing in this book an integrated framework for understanding executive development and by clarifying the assumptions that underlie it, I hope to provide a next step in our quest to understand how leadership is learned.

Obviously, the task is a big one. Fortunately, there are big shoulders to stand on; executive development is a field of inquiry that has attracted many outstanding thinkers and practitioners. The value of the ideas offered in this book has been enhanced greatly by the wisdom of those who invested time and energy in reviewing earlier drafts. I am indebted to Warren Bennis, Bill Drath, John Fulkerson, George Hollenbeck, Esther Hutchison, Richard Kimball, Mike Lombardo, Joel Moses, Neil Sendelbach, Tom Standing, Mike Vescuso, and several anonymous reviewers who successfully steered me clear of many dangers and tried valiantly to steer me clear of others.

I'm also deeply indebted to several people who indirectly influenced my thinking about executive development. David Hatch's belief in the value of the experience-based approach and constant nettling forced me to try out of some of the ideas that ended up in the book (and some that might have been here, except that trying them out blew holes in them!). Doug Ready encouraged, the International Consortium for Executive Development Research funded, and Gretchen Spreitzer and Jay Mahoney joined me in doing the research on early identification that filled a major gap in the framework. And, of course, I owe a great debt to my former colleagues at the Center for Creative Leadership and especially Mike Lombardo, for their contributions to the early work on derailment and experience that became a part of the foundation for this work.

Lelia Molthrop's talent and achievements inspired much of my thinking about the development of exceptional talent. I am grateful to her for allowing me to use her story and to her mother, Judy Molthrop, for telling it to me from her perspective. Craig Fenter—friend, composer, musician, and musical director—was very helpful to me in understanding how musical talent evolves over time. My personal guru, David Oldfield, did his best to help me understand the implications of ancient myths for executive development.

Putting a manuscript together is no small undertaking, and many times I was ready to deep-six the whole thing. I was extremely fortunate to have an editor, Marjorie Williams, who was both kind and patient, who never lost the faith, and without whom this never would have happened. Thanks, too, to the many people who worked behind the scenes. Barbara Roth worked tirelessly with design issues and bears responsibility for the overall good looks of the book. Wendy Jacobs is the extremely talented copy editor whose efforts saved me from a humbling by my former English teacher.

Anthony Turner spent many hours verifying quotations and the accuracy of various summaries from the business press, and Karen Smith helped track down elusive references and permissions. My son Morgan gave up some of his free time to help organize research materials and articles used in creating the manuscript.

A special acknowledgment is reserved for Esther Hutchison: colleague, friend, critic, cheerleader, and wife. Drawing on her experience as an executive coach and on her deep insight into human development, she provided countless suggestions and ideas. As valuable as that role was, it was her love, support, and encouragement that kept me going through the frustrations and disappointments that get in the way of writing a book like this. Thank you, Esther.

Finally, I have dedicated *High Flyers* to my mother, Ada Rowe McCall, who, with little interest in the subject matter but considerable interest in the author, carried the manuscript wherever she went throughout the course of her illness. Unable to concentrate for long at a time, she died with the half-read draft on her bedside table. Love like that can never be replaced, and I miss her unflagging support and the pride she always had in whatever I did. It made me fly.

MWM
Manhattan Beach, California

1

OF
ASTRONAUTS AND
EXECUTIVES

"WE DON'T DO VERY MUCH TO DEVELOP OUR PEOPLE," THE executive said, with more than a trace of guilt. Since I was there to give a seminar on executive development, this executive felt it necessary to apologize in advance that his six-billion-dollar international corporation hadn't paid much attention to this aspect of the business. His lament, though shared by many other executives, is based on a belief that is patently false. There is no question that this company—and all other companies—*are* developing their managers; in fact, they are doing a very effective job of it. Their managers are learning from their experiences, from the examples set by their bosses (good and bad), from the mistakes they make and what happens to them afterward, and from the challenges they face in their jobs. In this respect, it is impossible *not* to develop people. The development may be dysfunctional—managers may end up dictatorial and arrogant, cautious and indecisive, bureaucratic and political, entrepreneurial and results-oriented, or some other combination—but they are learning *something*, hand over fist.

In this company, as in others, development happens whether planned or not. The real issue is not that companies don't develop talent but rather that they aren't aware of how these unmanaged processes are working, of what their talented people are learning, or of what they could be doing to influence the kinds of leaders being produced.

The executive I spoke to, in averring that the firm doesn't do much to develop people, is making the common mistake of equating management development with visible "programs" (especially training programs) and "systems" sponsored by the human resources department or by outside vendors (career planning, rotational assignments, mentoring programs). Programs are tangible—they can be counted, their graduates surveyed, and their budgets adjusted. In the sense that this company had few development "programs" or "systems," the executive was right in asserting that they don't "do" development. The executive was wrong, however, to think that investing in these kinds of activities meant the company *was* doing development. Executive leadership skills, to the degree that they are learned, are learned primarily from experience and only rarely in the classroom. "Doing development" means understanding how experience teaches, what its lessons are, how to use it more effectively, and above all, how to link development to a company's business strategy so that people with the talent to lead the company are learning what they need to know.

The resurgent interest in developing executive talent has been stimulated in recent years by various events and a lot of wishful thinking. It was not lost on corporate America that the leadership styles that had seemed so effective in the twenty or so years after World War II were inadequate in a later, convulsive era characterized by global competition, deregulation, economic upheaval, technological revolution, the end of the Cold War, and other developments that ended the seemingly halcyon days. Wherever one looked, it seemed, there was a shortage of leaders who could navigate the storms, and company after company, legend after legend, stumbled, floundered, and sometimes died altogether.

Many factors determined the success and failure of corporate struggles, only one of which was the quality of leadership.

But it did seem that the inability of many companies to adapt was abetted by inadequate leadership, and it was at least plausible to assume that a different kind of leader was needed. Wisely or not, in times of crisis we want leaders to take charge, then we hold them perhaps more responsible for events, good and bad, than is actually merited. The massive dislocations of the last thirty years, driven by deregulation, globalization, and competitive pressures, led to a widely perceived shortage of leaders who had the skills to handle change effectively.

A second stimulus for renewed interest in developing leadership also resulted from corporations thrashing about as they tried to survive all the changes. Innocent-sounding euphemisms (right sizing, delayering, reengineering, total quality, restructuring) couldn't hide the decimation of human resources that ensued, leaving many organizations without much depth in managerial talent and with a new kind of organization—flat, customer-focused, team-based, entrepreneurial—that is even harder to lead effectively than the ponderous bureaucracies it replaced. When training programs—the first-thought development panacea—failed to transform the surviving managers into empowerment experts who could do more with less, increasingly Draconian measures were employed to *force* managers into changing their style: spans of control went from seven to forty or more;[1] everyone was fired, given personality tests, and forced to reapply for the jobs remaining;[2] full authority was given to people on the front line, and managers were held accountable not for controlling them but for supporting them.[3]

Drastic actions may have created more casualties than leaders with the requisite skills. Corporations still needed more leaders, with more sophisticated skills, and needed them *now*. And the leadership crisis was not just in corporations that had to retrench; for many firms, the leadership shortage threatened their ability to seize the opportunities that all the changes had created. To fix the shortage, busy executives turned to human resources staffs and said, in effect, it was time they started earning their pay.[4] Human resources departments had to figure out what characteristics these "new leaders" had to have and find ways to identify and develop leaders—fast. Thus was ushered in the age of competencies, leadership development programs, and belief in miracles.

Executives, even those who profess otherwise, usually make two fallacious assumptions about leadership talent that get in the way of actually developing leadership talent. The first is that leadership ability is, in essence, something that one either has or does not. The second is that the fires of organizational life will test the mettle of the contenders and that the fittest not only will survive but will also, more often than not, end up at the top. (This particular assumption is most firmly held by those currently at the top.) With these assumptions in place, it makes perfect sense to search for the finite set of characteristics that distinguish leaders from followers (sometimes called "competencies"); develop measures of those characteristics, which can then be used to identify leaders early (if the characteristics are innate, they should be identifiable in some form early on); and accelerate potential leaders' "development" by putting them on a fast track both to test and mature them ("trial by fire" accompanied by polishing). Calling these selection activities development is, of course, to dress the wolf in sheep's clothing.

Considering what development would look like if it were based on different assumptions is the real purpose of this book. Without intervention, the cream may eventually rise. But for reasons I will explore in detail, things other than cream rise, and considerable talent is wasted; the system is very inefficient. Some would even say that cream isn't good for your health anymore.

ORIGINS OF LEADERSHIP

Instead of assuming that leaders are mostly born, not made—an assumption Ron Heifetz claims "fosters both self-delusion and irresponsibility"—I start with the assertion that executive leaders are both born and made but mostly made, based on a significant amount of research showing that executives do learn, grow, and change over time.[5]

Instead of viewing experiences as tests that reveal whether

or not a person has the "right stuff" to lead, I suggest that experiences are the teachers of leadership and that a "passing grade" means learning the lessons of experience, not necessarily aceing the test. Research has not only established that experience can teach but has also identified what kinds of experiences are powerful teachers and what kinds of lessons they offer.

Finally, if executive leadership is mostly learned and the school from which it is learned is mostly experience, then the "competencies" that differentiate leaders from followers are the *result* of accumulated experiences, not their antecedent. Potential, I believe, is not the demonstration of acquired assets but rather is the demonstration of the ability to acquire the assets needed for future situations. No single set of characteristics or competencies can be meaningfully applied to all leaders, anyway. What matters is how well prepared people in leadership roles are to meet the challenges and overcome the obstacles posed by pursuing the organization's business strategy. In a world of rapid change, the real measure of leadership is the ability to acquire needed new skills as the situation changes.

Before elaborating on this alternative view, however, I will examine some typical assumptions and practices—what I call "right stuff thinking" about development—that characterize practice (if not theory) in many corporations today.

THE RIGHT STUFF AND EXECUTIVE "DEVELOPMENT"

In 1979 Tom Wolfe published his bestseller about the military aviators who flew the United States into outer space. His analysis of these unique individuals produced an unforgettable portrait of extraordinarily talented individuals facing and embracing increasingly demanding challenges, and proving to themselves and to the world that they had "the right stuff."[6] The underlying, pervasive belief that those who accomplish exceptional things have this innate quality seems to operate in the world of corporate executives as well, and its often unstated premises and assumptions seem to guide the practice if not the rhetoric of corporate leadership selection and development. If the implications of alternative points of view are to be considered, even as a straw man, it is important to establish first what is right stuff thinking and what are its implications.

THE ORIGINAL "RIGHT STUFF"

Trying to devise a precise definition of the qualities represented by the right stuff is an interesting exercise. One of the first conclusions to be drawn is that whatever "it" is, it is ultimately defined by performance. If someone consistently faces serious challenges and either wins outright or shows incredible fortitude in trying again and again until victory is won, then the "right" qualities are attributed to that person. There is clearly a masculine undercurrent to the heroic image that is conjured. As Wolfe put it, "A man should have the ability to go up in a hurtling piece of machinery and put his hide on the line and then have the moxie, the reflexes, the experience, the coolness, to pull it back at the last yawning moment—then go up again *the next day*, and the next day."[7]

When translated to the corporate world, this idea means that executive leaders demonstrate they have the right stuff by amassing a track record of performance under difficult circumstances. The stuff itself is whatever qualities seemingly were necessary for achieving that outcome. The heroic nature of the accomplishment suggests that the competencies that distinguish successful executives from their less successful counterparts involve resourcefulness, risk taking (courage), readiness to take action, flexibility, perseverance, creativity, and the like. Because these executives are exemplars, they are also likely to be described as inspiring others. The important part of the definition is not the particular list of competencies but that "right stuffness" is determined *after* remarkable performance has been achieved. The inference is clear that the challenge created a setting in which the presence of requisite qualities could be identified post hoc. Ergo, the presence of the right stuff is inferred from and contingent on continued achievement. The right stuff itself is whatever it needs to be to explain a result. It isn't necessarily tangible.

Although the presence of the desired qualities is inferred from performance, one performance is not enough to establish these qualities' existence for all time. Indeed, it would appear that the testing never ends—the presence of the qualities must be reaffirmed in progressively more difficult settings. Wolfe described it in graphic terms:

> Nor was there *a test* to show whether or not a pilot had this right-eous quality. There was, instead, a seemingly infinite series of tests. A career in flying was like climbing one of those ancient Babylonian pyramids made up of a dizzy progression of steps and ledges, a ziggurat, a pyramid extraordinarily high and steep; and the idea was to prove at every foot of the way up that pyramid that you were one of the elected and anointed ones who had *the right stuff* and could move higher and higher and even—ulti-mately, God willing, one day—that you might be able to join that special few at the very top who had the capacity to bring tears to men's eyes, the very Brotherhood of the Right Stuff itself.[8]

The notion was that at each step of this pyramid, judgments were made about who would continue to climb and who would not. In military aviation, judgment is often passed by fate—when things go wrong at Mach 1, only the lucky are later judged by a committee or their superiors. The corporate world has an unmistakably similar "what have you done for me lately" process that crowns and banishes heroes with some reg-ularity, one often precipitated by such external exigencies as changes in market share or stock price, or front-page stories.

SUCCESS AND THE RIGHT STUFF

With each test that is passed comes confirmation that this per-son does indeed possess the right stuff, and each success adds to the siren song of invincibility.

Wolfe's tale showed that continued progress up the ziggurat had several unintended consequences. First, it affected how the survivors viewed themselves. As they surveyed the increasing number of people who failed to make it and the even larger number who never found the courage to try, the "Knights of the

Right Stuff" began to look "upon themselves as men who lived by higher standards of behavior than civilians."[9] They began to see themselves as something special—as people who did not have to live by the same rules that everyone else did, who were in some way braver, stronger, smarter, or quicker than others. At the extreme, Wolfe writes, "The entire world below . . . [was] *left behind*. Only at this point can one begin to understand just how big, how titanic, the ego of the military pilot could be."[10] As I will demonstrate, successful executives are just as vulnerable to the effects of elevation (high position, high socioeconomic status, substantial power and prestige, perquisites and special treatment) that can amplify a tendency to lose touch with personal shortcomings.[11]

Along with its direct impact on a person's self-image, success can lead significant other people to contribute to inflating the ego. As high achievers begin to define themselves as special and as above the rules that guide others, their bosses (or instructors) begin to act as if they are right. According to Wolfe, "The message [was] that the man who truly *had* it could ignore those rules. . . . His instructor halfway expected him to challenge all the limits."[12] That is, going beyond normal boundaries becomes a part of the expected behavior of corporate right stuffers, leading in some cases to a belief that the input of other people is unnecessary, that their ideas and feelings can be ignored, and taken to the extreme, that other people can be devalued.

The third consequence of success follows from the first two. The subjects of Wolfe's analysis began to generalize their superior qualities into arenas other than the one in which they had been successful. It was, Wolfe says, "as if the right stuff, being indivisible, carried over into any enterprise whatsoever, under any conditions."[13] As we shall see, executives who have walked on water may think they also can walk on coals or air or anything else.

FAILURE AND THE RIGHT STUFF

Because one either has the right stuff or doesn't, failure (or reaching one's limits) indicates that one really didn't really have it after all. "There are no *accidents* and no fatal flaws in the machines," notes Wolfe. "There are only pilots with the wrong stuff."[14] When things go wrong, it is usually because of compound errors, so there is always room to find fault with the pilot.

Success has a way of creating extraordinarily high expectations. These expectations can create opportunities and freedom to act, but the higher the expectation, the greater the chance it will not be met. In the thin air near the top of Wolfe's ziggurat, one may easily lose one's sense of reality and stumble over the edge. The problem lies not in the stumble per se but in the assumption that one has it or not, which treats a stumble as proof of inadequacy rather than as an opportunity for learning. Fear of being "found out," in turn, can cause stumblers to attempt to hide their stumbles, not to take the risk of stumbling, or to blame their errors on something or someone else, all of which thus eliminates learning.

IMPLICATIONS OF RIGHT STUFF THINKING

Tom Wolfe's book suggests that there is something ancient, even primordial about the right stuff. In settings other than military aviation, where tests for the right stuff emphasize things other than physical challenges, the content—the "it" of the right stuff—is defined in different ways but is still something that one has or does not; the implication is that it is innate or in some other way predetermined. Right stuff assumptions underlie various ways of choosing leaders that over the years have included selection according to bloodlines ("it" is inherited, as with royal families), social class (being born into the right caste or strata), education (the right schools, the right degrees), or in more primitive settings, physical characteristics (such as strength or height).

In many societies, however, and especially in the United States, whether one has the executive right stuff is revealed through accomplishments, at least in theory. Specifically, those who ascend the executive ranks, like the pilots in Wolfe's tale, are expected to prove themselves by succeeding in a series of ever more difficult challenges. Having "it" allows them the leeway to break the rules and leads others to believe they (the right stuffers) *should* break the rules. So prevalent is the phenomenon that it has been given a name in leadership research—"idiosyncrasy credits," which grant a person who has made good judgments the latitude to deviate from group norms.[15] Expectations grow that those with "it" will have moxie, resourcefulness, and daring. There is tremendous potential to inflate the ego.

Apparently, a right stuff approach works well enough in military aviation and may also work well enough in the corporate environment. But at least two critical issues in right stuff thinking have implications worthy of consideration in the corporate context. The first is the assumption that for the most part, executive leadership ability is something innate. This assumption is especially easy for people who believe they have the right stuff themselves to make about other people; in corporate practice, the assumption translates into an emphasis on the identification and selection of people who have "it." A substantial investment of time and money may then be expended in an effort to identify the attributes constituting the right stuff in the hopes that a more precise definition will improve the accuracy of selection. After all, it is time-consuming and quite expensive to find people with the right stuff by waiting for them to survive a series of challenging experiences. It is much more efficient, if the right stuff of executive leadership is an innate quality possesed by some but not others, to translate "it" into something tangible, find a way to measure it, and identify the right people in advance. To do so requires assuming that whatever "it" is, it is present *prior to* the experiences that reveal it. That is, it exists in some form in people early in their careers and can therefore be measured and used to predict later success. This assumption is an important one: Talent (potential) is a desired end state (right stuff) in a primitive or disguised form (see Figure 1-1).

A second issue concerning right stuff thinking that is worthy of consideration follows logically from the first. Even if

FIGURE 1-1

THE CORPORATE ASSUMPTION ABOUT TALENT

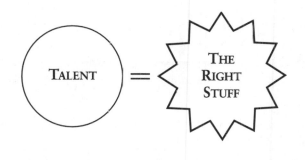

competencies are identified early, prediction is still imperfect, and subsequent experiences will still be important as tests (see Figure 1-2). Just as Wolfe's pilots faced progressively more difficult challenges, of which each level served to eliminate some of the people with the wrong stuff, executives and potential executives are progressively challenged as their careers unfold. These challenges should therefore test for attributes related to the final product (the competent executive) that the corporation hopes to find. Although it is revealing to know that a person has survived challenging situations, it is more revealing to know what skills the challenges actually required the person to demonstrate. Passing irrelevant tests, however spectacular, is not helpful.

CORPORATE SURVIVAL OF THE FITTEST

The word "development" has two meanings. From one perspective, development involves identifying and then realizing potentialities—strengthening and polishing what already exists. From another perspective, development is about the acquisition of abilities—bringing new things into being. Both processes obviously are at work, but underlying beliefs about leadership based on a right stuff premise are best served by an emphasis on finding people who have the abilities and then strengthening

FIGURE 1-2

EXPERIENCE AS A "TEST"

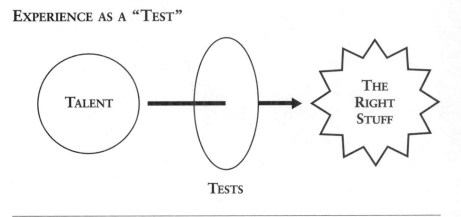

them. Because "it" is already inside, the same challenges simultaneously reveal its presence and develop its potential. This premise is suggested by talk of "seasoning," such as "she has the ability but needs to get some experience." If nature has done its bit, development is just a matter of adding the specific content, some practice, and maturity. The downside of the premise, however, is that if the natural abilities aren't there, acquiring them—though certainly a noble pursuit—is a long shot at best.

Implementing this premise gives development systems in most corporations a decidedly Darwinian flavor. Executive leadership ability is a gift bestowed, so the heart of development is *discovering* those qualities and then finding their limits through a series of progressively more difficult experiences. If "the system" believes someone has talent, it gives that person a challenging assignment (a "stretch") and then stands back to watch. If the person does well, the system's judgment and insight are confirmed, he or she gets a notch on the experience record, and the system assigns another, presumably more difficult challenge. This process continues until the person either fails or eventually reaches the highest levels of the corporate pyramid.

If the supply of raw talent is large enough, either internally or in external markets, and the corporate need for leadership small enough, the right stuff or survival-of-the-fittest approach may supply enough natural talent. Many of the same challenging assignments used to test for so-called inherent qualities can be used under different conditions to develop those same qualities. Talented people usually like thinking they have something special that makes them uniquely effective at the challenges they face. And the Darwinian approach "feels" right to those who reached high positions through trials by fire and who in turn believe others should go through the same process. True, a barbarian rises every now and then, and sometimes people can't handle a general manager role because their narrow technical expertise is too parochial for the problems to be faced. But as a rule, if one survives the gauntlet, it is assumed that one has proven oneself.

The natural processes of right stuff selection may be good enough, but they are by no means the best that we could be doing. Executive leadership in these times requires so many skills and so many complex skills that "natural ability" is nowhere near enough, nor are there nearly enough people with natural ability. Very talented people, very gifted people, unless they continually grow and develop, also have a high probability of ending up in trouble. The other perspective on development—acquisition of new abilities—leads to a different system for developing executive leadership and is more rational than hoping that the cream will rise.

AN ALTERNATIVE PERSPECTIVE

The differences between a selection (or survival-of-the-fittest) perspective and a truly developmental perspective are outlined in Figure 1-3, along with their attendant implications for development. Sometimes the selection perspective is a "wolf in sheep's clothing" because like the wolf in the fable, selection strategies can masquerade as development. On the assumption that executive leadership characteristics are finite and largely innate, companies build systems to identify people who might have the characteristics and then put candidates through a series of tests (in this case experiences) to see if they really do. The systems can look developmental because the assessments can be fed back and used to set developmental goals, and challenging assignments (which can be developmental as well) are the primary vehicle used in the testing. The espoused philosophy may even use developmental language. What reveals a system's true nature, however, is when talented people are given challenging assignments and the organization *stands back* to "wait and see" how they do. The responsibility for learning is on them, and the outcome to the system is whether they passed the test. The developmental perspective, in contrast, assumes that the skills needed for executive leadership depend on the directions in which the business is headed, that what approach works for a given individual is more important than inculcating "one best way," and that these skills are learned through experience. Although assessment and challenging assignments are part of the system, the telling difference is in the commitment to making people successful in acquiring new skills rather than testing them to see if they already have them. Metaphorically, one perspective is basically corporate Darwinism, with the "fittest" emerging from the series of tests, whereas the other is closer to an agricultural model, based on nurturing and cultivating the seed of talent.

Where someone ends up is often a function of where that person begins, and how development is viewed begins with assumptions about talent and learning. Few people are really at the extremes in the "born or made" argument, although most lean one way or another, and the direction of the tilt is not inconsequential. The "borners" recognize that raw talent, charisma, and whatever other gifts they possess must be practiced and honed. The "maders" recognize that people are not lumps of clay that are equally easy to mold into effective executives—some people are more likely than others to grow into effective executives, and that means there have to be underlying "gifts" that they bring to the party. It might be possible to prove that neither extreme is accurate, but once one gets into the

FIGURE 1-3

CONTRASTING VIEWS OF LEADERSHIP DEVELOPMENT

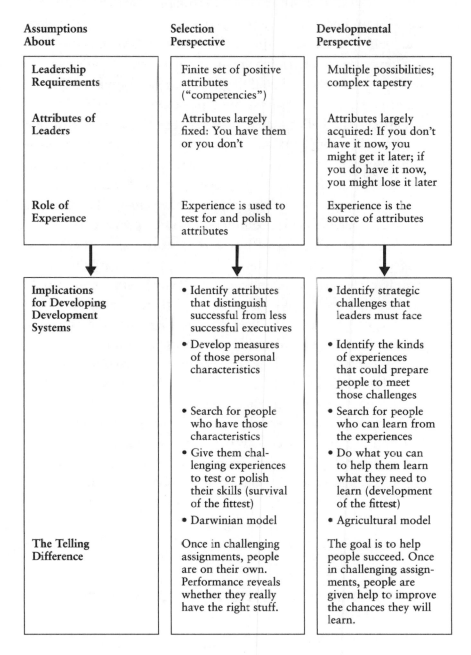

Assumptions About	Selection Perspective	Developmental Perspective
Leadership Requirements	Finite set of positive attributes ("competencies")	Multiple possibilities; complex tapestry
Attributes of Leaders	Attributes largely fixed: You have them or you don't	Attributes largely acquired: If you don't have it now, you might get it later; if you do have it now, you might lose it later
Role of Experience	Experience is used to test for and polish attributes	Experience is the source of attributes
Implications for Developing Development Systems	• Identify attributes that distinguish successful from less successful executives • Develop measures of those personal characteristics • Search for people who have those characteristics • Give them challenging experiences to test or polish their skills (survival of the fittest) • Darwinian model	• Identify strategic challenges that leaders must face • Identify the kinds of experiences that could prepare people to meet those challenges • Search for people who can learn from the experiences • Do what you can to help them learn what they need to learn (development of the fittest) • Agricultural model
The Telling Difference	Once in challenging assignments, people are on their own. Performance reveals whether they really have the right stuff.	The goal is to help people succeed. Once in challenging assignments, people are given help to improve the chances they will learn.

muddy middle, it is unlikely that any research will provide a definitive answer on which way to lean. The battle rages even among researchers who study personality, with the ebb and flow of argument moving from stable personality traits to environmental forces as predictors of behavior.[16] Within the much narrower frame of management and executives, the cycles are no less pronounced. Even though it has been known for decades that no single set of traits defines all successful executives in all situations, the belief that it does has been resurrected in one-size-fits-all competencies.[17] (Ironically, leadership development began with "Great Man" theories that were debunked by contingency theorists, only to reemerge as "competencies.") Entirely new personnel bureaucracies have emerged to translate these competency lists into human resource programs.

For those who lean toward the "born" side, there is an appealing logic and orderliness to identifying the attributes that characterize successful individuals. If such attributes can be identified, then the people possessing them can be found—a much quicker solution to the talent shortage than trying to nurture the attributes. Nevertheless, the assumption that all successful leaders have one set of a dozen or so characteristics or behaviors denies everyday experience, which shows that effective leaders come in various shapes and sizes (contrast Roberto Goizueta of Coca-Cola with Jack Welch of General Electric, for example, or for World War II followers, Omar Bradley with George Patton); that there are usually several equally effective ways to achieve the same outcome (different styles may achieve the same ends or, in the jargon, "equifinality"); and that leaders are dependent on the strengths and weaknesses of their followers as well as their own resources.[18]

FROM "SURVIVAL OF THE FITTEST" TO "DEVELOPMENT OF THE FITTEST"

Even Chuck Yeager—ace test pilot, conqueror of the sound barrier, folk-hero inspiration and personification of the right stuff—was skeptical of the idea that successful pilots were "born that way." Obviously perturbed by the notion that his piloting skill was innate, he said in his autobiography that "I am the sum-total of the life I have lived. . . . There is no such thing as a natural-born pilot. Whatever my aptitudes or talents, becoming a proficient pilot was hard work, really a lifetime's learning experience. For the best pilots, flying is an obsession, the one thing in life they must continually do. The best pilots fly more than the others; that's why they are the best."[19]

Whether the truth is found in Chuck Yeager's homespun wisdom or in the research on why talented people fail, the "right stuff" is not simply a catalog of natural gifts.[20] Instead, it is the result of talent honed by experience over a long period. If learning leadership is a lifelong journey, with its lessons taught by the journey itself, then neither the sink-or-swim approach of corporate Darwinists nor the programs approach of human resources specialists addresses the core issues of development. The former takes advantage of the power of experience but leaves to chance the direction that development will take and whether all that could be done has been done to help people realize their potential. The latter relies on short-term interventions often far removed from strategic objectives that lack the power of on-line experience to affect individual growth. The first step in executive development, then, is to move away from "survival of the fittest" to "development of the fittest." This shift requires an alternative to both the short-term "throw-'em-in-and-see-if-they-can-do-it" and the "send-them-to-a-program" approaches.

The ultimate implication, then, is that executive development, more so than most human resource systems, must be anchored in and driven by the business strategy—not by immediate business needs or crises, or by human resource practices, no matter how elegant or which admired companies use them. The available technologies for training, selection, succession planning, assessment, and other activities related in some way to executive development are quite sophisticated, but the undoing of development lies in its perceived noncentrality. When viewed as a "human resource program that's nice to have," even the most refined executive development program is a budget item waiting to be cut.

To suggest that executive development begins with experience and is driven by strategic business needs immediately puts the focus on a different series of questions that guide the remainder of this book:

- How important is the context within which development takes place? Chapter 2 sets the stage by exploring what happens when things go wrong. The dynamics of corporate derailments suggest an unintended conspiracy between the individual and the corporation that works against development and results in unrealized potential and wasted talent.

- If leadership is developed through experiences and is not just a gift, what experiences matter? What do they teach? How do they teach it? These are the topics addressed in Chapter 3.

- Given that many experiences can teach valuable lessons, how can you choose among them? Chapter 4 tackles the issue of how business strategy relates to the kinds of experiences that talented people need to have by showing how strategic business challenges can be translated into specific developmental needs.

- If talent is not a static asset—if people change for better or for worse over time—then how should we think about potential? Chapter 5 explores the dynamic nature of talent and potential, suggesting that if experience is the key to development, then the ability to learn from experience may be the most important attribute of potential leaders.

- If developing leadership requires a variety of experiences over time, and if people with the potential to develop executive leadership skills can be identified, how do we get the "right" people into the "right" experiences at the "right" time? Chapter 6 looks at the mechanisms, such as succession planning, available for matching talent with needed experiences.

- Even when talented people are exposed to potentially developmental experiences, there is no guarantee that they will learn from their experiences. Can anything be done to improve the chances that what could be learned will be learned? Chapter 7 explores how many traditional human resource practices, including 360° feedback and coaching, can be used in conjunction with managerial techniques like goal setting and appraisal to enhance learning.

- The answers to these questions lead to a framework presented in Chapter 8 for understanding how organizations can select high-potential candidates and give them the experiences they need to develop their talent as the next generation of leaders.

- Finally, for managers and executives concerned with their own development, the appendix provides specific action steps for creating and implementing a personal development plan.

2

THE DERAILMENT CONSPIRACY

IN TRYING TO UNDERSTAND EXECUTIVE DEVELOPMENT, IT IS tempting to draw conclusions only from those who have exemplary achievements. Sometimes, however, more can be learned from the stories of talented people who run into trouble. Consider the following account that appeared in the *Wall Street Journal*.

> Kellogg Co. President Horst W. Schroeder had looked forward to a relaxing weekend in Chicago with his wife after a visit to a Kellogg plant in Ontario last Sept. 15. Instead, the sleek Falcon 50 corporate jet in which he was riding was ordered to land at Kellogg regional airport near company headquarters here.
>
> Kellogg Chairman and Chief Executive Officer William E. LaMothe met the plane, ushered his 48-year-old heir apparent into a gray-wallpapered airport conference room, and told why he had diverted the plane: After only nine months as president, Mr. Schroeder was fired.[1]

By all reasonable criteria, this executive had been extremely successful and had demonstrated, over a long period of time, an ability to get results. In choosing him as president, Kellogg had every reason to believe he would be a success. Yet in only nine months, the chairman and the board of directors reached the verdict that he was not the right person for the job. In a most spectacular fashion, Horst Schroeder had derailed.

What happened here? George Will has observed that "few things are as stimulating as other people's calamities observed from a safe distance,"[2] so what can Mr. Schroeder's (or depending on how you look at it, Kellogg's) calamity tell us about leadership talent or executive development? If business results were the only marker for the right stuff, and if survival of the fittest were effective, then those who emerged at the very top of the pyramid would be—by definition—the best. There would be no need to worry about "development" because the system, by whatever means, was already doing it. If senior-level derailments like Horst Schroeder's were rare, it still might be that the system is working well enough, even though derailments at this level are quite costly. The way Schroeder's derailment was handled was unusual (diverting corporate jets for such purposes is a bit extreme), but the failure of managerial talent to live up to expectations is not. Because the corporate pyramid narrows as one moves up, many people, for a variety of legitimate reasons, simply reach their appropriate level and stop rising. By their own choice or by some perceived limitation on their ability, their organizations' expectations of them and their level of achievement align, and their ascent halts. For others, however, there appears to be considerably more potential than is realized—the expectations for them were higher than their achievement turned out to be, resulting in a derailment that was at least a disappointment and usually a surprise as well.

The patterns that describe why talented managers and executives derail are very useful in understanding how development takes place (or fails to take place) and the forces that any development system must contend with. These patterns not only show that the cream doesn't always rise but also suggest the reasons that it doesn't and what can be done about it. So our journey into the dynamics of developing talent begins with a look at what causes talented people to unravel.

Research into the processes of managerial derailment began in the early 1980s. My colleagues and I originally defined a derailed executive as a person who had been very successful in his or her managerial career but who failed to live up to his or her full potential, as the organization saw it.[3] How the organization reacted to the disappointment varied considerably, but whether the derailers were fired, demoted, forced to resign or retire, shunted aside, or passed over, the outcome was a non-voluntary cessation of career progress in that company.

Since then, across a series of subsequent studies, popular articles, and applications, the pattern of results has been consistent.[4] Managers and executives who later derailed were successful for similar reasons prior to derailing, which seemed to say something about how organizations judge performance, what expectations get set, and what is meant by "potential." Managers and executives also derailed for similar reasons and under similar circumstances, suggesting underlying patterns that recur across industries, organizations, and hierarchical levels.

To illustrate the principles involved, I have used published accounts of senior-level executive derailments, many of which appeared on the front page of the *Wall Street Journal*. I have called the people who derailed "front pagers," though not all of them were on the front page, and some of the stories were found in other publications.[5] These talented people had many significant accomplishments, ran into trouble, and eventually derailed. The magnitude of their success and the high levels they reached make the point well that failure and derailment are not synonymous. In life's terms, someone who becomes a senior officer of a major corporation is hardly a failure!

Few derailments are as dramatic as the one that began this chapter, but the tale of Horst Schroeder, as told by the *Wall Street Journal*, does highlight some of the dynamics that often occur when talented people derail. An obviously gifted executive, the German-born Horst Schroeder had been a Kellogg star for sixteen years. Starting out as a controller in West Germany, Schroeder accumulated cross-functional and cross-cultural experience, managing operations in Europe and then all of

Kellogg's overseas businesses. He consistently achieved impressive results, including the successful introduction into America, despite heated opposition, of a popular European cereal, Mueslix. Further demonstrating his deep understanding of the business as well as his articulateness, he impressed the board of directors with a vision for the corporation that promised "new heights" when market share had begun to erode.

Like almost all derailers, Horst Schroeder unquestionably had a lot of talent. His outstanding track record suggested he had more than a little of the right stuff, including a willingness to persevere in the face of opposition and to make personal sacrifices for the company. His diverse cultural experience and cross-functional background were a perfect match for the rapidly growing markets overseas, and his vision for the business, together with his decisiveness, augered well for waking up Kellogg's perhaps too-complacent midwestern corporate culture. Indeed, if Horst Schroeder's many strengths were listed on a flip chart, few could predict the turn of events that would follow.

If career success and repeated corporate recognition teach nothing else, they demonstrate to a person that he (in this case) is doing something right. It should come as no surprise, then, that Horst Schroeder might take on the presidency assuming that Kellogg wanted him to continue doing what he had done so well for so long. Perhaps underestimating the magnitude of the change to American, midwestern, and headquarters cultures, Schroeder proceeded in his accustomed autocratic style to implement his plans. Unfortunately for him, the external market demanded oat bran, whereas Kellogg's forte was in corn and wheat. Falling market share, coupled with a few of his errors in judgment, increased the pressure on Schroeder, who supposedly reacted by becoming even more dictatorial and demanding. The performance decline, the lowered morale, and the resignations of good people attracted the chairman's attention. In response to the chairman's inquiries, people apparently did not rise to Schroeder's defense. According to the *Wall Street*

Journal account, he was seen "as demanding and abrasive and often unwilling to listen to subordinates." Some subordinates said he "ignored their input and seemed intolerant of dissent," that he had a tendency to blame others when things went wrong but took the credit when things went right. In one instance, it was even implied that Schroeder had ordered company researchers to "keep their conclusions quiet" when their market data disagreed with his convictions.[6]

To make matters worse, Schroeder seemingly magnified the image of aloofness others had of him by driving a conspicuous foreign car (in Michigan, no less), living in a community away from that of other Kellogg executives, and not applying to become a U.S. citizen. All of this took place in a corporate culture that valued consensus and collegiality and under a chairman who favored teamwork and a willingness to challenge authority.

In contrast to the strengths listed above, the *Wall Street Journal* account presents a dark side of Schroeder that could fill a second flip chart. We see an executive portrayed as someone who was insensitive and abrasive; who had a dictatorial and autocratic style that grew more so under pressure; who blamed others for mistakes and took credit for successes (and may have been seen as untrustworthy because of it); who failed to recognize how the situation he was in differed from what he was used to; who compounded the error by his unwillingness to listen to or to tolerate dissent from those who did; and who apparently failed to build an effective relationship with his immediate superior.

As I will show, Horst Schroeder's list of "developmental opportunities" was not unlike those of other derailed executives. But the list of alleged flaws is far less interesting than the many questions the whole scenario raises and which will prove crucial to understanding the development of executive talent. For example, is there a relationship between Horst Schroeder's strengths and his weaknesses? Are the two truly separate? Or are the very qualities that made Schroeder successful for sixteen

Strengths	Flaws
Has a good track record	Is overly demanding
Is decisive/action-oriented	Doesn't listen
Has extensive international experience	Is intolerant of dissent
Perseveres in the face of opposition	Takes the credit for success
	Blames others for mistakes
Has cross-functional experience	Is untrustworthy—buried reports
Has a vision for the future	
Knows details of the business	Is aloof—seen as arrogant
Is loyal—16 years' service	Has a dictatorial style
Is articulate	Is abrasive/insensitive

or more years the same qualities that led to his undoing as president? Unless one is willing to assume that his insensitivity and autocratic style developed only *after* his final promotion, one is left to wonder how they figured in his past successes. As long as he was successful, his style might have been described as dedicated and committed, decisive and demanding, driven by high standards, and performance-oriented. When despite naysayers and heavy criticism, he introduced Mueslix successfully into the United States, he might have been applauded for his perseverance and insight. When he overcame opposition to introducing Pro-Grain by reportedly suppressing nonsupportive market data, however—and this time the product was not a market success—his integrity rather than perseverance and insight became the issue. In short, a case may be made that there is no such thing as an unqualified strength nor, perhaps, are "weaknesses" always dysfunctional. They may even be two sides of the same coin. If so, what does this imply about the endless pursuit of a finite list of characteristics that can accurately describe effective executives?

This question leads immediately to another critical question: specifically, why long-standing flaws suddenly become significant. What makes strengths turn into weaknesses or weaknesses into fatal flaws? Horst Schroeder's case raises several possibilities. He was in a new "culture"—actually three: the

United States, the Midwest, and corporate headquarters. He was in a new job—president—that was qualitatively different from his previous operational and staff assignments, so perhaps something about the difference became a trigger. His relationship with his boss was different, too, by virtue of his promotion to president. So we might conclude that he simply failed to adjust to the new environment and that his patterns of behavior no longer fit.

But maybe that explanation is too pat. Why didn't Kellogg anticipate that his style would cause problems? The *Wall Street Journal* account gives no indication that his CEO talked with Schroeder about the differences between the new job and the old one, or advised him of pitfalls, provided feedback along the way, checked in periodically to see how things were going, or otherwise intervened to help Schroeder change his approach. In fact, the only reference to corrective action given in the article is the CEO's lament that "perhaps he [Mr. Schroeder] could have made the adjustment, given more time." Apparently, time was not available. Why didn't Kellogg anticipate problems? The company may not have seen them coming—after all, most of Schroeder's career was overseas, and as some might argue, his style might have been effective there (or just more acceptable). Perhaps the company didn't have a very effective international performance appraisal system, so the flaws were never noticed until he came to the United States and could be watched more closely. Or perhaps the ability to get results was more important than how those results were obtained, and the company, even if aware of some of the downsides of his style, chose to underestimate or to overlook them.

Whatever the specifics, the companies themselves were always implicated somehow in all the derailment cases I and my colleagues have studied. It is never sufficient to say that only the derailed person was at fault. In Horst Schroeder's case it was Kellogg, after all, that called for a knight on a white horse when eroding market share became an issue. It was Kellogg, after all, that consistently rewarded Schroeder for his previous accomplishments, sending a powerful and perhaps unintentional message that not only were his strengths admired but that his weaknesses were also acceptable. In other organizations, talented people have sometimes been promoted within silos or functional specialties, in effect keeping their vision narrow and parochial, only to be derailed later when general management and executive positions required broader focus. So the question of what role or roles the organization plays in derailing talented people must be addressed.

And finally, the responsibility that individual executives bear for their derailment must also be considered. What, one might ask, could Horst Schroeder have done to prevent the events that overwhelmed him? In the absence of feedback, should he have sought it out? Why didn't he? To what extent do talented and successful people gradually come to believe their own press clippings, and is there an antidote to arrogance, which often springs from that siren song of success? Is this an unteachable "old dog" problem, or can people change their approach when new circumstances require it?

THE FIRST IMPOSTOR: SUCCESS

Rudyard Kipling recognized the similarity between triumph and disaster when he advised that the "two impostors" be treated just the same.[7] Although he gave this advice at the turn of the century, he might as well have directed it to modern executives en route to derailment. Like Horst Schroeder, the managers and the executives in the various derailment studies brought impressive attributes and accomplishments to the fateful job. Among those attributes (summarized in Figure 2-1), which varied from person to person, were some combination of building an exceptional track record of successes, being seen by others as uncommonly bright (whether that brilliance was reflected through a functional, technical, or even behavioral specialty), demonstrating remarkable commitment and drive, showing great personal charm, and being driven by ambition to seek out and fight for leadership positions. Only under the most unusual

FIGURE 2-1

SOURCES OF INITIAL SUCCESS

Track Record	Most people who make it into the executive ranks have a strong track record, consistently getting bottom-line results or making an impressive impact in a functional or technical area.
Brilliance	Being seen as uncommonly bright was a common reason for success. Brilliance might show in a technical or functional specialty, in analytic and problem-solving skills, or in a singular burst of genius in a specific situation.
Commitment/ Sacrifice	Many could list as a strength their loyalty to the organization, often expressed as a willingness to work long hours and to accept whatever assignments they were asked to take.
Charm	Some people are capable of considerable charm, charisma, or personal warmth when dealing with others. Sometimes this quality was used selectively, and often it was expressed upward toward those who made performance judgments.
Ambition	Although some were "drafted" into the management ranks, many others actively sought it out, doing whatever was required to achieve success.

Source: Adapted from M. W. McCall, Jr., and M. M. Lombardo, *Off the Track: Why and How Successful Executives Get Derailed,* Technical Report 21 (Greensboro, N.C.: Center for Creative Leadership, 1983), 2–3.

circumstances does a person rise to the senior leadership ranks of a major corporation without *significant* strengths (or at least strengths that were admired at some point). But for those who later derailed, past success and the attributes that had led to it were not enough to sustain it. Perhaps because they possessed one or more truly extraordinary strengths, the derailment was all the more shocking.

First among impostors, the characteristic most common among derailers, was a track record: either a long history of success or a singular, stunning accomplishment that propelled them up the ranks.

TRACK RECORD

A track record can take many forms, and the front pagers' accomplishments were nothing short of exceptional. They had built empires, saved failing enterprises, appeared on the cover of *Fortune* magazine, and otherwise drunk deeply from the fountain of success. Take, for example, the following cases:

- Richard Snyder began as a book salesman and worked his way up to chief executive of Simon and Schuster. In his thirty-three years with the company he was a key player in building it into "the most diversified book publishing company in the country," with bestselling authors and 1994 sales of $2 billion.[8] On June 13, 1994, he was fired from his job as head of Simon and Schuster.

- William Fife, Jr., inherited a company with a narrow customer base and rapidly declining sales. Through acquisition, expansion, endless hours of work, and a fanatic devotion to customers, in two years he turned the company around, achieving fifteen successive quarters that exceeded year-earlier results, doubling sales, and increasing earnings 61 percent. With stock up fourfold, he became a spokesman for the industry and made the cover of *Fortune* magazine. Despite his accomplishments, he was forced out by the board of Giddings & Lewis.[9]

- Paul Kazarian resurrected Sunbeam-Oster, taking it from bankruptcy to profitability before being visited in his room at the Hilton Towers by three board members who asked him to resign.[10]

- Robbie Ftorek coached the Los Angeles Kings hockey team to fourth place from eighteenth in their league—a feat that included the third-best regular season ever, packed houses, becoming the highest-scoring team in the NHL, and making it to the second round of the Stanley Cup playoffs by defeating the defending champions—before being fired.[11]

The list could go on, but achievement was clearly no stranger to these people. John Kotter, a leading expert on executives, described a recurrent pattern among successful general managers he called the "success syndrome:"

> They did well in an early assignment; that led to a promotion, or a somewhat more challenging assignment; that reinforced (or even increased) their self-esteem and motivation and led to an increase in their formal or informal power and an increase in the opportunities available to develop more power. More challenging jobs also stretched them and helped build their skills; that in turn led to an increase in their relevant relationships (including one or more with a mentor in top management), and an increase in their interpersonal and intellectual skills; that helped them once again to perform well in their jobs; that led to another promotion or challenging assignment; and that repeated itself again and again.[12]

In psychological circles, it is often said that the best predictor of future behavior is past behavior. In the case of derailed executives, a track record of success apparently is not sufficient. Although few get a shot at the executive swivel chair without significant past accomplishments, success alone obviously is not enough to anchor them there.

In some cases, it appeared that success was fleeting, and a "what have you done for me lately" organization passed them by quickly when results faltered. But in most cases, success was a bright marquee behind which a different kind of show was playing. As we will see, how the success had been achieved and the weaknesses it had masked eventually assumed center stage.

BRILLIANCE

A second common characteristic of executives who later derailed was unusual analytical or technical ability, often described by others as "brilliance." Paul Kazarian of Sunbeam-Oster, for example, was described by the *Wall Street Journal* as a "sort of a mad genius with 'incredible' business acumen." Intellectual capacity and "street smarts" were one kind of brilliance; another kind had to do with an uncanny ability to win people over. An example of such "genius" was William Fife's commitment to customers and the extraordinary lengths he went to earn their loyalty.[13]

COMMITMENT/LOYALTY/SACRIFICE/DRIVE

The success achieved by many executives who later derailed was not without a price, often a steep one. For some, it was a long career of devoted service (sixteen years for Horst Schroeder, thirty-three years for Richard Snyder); for many others, it was all-consuming workaholism. Paul Kazarian earned a reputation for working long hours and weekends, as did William Fife who, while at Giddings & Lewis, "worked seven days a week and expected no less from his deputies."[14] The road to the top was a lot of work for most of the executives who derailed, which made the rapidity of the subsequent fall all the more striking.

CHARM

Though not as common as the other reasons for success, charm was nonetheless a characteristic of some of these executives. Richard Snyder, whose "bullying" style contributed to his derailment, was also known for his "considerable charm and charisma."[15] Horst Schroeder's inspiring and articulate presentation to company directors earned him a standing ovation. Robert Stempel, chairman and CEO of General Motors until he resigned under fire in 1992, was so admired by the troops that one manager interpreted his derailment as "nice guy loses is the message here."[16]

An executive who exudes charm might be described as the kind of person who puts people at ease, who after a few minutes makes people feel as if they have known him for years. For some who later derailed, however, there was a more sinister twist. They were described as being charming, even ingratiating, when it served their purposes and the reverse when they saw no apparent personal benefit. Or they had a knack for getting their bosses enthused or supportive, exhibiting behavior toward superiors seldom displayed to those below them.

AMBITION

Of course, a select few may be born into high position or have it handed to them by some whim of fate. Most people who work their way up the corporate ziggurat, however, including those who derail, are an ambitious lot. The commitment and sacrifices required of them are such that only those with substantial ambition are willing to embark on the journey.

IMPERFECTIONS AND THE PATTERNS OF SUCCESS

No doubt other strengths characterized the managers and executives who later failed to live up to the expectations their organizations had for them, but the above list is not a bad one to start with. Most were bright, talented people who had achieved great things and gave every indication of continuing to do so. They were exactly the kind of managers an organization would put high on its succession list.

Obviously, their stories do not end there, and in the unexpected twists and turns of the tale lie the lessons that frame the challenges of developing talent. To begin with, the strengths that made the derailers successful had a darker side as well (see Figure 2-2). Seemingly stellar track records, for example, don't always reveal who (or what) actually played the major role in a successful outcome, nor do they always show how results were achieved. Corporate stars sometimes move so fast that the real impact of their actions doesn't catch up until much later, if at all. The potential for strengths to become liabilities is one of the common dynamics of derailment.

But the tale is not told entirely in the perfidy of strengths; even the eminently successful had flaws. Research has identified the fatal ones for corporate executives and for physician managers. These findings reveal that across time, samples, and cultures, the same flaws tend to reappear.[17] The impact of these flaws, however, is not always immediate, and just how these weaknesses can assume importance is another dynamic of derailment.

FIGURE 2-2

The Darker Side of Strengths

Track Record	Success can be in a narrow technical or functional area that later blinds a person to the broader context. Track records can be misleading: Other people or events may have had more to do with the success than the executive, success may have been achieved in destructive ways, or the executive may have moved too fast for the consequences of his/her actions to catch up.
Brilliance	Brilliance in and of itself can be intimidating to others, but brilliant people sometimes dismiss people they believe are less brilliant than themselves or devalue other people's ideas and contributions.
Commitment	Overcommitment may lead to defining their whole lives in terms of work and expecting others to do the same; being willing to do almost anything, including engaging in questionable activities for the sake of the business; or treating people as means to an end.
Charm	Charm can be used selectively to manipulate other people.
Ambition	Ambition darkens when people do whatever is necessary to achieve personal success, even at the expense of others or the organization.

Source: Adapted from M. W. McCall, Jr., and M. M. Lombardo, *Off the Track: Why and How Successful Executives Get Derailed,* Technical Report 21 (Greensboro, N.C.: Center for Creative Leadership, 1983), 2–3.

Ironically, those who derail and those who don't can look alike in many respects. The same strengths and their associated weaknesses exist among both derailers and those still on track. The same flaws also exist in each group, raising intriguing and important questions about the nature of talent that must first be answered before a model of development can be constructed. At the very least, these findings suggest that business results per se are a misleading indicator of the right stuff because they say little about the pattern of strengths and weaknesses a person has developed or how that pattern contributed to the success. If there are no unqualified strengths, if major strengths are not enough to ensure continued success, and if weaknesses may or may not be fatal, then the search for "natural" talent can become complicated indeed.

THE REVEALING DYNAMICS OF DERAILMENT

The world is too complex for a simple report card of strengths or weaknesses to explain what we observe about human behavior, talent, and the development of abilities. Overly simplistic models have created a shaky foundation upon which most executive development systems have been constructed. The dynamics underlying the derailment of talent (summarized in Figure 2-3) suggest starting with a different set of assumptions: every strength can be a weakness; blind spots matter eventually; success after success can lead to arrogance; and "bad luck" happens, but often what a person does when things go wrong is the determining factor.

EVERY STRENGTH CAN BE A WEAKNESS

Every strength, even those that have led to success, can be or become a weakness. For the brilliant, there are the potential downsides of dismissing others' ideas, not listening, or letting arrogance take root. Admirably adhering to principle can evolve into fanaticism or imposing one's beliefs on others. An extraordinary ability to build high-performing teams can seduce a person into ignoring other relationships that aren't going as well. How often is a leader who, at one point, is described as decisive and setting high standards, later seen as imperial, autocratic, or dictatorial?[18] How far is it to go from acting in a self-assured, self-confident manner to acting arrogant and cocky? From being broadly strategic and carefully analytical to being unfocused and indecisive?

The corporate version of the right stuff is built on the assumptions that there is a finite list of virtues that defines effective executive leadership, and that these virtues distinguish exceptional from average executives. If every strength is also a potential weakness, however, neither assumption holds. The list

FIGURE 2-3

The Dynamics of Derailment

Strengths Become Weaknesses	Remarkable strengths that made a person successful can become liabilities in situations where other strengths strengths are more important.
Blind Spots Matter	Weaknesses and flaws that didn't matter before or were forgiven in light of strengths/results become central in a new situation.
Success Leads to Arrogance	Success goes to a person's head, leading to the mistaken belief that he/she is infallible and needs no one else. This often occurs at precisely the time when these assumptions are least viable.
Bad Luck	Sometimes derailment results from a run-in with fate that is not an accurate reflection of the person's talent. Sometimes, however, bad luck is exacerbated by one of the other dynamics, suggesting that fate does not always act alone.

Source: Adapted from M. W. McCall, Jr., and M. M. Lombardo, *Off the Track: Why and How Successful Executives Get Derailed,* Technical Report 21 (Greensboro, N.C.: Center for Creative Leadership, 1983), 2–3.

of virtues in Figure 2-4 was adapted from an actual list of competencies developed by a large international organization— it is quite typical. In the right-hand column are potential dark sides for each strength. Take, as an example, the competency "customer-focused." How could anyone question the value of focusing on the customer's needs? *Fortune* did, in an article entitled "Ignore Your Customer," which described how Chrysler, Compaq, Fox Broadcasting, Motorola, and Steelcase have done just that to great success.[19] These companies believe that customer input can be confusing or wrong (remember New Coke?), and that breakthroughs may require faith in the product more than they require listening to the customer.

Among the front pagers, there are many examples of notable strengths becoming notable weaknesses. When Edward Lucente assumed second-in-command at Digital Equipment, he was said to have the toughness and discipline needed to change the culture. But he was later described as abrasive and

FIGURE 2-4

COMPETENCIES AND THEIR DARK SIDES

Competency	Potential Dark Side
Team Player	Not a risk taker, indecisive, lacks independent judgment
Customer-Focused	Can't create breakthroughs, can't control costs, unrealistic, too conservative
Biased toward Action	Reckless, dictatorial
Analytic Thinker	Analysis paralysis, afraid to act, inclined to create large staffs
Has Integrity	Holier than thou attitude, rigid, imposes personal standards on others, zealot
Innovative	Unrealistic, impractical, wastes time and money
Has Global Vision	Misses local markets, over-extended, unfocused
Good with People	Soft, can't make tough decisions, too easy on people

autocratic. Same story for Michael Gartner, who was brought in from the outside by General Electric presumably because he was tough enough to do whatever was deemed necessary to turn around the NBC news division. Later, after acting toughly, he was described as out of touch, prickly, an outsider.[20] In both cases, one has to suspect that the very attributes for which they were chosen became a part of their undoing.

Robbie Ftorek illustrates a different angle on strengths becoming weaknesses. As coach of the Los Angeles Kings, he was described as good technically and a good teacher—strengths perfectly suited to the Kings when they were a struggling team with a lot of young, inexperienced players. As the team matured and acquired veteran players, including superstar Wayne Gretzky, Ftorek's teaching style was no longer so well received. The more he attempted to tell the veterans how to play, the deeper his former strengths got him into trouble.

The problem with strengths that have led to success is a result of the success itself. It is difficult to abandon what has worked, even when circumstances change, and it may be nearly impossible to give up old patterns if no new skills have been developed to replace the old ones.

Being a tactical genius is hardly a flaw in a situation that calls for tactical skill. But a tactical orientation that results in a preoccupation with details or mires a person in technical problems can prevent an executive from grasping the big picture.

Learning tactical proficiency at the expense of strategic perspective is especially common in organizations and in jobs where performance is assessed by short-term (quarterly or even daily) results. Of the collection of front pagers, William Fife was hit the hardest by this particular malady. Described as a hard-working, down-to-earth, shirt-sleeve kind of guy—the positive side of tactical skill—Fife's "too-aggressive emphasis on short-term results" eventually led him into questionable financial deals in pursuit of short-term profits.[21] In this case, the flaw played out in two spheres: the short-term results were attained at the expense of long-term strategy, and immersion in short-term thinking blinded him to the larger consequences of his actions.

Technical expertise is another strength that is effective in some leadership situations, especially at lower management levels. When, however, a manager's superior expertise leads to overmanaging—telling people how to do their jobs rather than letting them do their jobs—it becomes a liability. This tendency is especially self-destructive when the people being overmanaged know more about what they are doing than their boss does—and sooner or later, a successful executive will end up managing people and functions outside of his or her expertise. Among other things, overmanagers can be guilty of meddling in things they don't understand, alienating people whose help they need, making a lot of mistakes because they don't listen to experts or because the experts don't care to help them, or getting mired in details and not thinking broadly. Some micromanagers get so busy doing everyone else's job that they don't do their own.

The point is that the value of a given attribute in an executive's repertoire is relative—to the immediate situation, to the organization's strategic direction, to the executive's other strengths and weaknesses, and to the observer's relationship to the executive. All too often, it seems that certain attitudes and behaviors are viewed positively (demanding, decisive, persevering, tough-minded) until things go wrong; then they miraculously turn into weaknesses (dictatorial, arbitrary, stubborn, bullying). In reality, people are complex tapestries of values, attitudes, beliefs, and abilities. It is misleading to believe that these ten or those ten virtues apply to all successful executives in all situations, even within the same company. How that tapestry is woven, not its individual threads, determines how it looks. The room it is hung in and the surrounding decor—not individual threads—determine whether the colors and patterns of the tapestry are a good fit.

Because there is no list of ultimate strengths, the perfect executive is a myth. Executive development and selection practices built on the assumption that the myth is true can never be completely successful. Development systems need to be built on some other foundation that incorporates the intriguing variety among talented people.

Blind Spots Matter Eventually

The world is not always fair, nor does justice always triumph in the end. Nonetheless, the stories of the front pagers suggest that flaws that have been overlooked or have lain dormant for long periods can and often do become a manager's nemesis. Weaknesses do catch up. Especially with derailed senior executives, it seems unlikely that the flaws that eventually did them in appeared suddenly. In most cases, the flaws that later were fatal had existed for a long time, if not in their pure form, then certainly as recognizable precursors.

Insensitivity was the most commonly reported flaw among

derailed executives in our research and was one of the sharpest differentiators between derailed and successful executives. It was also a dominant theme among the front-pager derailments.[22] Horst Schroeder was described as imperious, demanding, abrasive, unwilling to listen, abrupt, and intolerant of dissent, yet he had a sixteen-year track record of success.[23] It wasn't until he stumbled as president and needed the support of his subordinates that the consequences of his alleged treatment of others emerged.

Richard Snyder supposedly ruled Simon and Schuster by "intimidation and fear," becoming something of a legend within the firm. According to the *Wall Street Journal,* "Scores of former employees tell of meetings where he would threaten to lop off someone's hands or private parts, or tear out their throat for some failure to perform."[24]

Humiliating managers in front of peers or subordinates, cutting people off, demeaning others' ideas—everyone who has ever worked for an insensitive boss (and most of us have) knows the story and the incredible visceral response such treatment generates. Power and intimidation can produce compliance, but insensitivity can lead to lack of support at crucial junctures, failure of subordinates to pass on important information, active sabotage, loss of ideas from below, and a host of counterproductive activities. Organizations seem quite willing to overlook the flaw of insensitivity as long as someone gets results, but at the higher levels of management, alienating others in most cases assures that good results will not be sustained over time. It can't be very useful to have large numbers of people eager to see one fail.

The reason that formerly benign flaws become lethal usually involves a change in context. Talented people—people who get results, people who have visible achievements—tend to change situations often. They get promoted, are offered developmental assignments, find themselves assigned to important projects, are given increased responsibility, or otherwise move into new and often more visible settings. These opportunities typically bring with them a new boss, new job demands, or perhaps a new organizational culture (if the change involves a move to a different part of the organization or to headquarters), and these in turn call into question the continued success of a person's particular pattern of strengths and weaknesses. Finding themselves in situations that no longer play to their strengths, they are left with only their weaknesses to draw on.

Of course, successful people have many changes in jobs and bosses during their careers, and most of those transitions go smoothly. The deciding factor turns out to be the magnitude of the difference between what went before and what the new territory demands. Traditionally, boundary jumps have held the biggest threat: changing functional areas, for instance, moving from marketing to finance; moving from one division or business to another, such as going from a defense-related business to a consumer business; or switching from line to staff. More recently, however, organizations have been undergoing internal transformations that have led to derailments without a literal cross-boundary shift. The trend toward moving authority down and eliminating layers of hierarchy, for example, has shifted effective leadership from autocratic to empowering, with the resulting requirement that people successful with one style must shift to a new one. One might say that the territory changed underneath them.

Similarly, globalization, deregulation, consolidation, acquisition, and divestiture all create new territory that changes the relevance of existing patterns of strengths and weaknesses. Once again, the operative element is the degree of difference between what was and what is now. International assignments vary considerably in the degree of "difference" confronted— variations in climate, disease, political conditions, religion, language, and a host of other possibilities add to the normative and stylistic differences across cultures. The demands they impose are not inherently derailing, unless something in the new situation calls for strengths where a person happens to be weak.

Several implications may be drawn from the relative nature of weaknesses. First, two dynamic processes leading to derailment—strengths becoming weaknesses and weaknesses becoming important—strongly suggest that fixed-template models of executive effectiveness are inadequate. To reflect reality, they must incorporate context, time, and the interactions among strengths and weaknesses.

Second, defining effectiveness solely in terms of results masks significant developmental needs from both organizations and the managers. Understandably eager to achieve business results, organizations may be inclined to overlook how results are achieved—especially since judgments about differences in style are often subjective, and as we have seen, similar actions can be viewed as positive or negative depending on the context and outcome. An individual rewarded for results alone might reasonably conclude that the means for achieving those results were acceptable or admirable, even if they weren't. Unfortunately, ignoring or rewarding weaknesses sets the stage for future derailments, and ironically, the individual and the organization are co-conspirators in writing the script.

Given the obvious danger that weaknesses present in a changing world, why don't people—especially talented people—correct their weaknesses before they cause havoc? There are perhaps several reasons, but the bottom line is that they haven't yet been hurt by them. Because of the confidence built by success and the presence of demonstrated strengths, it is possible to dismiss potential weaknesses as unimportant or as nonexistent. John Steinbeck observed a biological parallel during his exploration of the Sea of Cortez. He wrote, "If an animal is good to eat or poisonous or dangerous the natives of the place will know about it and know where it lives. But if it have none of these qualities, no matter how highly colored or beautiful, he may never in his life have seen it."[25] So it may be with weaknesses, so easy to overlook unless they bite. What is even more dangerous developmentally, weaknesses may be seen as strengths, as "good to eat," because indeed they are in some situations.

This observation suggests a third and less obvious implication involving the situational nature of weaknesses. Because changing context can make weaknesses matter, well-intended promotions or developmental moves can turn into lethal situations. Many executive leadership skills are learned through exposure to challenging new situations (see Chapter 3), so a major challenge to any executive development system is managing these crucial moves effectively. The goal, after all, is to enhance and preserve talented people, not to destroy them. Putting talented people in situations that expose their weaknesses can be developmental or fatal, depending on how both the person and the organization handle the situation.

SUCCESS AFTER SUCCESS LEADS TO ARROGANCE

William Hazlitt aptly described the dangers of arrogance: "Do not imagine that you will make people friends by showing your superiority over them; it is what they will neither admit nor forgive."[26] Most of the front pagers were said to have been arrogant at least to some degree, sometimes to an extraordinary degree, and arrogance often figured prominently in their derailments. Self-confidence, so important to success, sometimes grew bloated by the success that fed it. Blinded by the bright light of their own achievements, immensely talented people can fly too close to the sun, like Icarus. Forced out of the top spot at Ford Motor Company, Don Petersen was described by his detractors as believing his own press clippings.[27] According to *Fortune* magazine, a competitor said of the Mars brothers, "Their own hubris was their downfall. They are arrogant, and when your arrogance exceeds your intellect you've got trouble."[28] *Business Week* even devoted a cover story to the phenomenon as it relates to chief executives, dubbing their (mis)perception that they can do no wrong as "CEO disease."[29] The article implied that the pampering and power of high office is the culprit, and certainly that is part of the story. But in studies of derailment, aloofness and arrogance among successful people is not restricted to those who make it to the very top. Each successive success, whether a technical accomplishment or a business result, adds to the opportunity to believe one's own press clippings or to admire the trophy case. Whether they were military aviators, physician managers, or executives, none were above interpreting accomplishments as further proof that there was something special about them (as indeed there was). For some, that specialness translated into egotism, resulting in behavior that served to alienate those on whom they depended.

In a complex environment characterized by interdependence, arrogance has the unfortunate outcome of depriving a leader of the loyalty needed to operate effectively. People usually aren't eager to go the extra mile to help such a person succeed, as Robert Schoellhorn, removed by the Abbott Laboratories board, found out. Even though he led a major comeback of the company, presided over steady and uninterrupted increases in revenue, earnings, and profits, and basked in external admiration, such achievements did not save him after he reportedly lost the respect of his executives. Described as "the grandiose man who ruled over his company as if it were a private fiefdom," Schoellhorn went from being one business magazine's 1986 Executive of the Year to becoming a case study of egotism in the 1991 *Business Week* cover story.[30] The reason? He became a victim of his own success.

Arrogance has some special qualities that merit separate treatment. One is that arrogance grows over time with success. Unlike preexisting strengths that become weaknesses in a different situation or preexisting weaknesses that become important later on, arrogance develops over time and causes people to lose their bearings. In effect, it sets up the other derailment dynamics by creating a feeling of invincibility and a blindness to one's impact and its potential consequences. The derailment cases were filled with people who were unaware of important information, failed to see the significance of crucial events, couldn't understand why their behavior had negative consequences, or ignored the obvious disrepair in critical relationships.

In some cases where total "blindness" was not possible, the importance of what was seen was diminished. It appeared that NBC's Michael Gartner accepted that his behavior was arrogant and aloof—he had been told repeatedly that it was—but he dismissed it with a shrug, saying "I don't try to be, but I am who I am."[31] At the extreme, arrogance feeds a belief that a person is immune to any consequences, as William Manchester's account of Douglas MacArthur's defiant confrontation with President Truman suggested.[32] Disagreeing with Truman's decision to settle for an armistice in the Korean conflict, MacArthur criticized and embarrassed his commander-in-chief publicly, forcing the showdown in which Truman removed him from command.

The net effect of arrogance as it grows over time is that once-effective people become increasingly out of touch and less effective. This may be the result of one or both of two dynamics. The first is that arrogance is associated with attributes that contribute to success (and therefore is at least partially justified); the second is the tendency to believe that exceptional attributes exempt their possessor from "normal" constraints.

It has been observed that "great egoists are almost always optimists."[33] In the case of MacArthur (and some of the physician managers we studied[34]), this dynamic played out as a misplaced belief that expertise in one area made him an expert in others. As one historian noted, "MacArthur's qualities are so indisputably great in his own field that it comes as something of a shock to explore the record and find that in others he can be narrow, gullible, and curiously naive."[35] Nonetheless, it is confidence—even if misplaced—that allows a person to be daring and to take on challenges that others avoid. The difference between boldness and foolish bravado may be determined by the outcome rather than the circumstances, so successful people may well come to believe that arrogance (pronounced "optimism" or "willingness to take risks") is actually a reason for their success.

The second way that arrogance erodes effectiveness is by creating the perception that the normal rules do not apply. Pursuit of results sometimes raised the specter of Faustian temptation—how far are you willing to go, what are you willing to sacrifice, to achieve success? Power and a long track record of success conspired to blind some executives to their dependence on others, sometimes to the extent of believing that their actions were above scrutiny. Like the pilot heroes of *The Right*

Stuff, they may have been treated as if they were expected to bend the rules, eventually coming to see themselves as living by a different set of standards.

This blindness is seen in the corporate world as well. According to Mitchell Engel, executive vice-president of Foote, Cone and Belding Advertising, who sued Paul Kazarian for breach of contract, "Kazarian revels in being a renegade. He's a . . . self-perceived boy wonder. Rules have never been important to him."[36]

The psychologist Harry Levinson, who has spent many years observing executives as they ascend to power, reports that it is not uncommon to see a grandiose self-image develop. Levinson described the phenomenon for *Business Week:* "They think they have the right to be condescending and contemptuous to people who serve them. They think they are entitled to privilege and the royal treatment."[37]

In summary, the development of arrogance is one of the most insidious of the derailment dynamics. It is a negative that grows from a positive, deriving as it does from actual talent and success. It not only has an immediate and direct negative impact through the overt behaviors it spawns, but it also blinds people to the impact of other behaviors as well. It shapes the expectations of the egotist and of those supervising him or her in ways that further separate behavior from direct consequences, especially through bending rules and special treatment. The erosion of talent, as well as its development, is embedded deeply in the day-to-day context of work. Any process aimed at the development of executive talent must recognize the potential downside of success, build in reassessment over time, and provide mechanisms for dealing with talented people who lose their perspective.

BAD LUCK AND REACTIONS TO IT

The fourth dynamic of derailment involves what appears to be bad luck. Sometimes talented people are just unlucky. Through no fault of their own, they lose a run-in with fate. There are victims of capricious circumstances, risk takers in corporate cultures that don't tolerate mistakes, scapegoats for others' errors, and innocent targets of "personal chemistry." Talented people can be swept out in large-scale corporate housecleanings, outplaced by generic agreements resulting from mergers or acquisitions, tainted by association with a regime that loses favor, sabotaged by jealous rivals, or dragged down despite personal achievement by uncontrollable market forces or others' mistakes.

Many factors that affect performance are out of the actor's control, and poor performance is surely a major derailing factor at the senior levels. For example, when the ousted General Motors chief Robert Stempel took the helm, he not only inherited the poor decisions of his predecessor but was also greeted by a recession that sent the economy into a nosedive.[38] Ironically, it may not matter whether the trouble is the result of forces outside of the person's control or a product of the person's errors or actions. In the case of Horst Schroeder, for example, eroding market share caused by a shift in consumer preferences to oats, when Kellogg's products were based on corn and wheat, could hardly be blamed on Schroeder. Nonetheless, the expectation was that market share would increase during Schroeder's watch; when it didn't, his boss wanted to know why and began to look more closely into what was going on. It was then that Schroeder's own mistakes and counterproductive behavior got serious attention.

But to say that bad luck is one dynamic of derailment is at once to acknowledge the obvious while obscuring the significant. The people who most believe bad luck is the cause of derailment are the derailers themselves. This "it wasn't my fault" interpretation of history sometimes masks an individual's contribution to the resulting ill fortune. Accepting responsibility for one's actions, even when external circumstances play heavily, is a prerequisite for learning.

Another way of looking at "bad luck" is to consider it broadly as a change in circumstances. Successful executives sometimes attribute their success to good luck. Beneath this superficial explanation, however, effective executives are prepared to take advantage of changes of fortune when they appear.[39] Those who derail represent the other side of the coin, lacking an ability to respond effectively when circumstances turn against them and then blaming the outcome on the circumstances.

As career success translates into increased responsibility, the potential ramifications of mistakes or poor business performance, whether internally or externally caused, increase as well. The final scenario of many derailments begins with some kind of performance problem (which may be unusual, given the prior success of the manager), and that "trouble" launches events that can take several different courses. Trouble can be a lone assassin, especially in organizations that are unforgiving, when the executive is in a highly visible position and has to take responsibility, or in cases where ethics or the law may be violated. But more often, trouble is only a backdrop against which something is revealed about a person's temperament or character by the way the situation is handled; attention is drawn to the person, with flaws surfacing that had not been considered as such before; long-standing weaknesses become central to resolving the situation; or pent-up anger finds release (people are ready to get revenge by pushing the perpetrator out of the revolving door).

For some, "bad luck" in the form of a setback revealed a sheer lack of experience with failure—many talented and successful people have not had many flops and therefore have not had an opportunity to learn how to deal with them. When a setback is major and highly visible, the inadequacies of talented people may be seen in the harsh and revealing light of adversity. By failing to admit the problem, covering it up, or trying to blame it on others, some managers display an inability or a refusal to take responsibility for their actions. Others under duress may let their frustration exaggerate their existing flaws and end up lashing out at other people, withdrawing, or otherwise behaving in unproductive ways. The reaction to trouble, not the reason for it, becomes a defining factor through what it reveals about the person on the spot.

Another way bad luck in the form of trouble plays out is in its effect on attention. Successful, talented people have track records composed of many more successes than failures. Whereas success after success can lull the successful person into overconfidence and an inflated self-image, it also affects the behavior of outside observers vis-à-vis the star performer. Just as squeaky wheels may get the grease, smoothly running machines may be ignored. For example, the boss of a successful performer quite naturally might spend more time and energy on other matters rather than on monitoring where there is no problem. As noted earlier, this was clearly the case with LaMothe at Kellogg—he fully expected Horst Schroeder to continue his excellent performance, so he spent his time dealing with other matters. It appears that only when the situation began to deteriorate did he begin to pay close attention to his subordinate's actions. So it was in many of the derailment cases. Because things were expected to be right, it was sometimes quite a while before problems were detected. But when they were noticed, problems were highlighted starkly against the backdrop of prior success. Whatever gain there may be in the freedom from scrutiny bought with success is more than offset by the possible overreaction to the appearance of failure.

Sometimes bad luck is a change in situation that brings a weakness to the forefront, not just through increased attention but because the skill deficit prevents solving the problem or makes it worse. One weakness frequently exposed when "luck" changes the situation is the inability to build and maintain effective working relationships with key players. Someone unable to deal with a boss with a different style might, by bad luck, get a boss with a different style and find that building the relationship is the most important task.

One account of Richard Snyder's story offers a detailed look at a relationship with a new boss that unraveled rather quickly after Viacom bought Paramount. Snyder had managed to maintain a workable relationship with a difficult boss for years before the acquisition brought him Frank Biondi, a boss with a different set of values and style. Perhaps lulled by relief at the change, it may have been Snyder's weaknesses in conjunction with the new boss's expectations that eventually did him in.

As chairman of Simon and Schuster (a Paramount subsidiary), Snyder for ten years reported to Paramount chairman Martin Davis, in what could only be described as a very demanding relationship to manage.[40] Davis, according to the *Wall Street Journal* report, disliked Snyder intensely and showed it by countermanding decisions, constantly looking over his shoulder, at times publicly humiliating him, and eventually choosing his own executives for key roles in Snyder's operation.

The contrast in styles when Viacom took over had a dramatic effect. Where Davis had micromanaged, Viacom preferred to stand back and let Snyder run the operation. Apparently he did so with gusto, intensifying his own predilections to overmanage and intimidate, at the same time neglecting the relationship with his new bosses, particularly his immediate superior, Frank Biondi (who, ironically, was himself ousted as CEO of HBO because of a disagreement with his boss, according to *Fortune*[41]). The quid pro quo for autonomy was keeping headquarters informed, and particularly not surprising top executives with bad news. It appears that Snyder enjoyed his autonomy too much to spend a lot of time making sure the brass stayed informed and they began to feel that information was hard to come by, superficial, and even misleading. They were hit several times by unanticipated decisions and events, sometimes finding out about them from the newspaper instead of from their own executive. As word of Snyder's heavy-handed and dictatorial leadership style filtered up, there were rumblings of mass resignations. Finally, the tumult was too much for Biondi, who fired him.[42] In retrospect, it might be said that Snyder was unlucky in getting Biondi for a boss. The reality was both more complex and more interesting.

In still other cases, bad luck simply provided the opening through which accumulated animosity could be released. "Friends come and go, but enemies accumulate," and many derailments result when successful executives find themselves confronted with their past.[43] It goes without saying that we tend to remember—vividly—people who achieve their success at our expense. So it was with some of the derailed executives, whose "bad luck" appeared when someone they had mistreated reappeared at a later date as their boss, a member of their board, a major customer, the union leader, the technical person on whom a project depended, or the head of a competing company.

It is almost impossible to live life without making some enemies, and leadership requires making decisions that sometimes leave resentment. But some people behaved in needlessly callous ways, and even though they got away with it for a long time, they ended up paying a stiff price. Believing they didn't need anyone else and treating people that way, they set themselves up for a fall. When the chips were down, no one stepped forward to bail them out. On the other hand, when they stumbled, there were many eager hands to help them out the door.

To summarize, when things go wrong for people who have a track record of success, trouble causes other people to look more closely. Even when the decline in performance is not directly their fault, the scrutiny often calls attention to various flaws that may have been there all along. In looking for an explanation for why things are going wrong, these flaws may assume greater importance than they have in the past or sometimes more than they actually merit.

When performance decline is caused by someone's own mistakes and not by external forces, derailment still is not automatic. Although there are unforgiving environments where one mistake is too many, most of the derailments resulting from trouble were less the result of the mistake than of the way people handled the mistakes they made. Often people's flaws caused them to make ineffective responses to the trouble they faced, so it was the interaction of trouble and weaknesses that got them derailed. Someone who was seen as untrustworthy might respond to a mistake by blaming others or trying to cover it up. Someone who was insensitive to others might strike out at people trying to help or make matters worse by further alienating those affected by the mistake.

Trouble, then, is often the context in which successful people's flaws assume an importance they never had while things were going smoothly.

The most obvious implication of the four dynamics of derailment is that there is no standing still. No one is immune to the dynamic forces that threaten career success—a current strength in danger of being overplayed, a weakness lying in wait, achievement inflating the ego, or fate lurking around the next corner. The relevance of these findings is not just that jeopardy is a way of life for the talented but rather that the painful lessons of derailment offer clues for development, certainly for individuals who aspire to careers in leadership but also for organizations that hope to create a context in which talent is preserved and enhanced.

THE UNINDICTED CO-CONSPIRATORS

Whether failing to listen to advice and feedback, refusing to change when change was needed, behaving in ways that alienated other people, or some other act of self-destruction, individuals who derailed *always* played a significant role in their own demise. Even when the organization, bad luck, or other external forces were heavily involved, which made placing blame difficult, individuals still contributed wittingly or unwittingly to the sequence of events. Because those who derailed were often unaware of their own role or actively denied it, they could be described as conspirators in their own misfortune.

But knowing that individuals always played a part in their derailments tells only part of the story. Their organizations also were responsible to varying degrees, as appeared to be the case for Horst Schroeder's misadventure at Kellogg. Organizational practices and reactions—from failing to provide clear feedback to rewarding counterproductive behavior—set the stage for what was to come. If one accepts the premise that talented people who later derail represent a loss to the organization and that the loss is at least in part the result of the organization's actions, then the organization has a great deal to gain by improving the context it creates. What makes it difficult is that the ways in which organizations undermine development and contribute to derailments are often subtle and hard to detect. Often, in fact, the most deleterious actions are the best intended, resulting in an "unconscious conspiracy" between an organization and an individual who together, in pursuit of effectiveness, produce a derailment.[44]

The organization creates a climate that can make learning and change harder or easier, depending on prevalent assumptions about development; on what is valued, measured, and rewarded; on how the inevitable mistakes of learning are treated; on how developmental opportunities are distributed; and on what is done to assist people in their development efforts. In short, the way an organization is designed and run creates the soil in which the seeds of both development and derailment are sown. Although it cannot directly determine how any given individual will turn out, it does directly affect the developmental environment in which individuals make their choices.

Even well-managed and successful organizations may have a difficult time balancing the drive for results and the need to develop talent. The "organizational complicity" that may lead to the derailment of talented people is not the result of maliciousness or opposition to the idea of development; it would be easier to confront if it were. Instead, organizations *acting rationally* create the very forces that eventually lead to derailments. This rationality, of course, is defensible from the point of view that executive ability is something one has or does not. The kind of rationality that results in wasted talent is ultimately not rational, although it may make sense in one frame of reference. The ways in which complex organizational forces can undermine good intentions and lead to derailment rather than development—even in the most successful companies and in companies with very sophisticated human resource systems—is best demonstrated by a case example.

A CASE IN POINT

The organization involved was a multibillion-dollar, U.S.-based, multinational company often held up by others as a benchmark for human resources practices. Its management and executive development systems were particularly admired, and this company already had incorporated two fundamental principles that most other organizations only envy. First, development was considered a business priority, so senior management invested a significant amount of time and energy on various activities associated with succession and development. Second, the organization used challenging assignments—not training programs—to develop executives, so it had created sophisticated systems for getting its "high potentials" into the experiences considered important for their development.

Derailments were common among those in the high-potential pool, but historically the supply of talent had always been sufficient to make up for the losses. Things changed, however, when competitive pressures led the company to implement an aggressive business strategy that was driven by dramatic growth. Projections of the numbers of executives needed to achieve the plan showed a staggering shortfall in the years ahead. Between the managers the company was already losing through firing and voluntary quits (many of whom were joining competitors and doing quite well) and the projected growth, current practices could not produce the needed supply of executive talent.

In an effort to fill the widening talent gap, the company employed two strategies. The first, consistent with its preference to "grow its own," involved various efforts to *accelerate* the development of talent by moving people more quickly through key assignments and by reducing the variety of different assignments to which they were exposed. The second strategy was to increase the number of executives hired from the outside, even though that was inconsistent with prior practice and preference.

The effort to accelerate the development of internal talent by speeding up the movement of high potentials had the opposite of the intended effect—derailments actually increased. To make matters worse, executives brought in from the outside, though carefully screened and extremely successful in their prior positions, failed at an even higher rate than the company's own internal talent.

At this point, the company took a closer look at derailments and at how its development practices might be adjusted to the new situation. Recent derailments of internally promoted candidates followed many of the same patterns described earlier in this chapter; the effort to accelerate development had simply exacerbated the existing dynamics. Those who derailed had been very successful at earlier assignments, and most were extremely bright or got impressive results, or both. As Figure 2-5 shows, derailers who had been assessed as exceptionally bright but lacking in line experience sometimes got bogged down in thought or mired in process at the expense of action. Action-oriented managers with great track records, in contrast, often derailed when the job got too complex or they were unable to develop a strategic perspective. Derailers who were seen as both smart *and* action-oriented sometimes were flawed by an inability to develop effective relationships, by ineffective responses to change or feedback, or by the arrogance produced by their successes. Though these flaws were usually identified in advance by the elaborate assessment process used on all managerial personnel, they were frequently overlooked or forgiven in high potentials because their strengths were highly valued and because of the pressure to accelerate the development process.

The study revealed that the organization contributed in several ways to the derailments that occurred. For example, challenging assignments were used for development, but high potential managers were moved rapidly and typically within narrow functional channels or business unit silos. When they inevitably hit a situation requiring dramatically new or different skills and their performance subsequently declined, the unforgiving, performance-driven culture emerged and derailed them. Though such difficult situations represented seminal opportunities to develop new skills, efforts to "rehabilitate"

FIGURE 2-5

DERAILMENT PATTERNS OF HIGH POTENTIALS

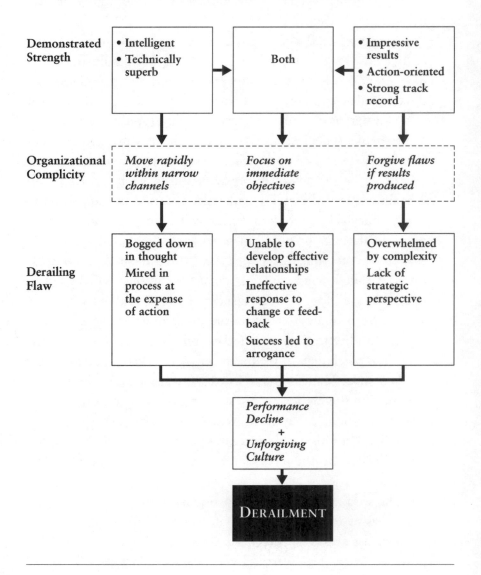

managers who ran into performance problems were relatively rare. This loss of potential development opportunities was compounded because the unforgiving side of this corporate culture was widely recognized, and managers and executives were reluctant to risk a stumble on the bottom line for the sake of their own or others' development. In fact, the culture seemed to consider "taking no prisoners" as a sign of effective management, resulting in perceived pressures not just to avoid developmental risks but to act decisively when performance declined—regardless of the reason.

A closer look revealed that the culture strongly emphasized and subsequently assessed and rewarded *individual* achievement, when at higher levels many of the skills needed for success shifted toward teamwork, coordination and cooperation with others, and working through others to achieve synergy. Talented managers found few incentives to develop skills that did not lead to the achievement of their immediate objectives and preferred objectives that were clearly within their control. As a result, the skills needed for achieving spectacular short-term results were honed to the sharpest edge, but when these people reached positions requiring different skills, flame-out was quick and dramatic.

Like the company's internal promotees, the people hired from outside at senior levels were extremely bright, results-oriented, and had impressive track records. Because these outside hires were screened thoroughly and given attractive signing bonuses and compensation packages, the company expected them to get immediate results. Unfortunately, people this talented still needed to learn the new culture and develop workable relationships—time-consuming tasks that had to be undertaken before sustained results could reasonably be expected.[45] With little developmental guidance from the organization and even less organizational patience given the high expectations, the new hires faced stiff odds.

Turning the situation around involved far more than altering management development practices, adding training programs, or urging high potential managers to "take charge of their own development." The problems were deeply embedded in the culture of the organization, and a piecemeal approach to change would not solve them. In this company, an emphasis on results, strongly coupled with rewards based on results, impatience with mistakes, and pressure to increase the managerial pool added up to a culture of a "survival of the fittest." Unfortunately and unintentionally, the elements that had made this driven company so successful had become part of the problem.

The paradox of wanting people to learn from experience, which by definition involves trial and error, yet punishing them when trial resulted in error, highlights a fundamental dilemma for development. That is, for learning to occur, the context must support learning. This is an issue of executive leadership, not just a human resources problem. At the most basic level, development is directly affected by the organization's business strategy (what it is trying to achieve) and by its values (what it is willing to do to get there). These organizational issues determine what is desired, what is rewarded, and what is tolerated. As we shall see, they also have significant implications for which kinds of learning experiences are important and how talented people are treated.

The answer to developing executive talent therefore does not lie in tinkering with human resource systems. This is not to say that compensation, succession, training, performance management, and other human resource subsystems are not essential but rather that if the larger context in which executive development is embedded is hostile to it, the most polished human resource subsystem has little chance of overcoming it.

THE STAGE IS SET

To know that the individual and the organization share responsibility for wasted talent and unfulfilled potential, and that many of the actions that lead to undesirable consequences often are unintentional, does not in itself suggest a solution. But it does suggest a starting point, and it underlines the reality that neither the organization nor the individual alone can guarantee successful development. From an organizational perspective, the task is clear: To create a context in which development is supported or, at the very least, in which it is not subverted. Clearly, this task involves strategic and philosophical concerns in addition to the development of effective systems and practices. Above all, the development of leadership is a leadership issue. The derailment research shows that, ironically, the very situations that most often lead to derailment can as readily lead to development. Put another way, experience can do one in or it can teach important lessons. The trick is to know how to influence which way it goes.

From an individual perspective, the implications are also clear. When it comes to development, most organizations are a little like the dinosaurs, lumbering along with a brain the size of a peanut. Operating on implicit assumptions that the cream will rise, they continue on their way until a problem emerges— usually a strategic change caused by environmental convulsions or a shortage of needed talent, in response to which they act precipitously to replace existing people or to promote or recruit new talent without adequate scrutiny. The bottom line for individuals is that no one cares as much about a person's development as the person. Whether the organization supports development or inhibits it, individuals need to take responsibility for achieving their potential.

3

EXPERIENCE
AS
TEACHER

WHEN YOU THINK ABOUT YOUR CAREER AS A MANAGER, certain events stand out in your mind, things that led to a lasting change in the way you manage. Tell me what happened. What did you learn?

> I had my own business and had to learn to manage every aspect of it. I started from scratch, developing the property, learning how to run everything from cash flow to people. It was a tough business, and I learned to focus on a few factors that could be leveraged to make it successful. I learned how important it is to get to know your customers and your employees inside and out. I learned to be resourceful in everything from custodial chores to strategic planning. It was an invaluable experience.
>
> —From an interview with a corporate executive

They made me the head of sales. I had to manage a very large and very complex organization. It was quite a shift from what I had done in the past. I learned to manage 3000 people, which requires a set of skills most managers never develop unless they are forced to. I had to learn how to keep people focused on a few key priorities. I also got to understand the customer side of the business—a key to effective leadership.

—From an interview with a corporate executive

The intellectual repartee of the classroom has a certain appeal, but when asked to recount events that changed them significantly, successful executives like the ones quoted above overwhelmingly described powerful, challenging experiences, the vast majority of which occurred anywhere but the classroom.[1] Although development is most commonly thought of as what occurs in training programs—and much of what corporations describe as development takes place in a classroom—most of the development described by successful executives occurred through on-the-job experiences.

To say that development is the result of experience leaves a lot open to interpretation. In the broadest sense, experience is what happens every day. Each Monday morning is an experience, but not all are equally powerful. Though most people emerge from the vast majority of our experiences unchanged in any significant way, some experiences do have a significant impact on one's understanding of oneself, one's view of the world, one's sense of right and wrong, and one's subsequent behavior. All experiences are not equal.

Experiences that create lasting change are rarely the product of routine daily fare or of minor turns in an otherwise straight road. The experiences that changed executives were hairpin curves or stomach-turning drops that forced them to look at themselves and their context through a different lens. Transformational experiences almost always forced people to face something different from what they had faced before. In a real sense, the challenge lay in what they weren't already good at, not in what they had already mastered. The harder the test, the deeper the eventual learning, even though for a time afterward, the full significance of the experience might be unclear.

Experiences that have a strong personal impact are almost always loaded with adversity. Because people often prefer to avoid adversity, many of the most developmental experiences happened as a result of fate rather than volition; still others were more or less forced on people by a boss or the organization. Of the experiences entered into willingly, even eagerly, executives sometimes had to admit in retrospect that they hadn't realized what they were getting into—they might not have done it had they known, although having survived it, the expereince was invaluable.

Experiences that teach are like that. Whether entered into voluntarily, or voluntarily but poorly informed, or involuntarily, there was little choice once there but to learn. President Steven Sample of the University of Southern California is fond of telling a story he attributes to Abraham Lincoln that captures the flavor of learning from experience. A frog fell into a deep rut in a dirt road not far from his pond.[2] Wagons had passed along this road in the deep mud left by heavy rain, leaving a now-hardened and cavernous—to a frog—rut that this particular frog was unable to hop out of. After numerous tries and several creative efforts, the frog gave up and sat in the rut, exhausted. After a while the frog's friends and family became worried and began to search for it. Eventually they heard its weakened croaks and, peering over the lip of the rut, saw the frog huddled sadly at the bottom. All of their creativity and efforts to help proved futile, and eventually, being frogs, they abandoned the frog to its fate.

The next day friends and family awakened to a hearty croaking, only to find their trapped companion jumping happily across the lily pads. "We thought that you were trapped in a rut and couldn't get out," they said with surprise. "I was, and I couldn't," replied the frog. "Until a wagon came along and I had to."

Like the frog in the rut or the hero facing the mythical tests, adults seem to learn best when they need to acquire a new skill in order to achieve something that matters to them. Executives found themselves facing situations for which they were ill prepared, that tested their assumptions and beliefs, and in which what had worked for them before no longer worked. What they already knew or believed was insufficient, so development was the only acceptable alternative.

In considering the elements of a systemic model for executive development, it is apparent that the driving force is experience. As Figure 3-1 suggests, a person with talent, given the appropriate experience, might develop the right stuff for effective executive leadership. The quest begins, then, by trying to understand what is meant by an "appropriate experience."

WHAT MAKES AN EXPERIENCE POWERFUL?

For managers who eventually emerged as successful executives, the experiences from which they grew the most contained significant challenges, most of them quite adverse. At their core lay one or more potent elements, such as managing difficult relationships with superiors or key staff members (recall from Chapter 2 that inability to resolve such conflicts often led to derailment), playing for high stakes, facing extremely harsh business situations, struggling with complexity of scope and scale, having the wrong background or lacking a needed skill or credential, and having to make a sudden, stark transition (see Figure 3-2).

As it turns out, certain jobs and events bring various of these "core" challenges together and, depending on which combination of challenges is present, potentially teach one or more of the lessons that executives need. Learning is driven by the things a person has to contend with in handling a particular experience, and the potential lessons in each kind of experience are determined by the overlap between what the experience demands and what a person does not yet know how to do. If, for example, a particular assignment involves leading a highly motivated group (typical of a start-up venture), it cannot teach the lessons that come from trying to motivate a demoralized group (typical of a turnaround situation). The learning possible from being in charge of a large-scale operation is simply not available to a member of a small project team. An experience can only teach what's in it, and as I will show, even that is not guaranteed.

FIGURE 3-1

THE ROLE OF EXPERIENCE: TO DRIVE THE DEVELOPMENT OF
EXECUTIVE TALENT

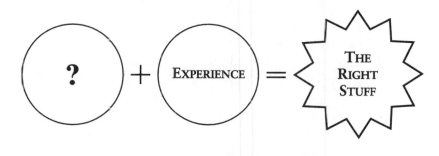

SIGNIFICANT DEVELOPMENTAL EXPERIENCES

There is now a substantial amount of research showing which specific experiences, by virtue of the demands they make, have the most developmental potential.[3] Putting these findings into practice has generated even more possibilities.[4] These experiences fall into four broad categories: job assignments; other people (specifically hierarchical superiors); hardships and setbacks; and "other," which includes formal programs and non-work experiences. The sixteen experiences identified in the first such study are presented in Figure 3-3. Because they are described in detail elsewhere, I will review them only briefly here and then discuss in more detail how they fit in the larger context of executive development.[5]

ASSIGNMENTS

Seven kinds of job assignments were identified as having unique developmental possibilities: early work experiences, first supervision, starting from scratch, fix-it (turnaround), changes in scope, special projects and task-force assignments, and a line-to-staff switch.

EARLY WORK. The potential developmental importance of early (pre-supervisory) work experiences underscores the reality

FIGURE 3-2

The Core Elements of Powerful Experiences

DIMENSION	DESCRIPTION
Job Transitions	
Unfamiliar Responsibilities	The manager must handle responsibilities that are new, very different, or much broader than previous ones.
Proving Yourself	The manager has added pressure to show others that he or she can handle the job.
Task-Related Characteristics	
Creating Change	
Developing New Directions	The manager is responsible for starting something new, making strategic changes, carrying out a re-organization, or responding to rapid changes in the business environment.
Inherited Problems	The manager has to fix problems created by the former incumbent or take over problem employees.
Reduction Decisions	Decisions about shutting down operations or staff reductions have to be made.
Problems with Employees	Employees lack adequate experience, are incompetent, or are resistant.
High Level of Responsibility	
High Stakes	Clear deadlines, pressure from senior management, high visibility, and responsibility for success or failure in this job are clearly evident.
Managing Business Diversity	The scope of the job is large, with responsibilities for multiple functions, groups, products, customers, or markets.
Job Overload	The sheer size of the job requires a large investment of time and energy.
Handling External Pressure	External factors that impact the business (e.g., negotiating with unions or government agencies, working in a foreign culture, or coping with serious community problems) must be dealt with.

FIGURE 3-2

THE CORE ELEMENTS OF POWERFUL EXPERIENCES *(Cont.)*

DIMENSION	DESCRIPTION
	TASK-RELATED CHARACTERISTICS *(Cont.)*
Nonauthority Relationships	
Influencing without Authority	Getting the job done requires influencing peers, higher management, external parties, or other key people over whom the manager has no direct authority.
	OBSTACLES
Adverse Business Conditions	The business unit or product line faces financial problems or difficult economic conditions.
Lack of Top Management Support	Senior management is reluctant to provide direction, support, or resources for current work or new projects.
Lack of Personal Support	The manager is excluded from key networks and gets little support and encouragement from others.
Difficult Boss	The manager's opinions or management style differs from those of the boss, or the boss has major shortcomings.

Source: From C. McCauley, M. Ruderman, P. Ohlott, and J. Morrow, "Assessing the Developmental Components of Managerial Jobs," *Journal of Applied Psychology* 79, 4 (1994): 544–560. Copyright ©1994 by the American Psychological Association. Adapted with permission.

that executive development begins long before a person reaches executive level. Exposure to new things was the theme of Early Work 101, as future executives entered the world of organizations and began to be pushed out of their comfort zone. It was often in these pre-supervisory jobs that people got their first taste of the difficulties of working with other people, experienced the pressure and stress of organizational life, were exposed to the realities of getting things done in a complex system, discovered specialties different than their own, or sometimes got

FIGURE 3-3

SIXTEEN DEVELOPMENTAL EXPERIENCES

Assignments

Early work experiences:
early non-managerial jobs

First supervision:
first time managing people

Starting from scratch:
building something from nothing

Fix it/turn it around:
fixing/stabilizing a failing operation

Project/task force:
discrete projects and temporary assignments done alone or as part of a team

Scope:
increase in numbers of people, dollars, and functions to manage

Line to staff switch:
moving from line operations to corporate staff roles

Hardships

Business failures and mistakes:
ideas that failed, deals that fell apart

Demotions/missed promotions/lousy jobs:
not getting a coveted job or being exiled

Subordinate performance problem:
confronting a subordinate with serious performance problems

Breaking a rut:
taking on a new career in response to discontent with the current job

Personal traumas:
crises and traumas such as divorce, illness, and death

Other People

Role models:
superiors with exceptional (good or bad) qualities

Values playing out:
"snapshots" of chain-of-command behavior that demonstrated individual or corporate values

Other Events

Coursework:
formal courses

Purely personal:
experiences outside of work

Source: Chart adapted from M. McCall, "Developing Executives Through Work Experience," and reprinted with permission from *Human Resource Planning* 11, 1 (1988): 1–12. Copyright © 1988 by The Human Resource Planning Society, 317 Madison Avenue, Suite 1509, New York, N.Y., 10017, Phone: (212) 490-6387, Fax: (212) 682-6851. Detailed descriptions of these events were originally published in E. Lindsey (now Hutchison), V. Homes, and M. McCall, *Key Events in Executives' Lives* Technical Report 32 (Greensboro, NC: Center for Creative Leadership, 1987) and M. McCall, M. Lombardo, and A. Morrison, *The Lessons of Experience* (New York: Free Press, 1988).

to go overseas and learn a new culture. It was in these early experiences that the groundwork was laid for later challenges, often including a broadening of horizons and an increase in self-confidence.

FIRST SUPERVISION. Supervising people for the first time was usually the second key event chronologically. When it was developmentally powerful, it was usually because the young manager had to learn the hard way that it was people, not the technical issues, that were the most difficult. By definition, the leap from individual contributor to manager involved a change in the scope of work, and learning to build constructive working relationships with subordinates (who may have been peers or had more experience than the new manager) became a central developmental challenge.

The transition from individual contributor to effective manager is documented fully in a thorough and enlightening book by Linda Hill.[5] Becoming a manager is, Hill concludes, no less a challenge than mastering a new identity. The result is the realization that one can be challenged by and enjoy leading others.

START-UPS. Three developmentally significant line leadership assignments were identified. One of them, start-ups, requires a manager to bring something new into existence. These experiences require taking action without really knowing how it will come out—after all, the task is by definition the creation of something new. Others look to the leader to tell them, in the face of uncertainty and inexperience, what needs doing. The leader has to learn the art of making do, of doing whatever it takes to get the job done, often with minimal or no direction from above. These assignments can be so demanding and at the same time exciting that they become addictive, and their "graduates" may not do well in the more sedate aftermath.

TURNAROUNDS. The turnaround is another of the major line leadership assignments. Sent in to fix an operation besieged with difficulties, the manager must work under intense time pressure, deal with demoralized and perhaps hostile or incompetent subordinates, untangle Byzantine complexities that underlie the mess, repair relationships within and outside of the organization, and do it all under scrutiny and with a tight budget. From these experiences managers potentially learn something about when authority works and when it doesn't, how to diagnose organizational problems, how to build credibility, make tough decisions, redesign systems, and a host of other invaluable lessons.

A comprehensive description of the demands of a turnaround, the lessons it can teach, and the process of learning those lessons is found in Jack Gabarro's book about general managers taking charge.[7] His description of the learning process provides invaluable insight not only into the challenges and the learning possibilities of turnarounds but also into the *process* of learning as the experience develops. In this kind of experience, there are distinct phases that an individual goes through as he or she "takes charge," and these phases dictate the learning possibilities in the event. The early phases of data gathering and action, for example, involves mostly application of what a general manager already knows how to do to the novel situation at hand. This approach usually improves the situation temporarily, but it begins to unravel because the initial "fix" is usually a Band-Aid. If the general manager doesn't get promoted immediately after the quick fix, the later phases force him or her to learn and act at a deeper level, which is where the majority of development takes place.

CHANGE IN SCOPE. The nature of management is such that continued progress up the hierarchy almost always carries with it increases in the scope and scale of what is managed. The complexity resulting from the scope of senior executive jobs is one of the most widely discussed aspects of executive leadership, and transforming a large organization may be one of the greatest challenges a leader can face. It can also be one of the most powerful and important developmental experiences.

Change in scope may be relative to an individual's previous

responsibilities, or it may be relative to other managerial jobs within the corporation in terms of the number of people, dollars, or functions. A career usually involves several changes in scope, but the most developmental ones tend to be those that have "first time" components. These elements, involving such things as first time managing multiple functions, first time managing a bottom line, or first time managing managers, are the grist of the potential learning. One rule of thumb from the research is that "a little more of the same" is rarely powerful for development.

A thorough treatment of the variety and demands within large-scope managerial jobs can be found in a study by Jon Bentz.[8] Although his emphasis is taxonomic and performance-based rather than developmentally focused, he points out that expanding one's perspective and then learning to integrate across perspectives is key to these kinds of jobs.

Our research showed that changes in scope can teach a variety of lessons, including learning to manage the unfamiliar (functions, businesses, people), learning to manage "by remote control" by carefully selecting and developing subordinates, delegating responsibility, learning to accept responsibility for the actions of others, and learning to develop structure and reward systems that move the organization forward.

SPECIAL PROJECTS AND TASK FORCE ASSIGNMENTS. The obvious developmental opportunity in a special project or task force assignment comes from its focused objective and short timeframe. Properly designed, such assignments provide untold opportunities to learn about products, processes, functions, customers, acquisitions, financing, joint ventures, new technologies, or almost any other aspect of the business that can be defined by a concrete set of objectives. These kinds of temporary assignments can, under the right circumstances, be just as developmental and a whole lot more cost effective than permanent job reassignments. In addition to providing a crash course in content, task forces also can provide opportunities to learn to work with different kinds of people, to negotiate with various parties, to influence without formal authority, and to present to and get to know senior executives.

Unfortunately, the potential developmental value of a task force assignment is often overlooked. High-profile projects are often staffed with only proven experts, even though some people with less expertise could probably do the job and at the same time develop more. At other times, task forces and commissions are convened over trivial issues, or the recommendations of the task force are not taken seriously by senior management—either of which has a decidedly negative effect on the willingness of talented people to be a part of one or take such an assignment seriously.

STAFF JOBS. To watch a jaw drop or a heart stop, tell a line executive he or she has just been given a staff assignment. Although they'd rather have a root canal, successful executives who have had certain kinds of staff jobs report that they have learned vital lessons from them. The developmentally powerful staff jobs usually had three characteristics: they involved analyzing a major product line or business, often from a marketing, financial, or strategic planning perspective; they involved a move from a field operation to headquarters, requiring the manager to adjust to the "culture" at the home office; and the manager worked for more senior—often quite a bit more senior—executives.

The lessons potentially learned flowed directly from these demands. Looking at whole parts of the business from a strategy perspective lifted the manager out of day-to-day, tactical concerns and led to an understanding of the infamous "big picture." Living in the usually unique corporate culture and working with top executives taught numerous lessons in how the corporation viewed the business, how to deal with executives, and how to exert influence without formal authority.

OTHER PEOPLE

Sometimes the potential for growth comes not so much from the content of an assignment as it does from something incidental to the task. Such was the case with exceptional bosses, good or bad, because they could influence development regardless of the assignment. Inability to adapt to a boss with a different style was a prominent derailment factor, so logically one of the most important lessons from exceptional bosses was learning to work effectively with them. Over time, exposure to bosses with a variety of styles and approaches is a key developmental factor.

Although there is no question that a developing manager can learn from anyone, perhaps because of the power vested in their positions, bosses and superiors in the hierarchy held a special place in successful executives' lives. Those with a lasting impact were exceptional in some way—about two-thirds were positive; about a third were seen as extremely negative. Of these heroes and devils, the most powerful teachers of all were, like the tragic heros in the ancient Greek plays, individuals of great accomplishment brought down by a fatal flaw. There were few natural coaches or mentors.

Learning from bosses, then, took several forms. One aspect was learning to adapt to their styles or, in the case of the ogres, to cope with their style. From another angle, one could learn from whatever expertise the exceptional boss had—and that could range from technical knowledge to interpersonal skill. Finally, and perhaps most importantly, developing executives learned what was truly valued by the organization by observing the behavior of these role models and the consequences of that behavior.

HARDSHIPS

Five of the potentially developmental experiences had little to do with a particular job or assignment but instead involved a jarring or even traumatic event that took place during that assignment (or, in some cases, off the job entirely). The hardships identified as having important developmental consequences for successful executives were business failures and mistakes, demotions or missed promotions or lousy jobs, taking the risk of changing career direction (what we call "breaking a rut"), confronting a subordinate performance problem, and personal trauma.

Whereas most of the experiences reviewed so far built self-confidence, the hardships were about personal limits and learning to cope with life's darker side. Ranging from the death of a loved one to giving up a secure job to seek a new direction, a common theme was getting through the tough time and emerging the wiser for it. These events had three elements in common: "Managers accepted appropriate responsibility for the mess they were in; during the worst of it they experienced a strong sense of aloneness or lack of control over events; and the situation forced them to confront themselves. It was this struggle with 'who (or what) I am' that made these events unique and triggered intensely personal learning."[9]

Most of the hardships are not amenable, physically or morally, to organizational manipulation for developmental purposes. The organization's handling of business failures and mistakes, however, is such a critical part of development that it deserves special attention. Most learning involves trying something, making mistakes, correcting them, and trying again, until one gets it right. Managers tend to be action oriented by nature, so trial and error, more than reflection, is a critical learning strategy. Yet error is not always embraced in results-oriented companies, despite widespread recognition that mistakes are an essential part of learning and growth.

The data on the developmental impact of failures and mistakes as reported in *Key Events in Executives' Lives* does not imply that organizations should be soft or cavalier about mistakes. The greatest learning seems to occur when the person making the mistake accepts responsibility for it and the consequences. Responsibility and accountability are key components, as is valid feedback. But there is a difference between living with the consequences of a mistake and having one's career at risk because the organizational climate is overly harsh. When an organization is perceived to be intolerant of mistakes, it doesn't necessarily reduce the number of mistakes made. Rather, it can very effectively reduce the number of mistakes discovered and analyzed and the willingness of perpetrators to accept the responsibility for the mistakes they make. In short, intolerance of mistakes wastes important developmental opportunities that have already been paid for.

FORMAL PROGRAMS

Company-sponsored training and external programs have been for too long the focal point of management and executive development. Although formal programs can be significant developmental events, educational programs are clearly complementary or supplementary to on-the-job experiences, which in turn are only part of a much larger and more complicated process of development. To define executive development in terms of the amount of money spent on internal and external education, the size of the training staff, the external reputation of the training programs, or related criteria is to shine a spotlight on an empty lot. Organizations that do a good job of developing leadership often have a strong commitment to formal education as well.[10] Nonetheless, it is important to keep in mind that programs are but a small part of the whole.

Despite all the attention training receives, it is not always used effectively. A great deal of energy may be spent on developing the content of programs, but the most frequent lesson learned from significant formal programs was self-confidence.[11] Unless it is integrated into the larger context of experience, training can end up an expensive but isolated set-piece with little, if any, lasting impact. Later in this book I return to how training can play a pivotal role as a substitute for experience and as a vehicle for helping people learn more from the experiences they have already had.

NONWORK EVENTS

It is surely not the case that all development or even all executive development takes place at work. Life is an interesting place with a multitude of developmental opportunities, from raising children (nothing is quite as developmental as a teenage child!) to spiritual discovery. The non-work ("purely personal") experiences with developmental impact on successful executives were diverse, "from athletics to politics, from early family life to running volunteer organizations, from private inspiration to military leadership—the developmentally significant personal events shared the same characteristics as job-related ones: diversity, working with other people, getting a job done in the face of obstacles."[12]

Although many organizations encourage involvement in community activities, the developmental potential of these opportunities often is overlooked by managers. Busy people are naturally inclined to make their voluntary service as efficient as possible, so they often choose activities consistent with existing expertise, when development results from doing something *different* from one's current strengths. For example, a person comfortable with finance might volunteer to keep the books for the church, when he or she would learn more by leading the fundraising campaign, managing the new building project, or taking a role in the next play. It is not unusual that the risk involved in trying something new at work is too high, so non-work options can be crucial to personal development.

PERSPECTIVES ON EXPERIENCE

Historically, organizational experience has been thought of in terms of generic job titles and types, and learning from them approached as stepwise sequences of increasing responsibility and exposure through rotation. For example, following a typical career path, a person might start as an accountant in a small plant, move up to accounting manager, then plant controller, then plant controller in a larger facility, and so on. An engineer might progress from individual contributor to project manager of a small project, to project manager of a larger project, to functional engineering manager. These are logical, small-step developmental sequences similar to the military model of progress through ranks.

To counter the limited development that can result from small steps within narrow corridors, people considered high potential for more senior managerial jobs are sometimes "rotated" across functional or business lines to give them "exposure" to other parts of the business considered important to senior-level perspective. A person who has spent most of a career in operations, for example, might need exposure to marketing or finance and therefore be given a rotational assignment in one or both of those functions.

Based on the kinds of experiences that resulted in significant development, these traditional approaches have serious limitations—at least for the development of executive leadership talent. In a longitudinal study of management progress, Ann Howard and Doug Bray reported that "the men who advanced furthest tended not to be promoted in a straight line through the same type of function. Movement between departments was common, as was movement to different geographical locations."[13] Their data support the observation that more of the same (small steps up in responsibility), assignments with little or only modest challenge (exposure), and bosses who were pretty much alike got little attention and had relatively small developmental impact.

INTERNATIONAL ASSIGNMENTS

As business has become more globally competitive, the traditional approach has been applied to the development of "international" executives. It is now de rigueur for high-potential managers to be given an international assignment, but often the rationale goes little beyond an assumption that a "stint overseas" can be quite developmental. Figure 3-4 lists a variety of lessons expatriate managers said they learned overseas, including managerial skills, tolerance of ambiguity, multiple perspectives, and working with others. Yet the sixteen developmental experiences summarized earlier in this chapter has no category labeled "international." The reason for this provides an opportunity to contrast the traditional approach to on-the-job development with the implications of more recent research.

The absence of a separate category for international experience does not mean that none of the experiences were

FIGURE 3-4

WHAT MANAGERS LEARN OVERSEAS

Managerial Skills	Asking questions
	Reaching compromise
	Being more open-minded
	Being able to deal with a broader range of people
Tolerance of Ambiguity	Making decisions with little information
	Taking action without understanding how everything works
Multiple Perspectives	Seeing things from other people's points of view
	Anticipating others' actions
Ability to Work with Others	"Tolerating" different kinds of people
	Communicating more
	Anticipating own impact more

Source: Adapted from N. Adler, *International Dimensions of Organizational Behavior,* 2nd ed. (Boston: PWS-Kent, 1991), 240.

international. In fact, many of the experiences reported in *The Lessons of Experience* were international assignments, and frequently, doing whatever they had to do in a country other than their own was just another element that made the managers' experience challenging.[14] So, for example, a turnaround in a foreign country or a start-up overseas would present an additional challenge—*if* the location created significant demands. The key, as always, is what the talented person is challenged to do, not where the challenge takes place. Twenty percent of foreign assignments are start-ups, for example, and I would argue that that aspect is the heart of the developmental experience. The location can make the start-up even more challenging, thereby enriching the learning, or it can be irrelevant.

A recent survey of expatriate assignments indicated that people are usually sent for one of three reasons: there is a need for technical expertise; the assignment is seen as a developmental opportunity; or there is a perceived shortage of local talent. Having had an international assignment does not necessarily create an international manager, especially if what a person does overseas is "more of the same" and the challenges presented by the location are mild.

TRAINING

As with international assignments, this larger perspective on how various on-line experiences develop leaders also brings the real potential for training interventions into sharper focus. By viewing training as an experience and by trying to construct training interventions so they have elements similar to powerful experiences, training can serve very important roles in the development of executive talent. Training can be used as a substitute for experiences that are not widely available or are too risky for "rookies" (e.g., simulations, action learning). Training can be used as a supplemental experience to provide learning opportunities that are useful in addition to what is already happening on the job (e.g., a university-based strategy program simultaneously with a staff assignment in strategic planning). Training can also be used to create new experiences to prepare people for future states that do not yet exist within the organization (e.g., simulations based on future scenarios or new structures).

DEVELOPMENT IS A SUNK COST

It should be obvious that in at least one important way, development is a sunk cost for the organization. Assignments exist and are filled. People are sent overseas. Exceptionally good and bad bosses exist in the system, and somebody works for them. Mistakes happen and things go awry. Some kind of training is going on, somewhere. The question is, are all of these experiences being used in ways that develop needed leadership skills efficiently, or is the outcome left to chance (or worse, is the system producing ineffective leaders). Development is not so much about building new systems (the inundation-in-bureaucracy approach) as it is about using what already happens in a wiser manner.

There is a direct link between the kinds of experiences that prove to be most developmental and the "dangerous situations" that precipitate many derailments. New assignments can carry with them various kinds of trouble, difficult bosses and relationships, unfamiliar job content, and a host of other elements that can be seen as challenges or as threats. Risk is involved in growth, especially in taking on the unknown. The challenges of individual transformation are the stuff of myth and legend.

Homer tells the story of Ulysses' journey in his epic poem the *Odyssey*. Having survived imprisonment by a sea nymph, the magic spell of the lotus-eaters, capture by a one-eyed Cyclops, seduction by the enchantress Circe, the horror of the underworld, sea monsters and the Sirens, a thunderbolt that destroyed his ship, and noblemen who attempted to take his throne and his wife, Ulysses is portrayed as a model of courage and determination who overcomes obstacles and setbacks and is transformed forever by his experience. For all that, Tennyson has said, "Yet all experience is an arch wherethrough gleams that untravelled world." Ulysses was not forged by an executive development program.

David Oldfield, drawing on the classic work of Joseph Campbell[15] as well as on his own extensive scholarship,[16] describes the myth of the hero's journey as common to all cultures around the world and reflecting something deeply embedded in the human psyche. The journey consists of four parts:

The call to adventure (leaving the comfort of the known for the danger of the unknown, usually out of desperation).

Finding your path (choosing how to navigate the unknown— the path of convention or the path of individual quest—by deciding what it is you seek, and by articulating by what principles you will seek it—a code of honor).

The road of trials and obstacles (facing challenges that test the undeveloped parts of you).

The return journey and ceremony of passage (returning to share—to give away—what has been gained or learned from the quest).

The developmental experience of choice has always been the one that takes people beyond their current strengths. An old Viking saying reflects this reality: What doesn't kill you outright will make you stronger.

WHAT EXPERIENCE?

Unfortunately, using experience for development is not as simple a matter as it appears, else one could give a talented manager a start-up, a fix-it, a miserable boss, a divorce, a few sea monsters, and *voilà*, he or she would emerge a leader. If nothing else was learned from the halcyon days of career paths, it was that the development of talented leaders could not be programmed by a standard series of sequential jobs. Given that many different experiences can be useful, and given that no one lives long enough to have all the experiences that would be useful, are there any guidelines for practice? Fortunately, the longer-term best interests of the business are consistent with rational use of experience to develop the leadership needed to meet the challenges critical to strategic success.

LINKING BUSINESS STRATEGY AND EXECUTIVE DEVELOPMENT

THE PURPOSE OF EXECUTIVE DEVELOPMENT IS TO PREPARE leaders for the challenges put forth by the business environment and a corporation's strategic intent. Achieving this purpose does not mean starting over or from scratch because organizations, intentionally or not, are already developing some of the required leadership skills, or they would cease to exist. To improve the "natural" process that has already evolved, the business strategy must be defined sufficiently so that critical leadership challenges can be identified. In short, the development of future leaders requires that current leaders have a tangible vision for their organization against which to assess the kind of leaders already being created and to determine what the future will demand.

The first step in this process is to make explicit what is happening developmentally to talented people in an organization at the present time.

IDENTIFYING THE PROCESSES ALREADY AT WORK

Organizations develop people whether they mean to or not, and whether or not they have formal programs in place. What the current "system" produces may or may not be cream, but people who occupy key leadership positions were shaped by the experiences they had in their careers. If future executives are having similar experiences, they likely are developing similar skills, while maintaining or even developing similar deficits. How can existing developmental experiences and the results they are producing—some of which may be inadvertent—be identified?

From a developmental perspective, business units or divisions can be thought of as "schools," each with a "curriculum" consisting of the experiences and exposures common to people who are successful within that part of the business.[1] People who have successfully worked their way through a business unit are likely to have acquired certain predictable skills. (At the risk of pushing the metaphor too far, they might be thought of as "graduates" of a particular school, with a "degree" in the core competence of that unit.) For example, a division that manufactures high-volume products at low cost might produce "graduates" who have finely honed operational skills—who understand quality programs, process improvement, teams, cost control, and the like. At the same time, "graduates" of this hypothetical division who have not had other experiences predictably may be weak in such areas as marketing, strategic or financial analysis, or customer service. Each business unit or function (or other appropriate chunk) can be profiled in this way, creating a road map of implicit developmental pathways and the resulting learning, both positive and negative. Some "chunks" may have multiple pathways that are followed by successful people; others may have no common experiences, or the key experience might be working for a particular person in a system. The experience a person has may be determined by the phase of the business cycle the business unit is in at a given moment of time.

Although the particular patterns are subject to change, the analytical approach assumes that the nature of the business and the structure of work in each part of the organization determines the patterns of experience that talented people will have. The nature of those experiences in turn dictates what they could learn and what learnings they are not exposed to.

A Case Example of a Company's "Schools"

Mention company schools (or, as has become the popular phraseology, "corporate universities") and people usually think of Motorola University, General Electric's Crotonville, or one of the other benchmark corporate training centers. In reality, the more powerful education may be in the classroom of on-line experience in the various functions and business units of a corporation. One large U.S. company attempted to find out about its on-line classrooms by interviewing executives and human resource professionals involved in assessing high-potential managers in its business units and functional departments. A series of questions was asked about what "graduates" of the different divisions and functions were good—and not so good—at doing.[2] As is true of most companies, talented people in this one usually progressed up a chimney or silo, holding a sequence of key jobs at the core of that function or business. Those reaching the top in a particular chimney tended to have great depth in the relatively narrow range of skills required for effectiveness within the piece of the business they were in. Not surprisingly, what they did well reflected what they had been immersed in for so long; problems occurred later when these talented people took on multifunctional responsibilites or moved into a business with a very different character. Because these people had proven track records of success, albeit in particular chimneys, it was assumed that they wouldn't need any help making the transition to the new responsibility (a right stuff assumption), and the absence of any help sometimes spelled the difference between a developmental leap and a dramatic derailment (see Chapter 8).

Examples of business unit profiles showing the strengths and weaknesses of successful managers are provided in Figure 4-1 (details have been altered to preserve anonymity). Profiling the appropriate units of an organization (which might include geographic and functional segments as well as business units or

FIGURE 4-1

GRADUATES OF CORPORATE BUSINESS UNITS AS "SCHOOLS"

Division/ Function	Division A (market-driven)	Division B (operations-driven)	Division C (growth-oriented)	Function 1 (finance)	Function 2 (human resources)
What they are likely to be good at . . .	• Resourcefulness • Entrepreneurialism • Risk taking • Getting things done	• Execution • Using systems superbly • Efficiency • Teamwork	• Competition • Getting results • Working hard • Flexibility, changing quickly	• Analysis • Strategic thinking • Detail	• Resourcefulness • Technical issues • Persuasion • Teamwork
What they are *not* likely to be good at . . .	• Consistency • Disciplined action • Using corporate systems • Teamwork	• Responding to customers • Change • Seeing the big picture	• Taking a longer-term perspective • Balancing life and work • Sensitivity to people	• Getting results • Turning ideas into action • Influencing line managers	• Leading others • Risk taking

Note: "Divisions" consist of multiple business units offering similar types of products or services.

divisions) generates a "big picture" of how leaders in each of them develop from their experiences. The next step is to identify the specific experiences within each discrete segment that account for the lessons learned there. As was noted in Chapter 3, it is the clustering of developmentally powerful experiences created by a business unit or function that matters, not the business unit or function per se. By knowing what specific experiences make the biggest difference it is possible to make more efficient use of the prior career experiences of talented managers (potentially shortening the time they stay within a chimney) and to focus developmental moves more sharply on the most significant experiences within the array afforded by a particular part of the company.

A corporate profile (metaphorically, the "university" containing of all the schools) can be essential for determining which parts of the organization develop the skills needed for the future, what kinds of developmental opportunities are missing relative to the business strategy, which cross-boundary moves can be justified by strategic need, and where developmental interventions might be most useful.

SKILLS FOR THE FUTURE

As an organization gazes into its crystal ball to determine what it needs to do to fulfill its destiny, understanding where its talented people can learn particular skills takes on unique importance. In a large, diverse corporation like the one in this case study, "schools" for just about anything can be found somewhere within the organization. Where, exactly, may not be obvious (if the needs are for the future, the experiences may not yet exist in a high-profile division), and talented people might not readily accept developmental assignments in what they perceive to be a corporate backwater. Nonetheless, finding internal experiences to use to develop leaders for future demands can reduce the need to hire from the outside for new skills or to develop expensive new programs. For example, many corporations facing increased competition feel that their survival may depend on entrepreneurial leadership that can overcome bureaucratic inertia. One approach, and perhaps the first one thought of, is to hire executives from entrepreneurial firms—importing talent to implement the strategic mandate. The assumption (another "right stuff" one, at that) is that executives with a track record of entrepreneurial success will be as effective within a different organization—that their skills are transferable to a new environment. There is, however, a substantial risk that new hires may not be able to effectively use the skills honed elsewhere, because the culture of the firm, the people with whom critical relationships must be built, and the way business is conducted are all different. An alternative that reduces this possibility of failure is to find parts of the existing organization—no matter how obscure—where entrepreneurship is flourishing. Not only is it likely that the managers and executives within this unit are learning the skills the future requires but also that this unit is a valuable educational resource for other talented managers who could learn new skills.

MISSING DEVELOPMENTAL OPPORTUNITIES

It is certainly possible that an organization profile does not contain learning fields for some leadership capabilities foreseen in the crystal ball. To pursue the last example, analysis may fail to unearth a pocket of entrepreneurial endeavor within an ossified bureaucracy. This information, too, can be invaluable, because achieving the business strategy will require a different approach—perhaps justifying outside hiring as a short-term remedy but more importantly suggesting that the structure of the organization may need a fundamental change. The implication is that a "school" must be created where none exists, else the organization will be forever dependent on finding people on the outside. From a leadership perspective, this kind of redesign, driven by developmental needs, is itself a developmental experience for existing leaders. They now have to face some tough issues—how do managers learn to be entrepreneurs? What experiences do talented people need to get good at entrepreneurship?

The same reasoning can be applied to just about any aspect of a new strategic direction. Where do people learn how to create shareholder value? To operate with an international mind-set? To change an organization's culture? Solving a talent shortage created by strategic direction involves finding or creating experiences that can develop the needed leadership skills.

JUSTIFYING CROSS-BOUNDARY MOVES

As an analysis of "schools" makes very clear, organizations have many internal boundaries, some of which are impenetrable. Switching from one business unit or division to another with a different product or service, moving from line to staff or vice versa, leaving the field organization for a stint at headquarters, transferring from the domestic to the international organization, or otherwise moving talented people across organizational boundaries can be very expensive. There are basic out-of-pocket costs (as high as $500,000 to $1 million for some international moves) if relocation is involved. There is the cost of the inevitable learning curve as someone tries to adjust to a new environment—not to mention any business losses resulting from the learning curve. A business unit losing a talented, effective person has no assurance that a replacement will be as good. There is a reasonable chance that the change will be too dramatic and that the valuable person attempting it will not like it and leave, or may fail. With all these dark clouds, a reluctance to make cross-boundary moves is not surprising, even when the principle of broadening is accepted by a corporation. Viewing a corporation as a collection of "schools" and knowing the lessons each of them can teach offers a more efficient way to approach developmental cross-boundary transfers. First, there may be experiences within the current unit or within a more similar unit that eliminate the need to jump a major boundary. This possibility is particularly important to assess for expatriate assignments, wherein the cost is great but the learning objective may be vague. "School" thinking forces the question of why a person is being given a certain posting and whether the cost can be justified, given the availability of another assignment just down the road that has the right curriculum!

Second, when a boundary jump is necessary, for instance, to break out of the mind-set of a particular function, profiles can help focus the jump into an environment with strategic relevance. Once again, this kind of thinking forces the why and what questions—why am I moving this person, and what is it I want him or her to learn?

WHERE DEVELOPMENTAL INTERVENTIONS ARE MOST USEFUL

Perhaps the future is so different from the present that all bets are off. Maybe all of today's "schools" will be obsolete. To develop leaders with new skill sets may require new schools geared toward that future, and these may take the form of project or task force assignments that deal with specific issues anticipated as future challenges. If the problems of the future are not occurring naturally, a training intervention based on action learning—assigning managers to solve organizational problems as part of a leadership development program—might be considered. The point is that thinking of organizations as schools does not artificially limit what might be added to the curriculum.

"SCHOOLS" AND PATTERNS OF DERAILMENT

Understanding the de facto developmental implications of structurally determined "schools" also reveals some of the causes of derailment in an organization. In one company, for example, technically superior individuals were attracted to staff jobs where they performed brilliant analytical work but failed to develop the action orientation necessary to help line management implement the ideas or to help themselves carry out the ideas. They derailed either because their brilliance led to arrogance, which was not appreciated by their higher-level customers, or because they couldn't adapt to the nonreflective pace of a line operation.

High potential managers coming out of line jobs in the business units into strategic planning or support positions tended to show opposite patterns. They had learned that being action oriented, results oriented, and execution oriented led to effective performance, but the same behavior in a new role led to a neglect of more reflective strategic analysis. In addition, they were sometimes so abrasive in their single-minded fixation on results that they were unable to cultivate effective working relationships in the new context.

Both examples highlight how the learning from certain kinds of experience, determined by the nature of the job and rewarded by success, can result in patterns of behavior that eventually become counterproductive. Not all the lessons learned in "school" are constructive.

Understanding what an organization is teaching its talented people is only the starting point. Development is about the future, not about the past or even the present. What is working now may be relevant in the future, but business strategies almost always entail some change. Hockey legend Wayne Gretzky once observed that it's not as important to know where the puck is now as to know where it will be.[3] From a developmental perspective, the challenge is to translate strategic intent into leadership requirements. Put another way, an organization's ability to achieve strategic objectives will depend in large part on the leadership ability of executive leaders. That said, a significant part of the strategy must be concerned with how those leaders will be found, bought, or developed. If the implicit development system just discussed is already producing executive talent that has the skills needed for the future as defined by the strategy, then the strategic leadership issue is locating those people. If other corporations are developing the kinds of leaders this corporation needs for the future, then a short-term solution is to raid those companies for the needed talent. But if the goal is to develop a sustained strategic advantage through the quality of leadership, a rational organization will find a way to systematically develop its own talent.

TRANSLATING A BUSINESS STRATEGY INTO DEVELOPMENT ACTIONS

There are many reasons that organizations invest time, energy, and money in activities related to developing executive talent. For some, these activities are dictated by fashion or habit—after all, most of the benchmark-worthy companies have some kind of program. For others, it is a philosophical and moral choice: education, growth, and development are seen as good in their own right, whether or not they contribute to the bottom line. (As an educator, I'm rather fond of this reasoning.) For still others, the primary motivation is the belief that effective leadership is critical to organizational success.

"Keeping up with the Joneses" as a reason for executive development activities is as ephemeral a motivation as the latest fad. It is true that a few widely admired corporations have maintained a strong and long-term commitment to activities that can be called developmental, but far more have demonstrated an intermittent commitment to development or have themselves disappeared from the "most admired" list despite their development practices. There are no guarantees that the Joneses' programs are effective, that they would work in a different corporate culture even if they are effective at home, or that internal development practices are the reason a company has been successful for so long. As a result, companies that get involved in development "because good companies are doing it" can end up with programs that flit from fad to fad, have only superficial connections to the business strategy, and disappear rapidly when the fads fade or the benchmark companies run into trouble. They disappear even more rapidly when bottom-line performance goes sour and cost-cutting campaigns identify peripheral activities.

Development that springs from moral and philosophical grounds may be more enduring, or at least be supported with more passion by the senior executive(s) who believe in it. At the same time, however, many of the same problems described above may arise. Because development is a moral rather than business imperative, the activities do not necessarily integrate with or enhance business outcomes. Sole reliance on a philosophical rationale leaves developmental activities vulnerable to fluctuations in business performance, especially if the board of directors or financial analysts don't share the sponsor's moral convictions. In addition, moral and philosophical beliefs don't necessarily dictate effective practice. On the one hand, strong beliefs can translate into doctrinaire practices that may not be effective in developing people. (The T-group fad of the 1960s might be an example of a philosophically driven technique that did not fulfill its promise.) On the other hand, belief in the value of general educational experiences may not translate into specific, transferable leadership skills. Sending people to university programs, bringing in outside speakers, giving sabbatical leaves, establishing exchange programs with government, and a host of other activities might fulfill the philosophical goal of broad education, but they also may amount to a jumble of unconnected, sometimes contradictory, unevenly applied, extremely expensive, and largely ineffective programs. In short, a general moral imperative may result in a hodgepodge that is extremely difficult to justify from a business perspective and is therefore highly dependent on the commitment of the executive sponsor. Should the sponsor retire, leave the company, or have insufficient power to stave off nonbelievers, then the moral and philosophical foundation can crumble quickly, taking with it whatever programs were spawned.

The third reason for investing in development is that it actually is critical to organizational performance. Most senior executives will readily agree that effective leadership is important to an organization's success, if for no other reason than to justify their existence. But making the leap from "leadership is important" to "leadership can be developed by these activities" can be a substantial challenge. Part of the chasm results from the "right stuff" assumptions discussed earlier—there is skepticism about the possibility of developing leadership ability. Another part of the chasm is the vague connection between "leadership" and business performance, which is compounded by the vaguer connection between activities identified as developmental and their relationship to the quality of leadership.

The difficulty in showing believable connections between actions generally identified as "leadership" or "executive" development and business results has many contributing factors. First, neither term usually is defined well enough to indicate whether a connection *should* exist. Many programs and activities might be called developmental, and as Chapter 3 showed, many developmental experiences might never be classified as part of a developmental program. Not only are the components somewhat difficult to identify, it's often not clear how the pieces need to fit together for their impact to be felt. If an executive has had a few "developmental" opportunities, is he or she developed yet? Of course, one would like to think that "business results" are more concrete than development results, but obviously there is ambiguity about the "best" measures of business performance. Is it one or more of the Rs (ROI, ROA)? Stock price? Shareholder value? Profit? Growth? Market share? Quality? Service standards? If it is one or more of those things, over what period of time does it need to be sustained? Even if there is agreement on performance indicators, to which of them is it reasonable to expect that quality of leadership would relate? If there is an expected relationship, to what extent does leadership alone determine the outcome, or are other forces also able to affect the results?

The second factor making it difficult to connect executive development with business results is the common misconception of what real development consists of. Often defined as internal or external courses to which people are sent and as human resources programs, such as career planning, mentoring, diversity, or rotation, the evaluation of impact is limited to perhaps the least powerful components of development. In Chapter 3, a strong case was made that most powerful developmental experiences—the ones that cause people to change and therefore are most likely to influence business outcome— occur on the job rather than in a program of some kind. The probability of finding a connection between development and results increases dramatically if truly developmental experiences are considered in addition to human resource programs.

A third difficulty is that development activities are rarely linked to strategic business objectives, much less derived directly from them. Furthermore, they are rarely designed or controlled by people with strategic business responsibilities or experience. As a result, it is not uncommon for development to be viewed by line management as a disconnected set of programs run by the human resources department with little relevance to business performance. When viewed this way, executive development may end up treated like a luxury, something that is nice to have when you can afford it and to attend when there isn't something important going on.

That said, there clearly are benchmark companies (General Electric, Motorola, and PepsiCo, to name only a few) that make strong linkages between strategy and human resource development. But where this is not true, the single most important part of designing an executive development system well may be deriving it directly from the business strategy (not just trying to manufacture post hoc connections), involving senior line management in its creation, and making it an integral part of running the business. These principles are common to any kind of change where commitment of the users is highly desired and where the designers of a process are not the primary users of it. Knowing what needs to be done and doing it, however, are different things. Designing an executive development process integral to the business, putting teeth in it, and enforcing it require superb leadership from the human resources staff.

There are, no doubt, many equally effective ways to approach this daunting task, one of which is outlined in Figure 4-2 and was used in the case example that follows.

Figure 4-2 builds on the principles of development elaborated thus far, specifically the results of the derailment research that affirm that executive leadership ability is not an innate attribute and must be developed over time, and that on-line experiences are the primary source for acquiring these abilities. Beginning with the business strategy, Figure 4-2 weaves a tapestry

FIGURE 4-2

TRANSLATING BUSINESS STRATEGY INTO AN EXECUTIVE DEVELOPMENT SYSTEM

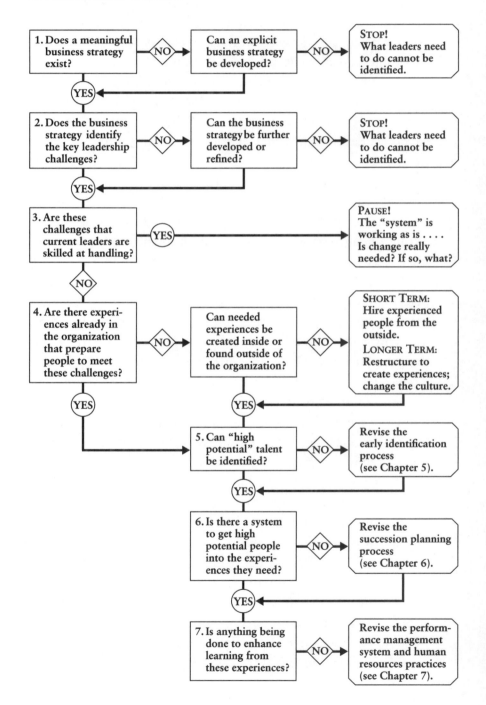

that ends with a specific process for developing the leadership talent the strategy requires.[4]

As the first box in Figure 4-2 indicates, executive development starts with the strategic intent of a business. There must be an explicit business strategy (or vision, mission statement, or "point of view") that provides meaningful (defined as actually affecting behavior) direction for the company into the foreseeable future. The strategy does not have to be elaborate, but it must have enough substance so that the leadership requirements for carrying it out can be inferred. Even if the business environment is largely unpredictable, making specific strategies impossible to determine, there must at least be a strategy for dealing with the uncertainty. Figure 4-2 suggests that if a strategy cannot be elucidated, there is no point in proceeding with executive development. There is no way to determine what leaders need to be able to do and therefore no basis for helping them learn how to do it.

If there is a business strategy, it still may not be easy to discover the leadership implications. Lofty goals like "best in the world" or "customer driven," and performance targets geared to market share, ROA, profitability, cost, stock price, and the like, say little about the leadership actions required to achieve them or the obstacles that may need to be overcome.

The second box in Figure 4-2 tackles the leadership implications of the business strategy. What challenges will leaders face as they try to enact the strategy? Put another way, what must they be able to *do* to successfully meet the challenges that lie ahead? What must leaders be able to *do* if the organization is to achieve a return on investment of 10 percent? Or 20 percent? What must leaders be able to *do* if the organization is to become a flat, lean, responsive, team-based competitor? What must leaders be able to *do* if the company is to successfully move into China, India, Vietnam, and the former Soviet Union?

Notice that the question in the second box is not about the attributes leaders must have but rather about the challenges they will face and what they must be able to do if they are to successfully meet those challenges. By focusing on situations and challenges rather than on personal characteristics, it is possible to avoid the "right stuff" trap of development. Asking about leaders' attributes generates the usual list of characteristics—flexible, smart, results oriented—but produces little useful information. If, for example, leaders must be flexible, then where do people learn to be flexible? Where do they learn to be smart? Most likely, the conversation ends with the conclusion that one really can't learn those things; one either has them or doesn't. Concluding that, the only rational approach is to select people with the needed attributes. If, however, the focus is on how to meet a particular challenge, then one can talk about experiences that prepare a person for the challenge. Suppose, for example, the strategy calls for alliances as a means of future growth. What can be done to prepare executives to effectively handle alliances? A list of possibilities might include experience as a team member on an alliance task force, leading a small negotiation with less at stake, or attending a training program on the nature of strategic partnerships.[5] The result, one hopes, is an executive who has developed the knowledge and skills to act in an appropriately flexible manner in putting together the alliance.

If the leadership implications of the business strategy cannot be identified, Figure 4-2 suggests that executive development would be an empty exercise. If the factors that affect business outcomes are all outside the control of the leaders of the organization, it doesn't matter whether or not they have developed a particular set of abilities.

If the central challenges facing leaders of the business have been identified, box three looks at how well the current (implicit) development system is doing at producing leaders who can handle those challenges. If the challenges are pretty much the same as they have been in the past, and if the organization is very good at meeting those challenges, then there would seem to be little need to meddle with existing development activities. More likely, however, step three will produce a mixture of challenges, some of which executives are quite good at handling but some of which represent new areas or issues that executives in this organization have not handled well in the past. It is these latter challenges that drive the developmental possibilities, bringing us back to the findings reported in Chapter 3. What kinds of experiences will talented people need to have to learn how to handle the strategic situations ahead?

That question leads to the fourth box in Figure 4-2, which asks whether those experiences exist now, somewhere in the organization, or whether they can be created or found outside of the organization. If they neither exist nor can be created, the chart suggests that there is little choice but to hire the skills from outside (which also may be the only alternative if there is not enough time to develop the needed abilities internally), at least for the short term. Resorting to hiring from the outside should, however, raise serious questions about why an organization cannot develop the people it needs for the strategy it has. Exploring this issue may uncover a need for restructuring so that developmental opportunities are created or for changing the culture so that developmental activities are given priority.

Boxes five, six, and seven take up the process after developmental experiences have been identified. Somehow, people with the talent to develop the needed skills must be identified, mechanisms must be found to get those talented people into the opportunities, and something must be done to help them learn from the opportunities. These ideas are developed in subsequent chapters. For now, I present a case study of a corporation that attempted to use the first four boxes in Figure 4-2 to refine its already effective executive development system in the context of its changing strategic priorities.

TRANSLATING STRATEGY INTO DEVELOPMENTAL NEEDS: A CASE STUDY

There are many ways the leadership implications of a corporate strategy can be determined. The CEO can dictate them; a consultant can draft them for executive approval; the latest management theory might be adopted. Like the formation of the strategy, however, the process by which developmental needs and a system for meeting them are identified has the potential to create important benefits beyond just the resulting system. One corporation's experience provides an example of how the process can be applied.[6]

More than almost any other U.S. corporation, this one believed in developing executives by providing them with challenging job assignments. Already in place was a sophisticated system of assessment that annually evaluated management potential from top to bottom of the corporation. From the assessments was generated a human resource plan and a high-potential pool of managers and executives that was reviewed regularly by the executive committee. The corporation exercised its authority to move "corporate property" across business and functional boundaries for developmental reasons.

The company also had a focused and ambitious business strategy. Like a great many large U.S. corporations, this one found its growth in its mature home market constrained. Yet its stockholders had come to expect the handsome returns generated by healthy growth, leaving management determined to find new ways to gain advantage in domestic markets and to better exploit the exploding but volatile international markets. The problem the company faced was not limits on the potential for growth but rather the limited number of talented executives available to take advantage of the many growth opportunities. Even though its human resource development practices had made it a benchmark company, the strategy required that it become even more efficient at developing needed executive talent. Hoping to "accelerate development," the executive committee, consisting of all the business unit heads as well as the heads of the corporate staff functions, met to reconsider the executive development process.

A variety of approaches was used in the reconsideration, but one of them followed the basic steps outlined in Figure 4-2, beginning with translation of the business plan. These executives had developed the strategic business plan and were accountable for achieving it, so they were in a unique position to identify the key leadership challenges. Although several major thrusts of the strategy were analyzed, only one will be considered in this example: sustained growth.

FROM STRATEGY TO LEADERSHIP CHALLENGES

As a first step, a group of executives well versed in the meaning and implications of the growth strategy identified critical situations that future executives would need to handle well if the strategy were to be successfully carried out. With the help of a facilitator, the lively discussion generated thirteen such critical situations, each described in sufficient detail to distinguish it from the others.[7] These situations included things like coping with the complexity resulting from growth, creating an environment and structure that treats change as normal, and providing superior value to customers in the face of rising expectations. An abbreviated sampling of these situations is displayed in Figure 4-3.

FROM CHALLENGES TO DEVELOPMENTAL EXPERIENCES

After agreeing on the critical situations dictated by the growth strategy, the executives had to assess whether dealing effectively with such situations was an existing strength of executives who had been successful in the organization, or whether it represented a new or untested ability that might require developmental attention. Assuming that executive capabilities already developed (whether intentionally or not) will continue to be developed, the new capabilities serve to focus developmental efforts and the next phase of the analysis on future requirements.[8]

Figure 4-4 provides some examples of the executives' conclusions. From their experience and given their understanding of the growth strategy, high-potential managers in this organization excelled at delivering value, reacting quickly to market changes, and effectively integrating acquisitions into existing businesses. They also were good at handling the complexity generated by growth, but the business strategy would increase that complexity by an order of magnitude, suggesting more

FIGURE 4-3

IDENTIFYING LEADERSHIP CHALLENGES

Strategic Intent	Leadership Challenges
Sustained Growth	Deal effectively with increased complexity resulting from growth: Adding new businesses, using different systems, using different distribution systems.
	Deliver value to customers in the face of rising expectations and increased competition.
	Create the ability to respond quickly, especially cutting lead time and time to market.
	Communicate business goals clearly and build consensus and collaboration on them.
	Take advantage of internal and external diversity.
	Effectively integrate acquired businesses.

sophistication was needed in this area and as well as more managers with that sophistication.

When it came to building commitment to the strategy and achieving collaboration across boundaries to achieve strategic objectives, the executives agreed that development was needed. Managers in the system had learned how to be effective in a more autocratic mode, but the style of leadership that had worked in a simpler era would not be effective in this situation. Further, existing managers had not learned how to make diversity in the marketplace or the workplace a driving force in the organization's potential growth.

Having identified the challenges, the executive committee was asked to identify the kinds of experiences people would need if they were to learn how to handle those situations. What kinds of experiences, for example, would prepare an executive to lead effectively in the face of the increased complexity resulting from rapid growth? Figure 4-5 shows some of the experiences from which these executives thought a person might learn to deal with that complexity: leading a turnaround

FIGURE 4-4

IDENTIFYING CHALLENGES THAT REQUIRE DEVELOPMENT OF NEW LEADERSHIP ABILITIES

Strategic Intent	Leadership Challenges
Sustained Growth	Deal effectively with increased complexity resulting from growth: Adding new businesses, using different systems, using different distribution systems.
	A current strength but needed much more
	Deliver value to customers in the face of rising expectations and increased competition.
	A current strength
	Create the ability to respond quickly, especially cutting lead time and time to market.
	A current strength
	Communicate business goals clearly and build consensus and collaboration on them.
	Not done well now
	Take advantage of internal and external diversity.
	A new challenge
	Effectively integrate acquired businesses.
	A current strength

---

that requires changing the direction of an organization; being exposed early in a career to running an entire business, as might be gained in certain international assignments; expanding an existing line of business by adding something new or different; adapting an existing business to a different country or market; starting up a new business; and for younger managers, working on a team doing any of the above. For handling complexity resulting from growth, these executives believed certain kinds of on-line experiences were most relevant, especially those that required changing an operation. There also seemed to be an emphasis on getting broad exposure earlier in a career.

FIGURE 4-5

IDENTIFYING EXPERIENCES FROM WHICH THE NECESSARY SKILLS COULD BE LEARNED

Leadership Challenge	Possible Experiences
Deal effectively with increased complexity resulting from growth: Adding new businesses, using different systems, different distribution systems.	• Lead a turnaround that requires changing the direction of an operation. • Gain general management experience early in a career (e.g., as country general manager). • Lead an expansion that requires adding something new or different. • Adapt a business to a new country. • Start something new. • Participate on a team doing any of the above (early in career).
Communicate business goals clearly and build consensus and collaboration on them.	• Work for an effective leader several layers up. • Let younger managers present to and work with senior leaders. • Champion an initiative involving people not directly controlled.
Take advantage of internal and external diversity.	• In an international assignment, work daily with non-U.S. staff. • Work with a diverse, cross-functional team on an important project. • Design or teach a program dealing with diversity issues.

The second challenge shown in Figure 4-5 elicited quite different developmental experiences. How to build consensus and collaboration apparently is learned in large part from working for and through exposure to senior-level leaders. There is also powerful learning in this regard in assignments that require influencing people over whom one has no direct authority.

The same themes appear in the third situation listed in Figure 4-5. Learning to make effective use of diversity results from experiences that involve working directly with diverse groups or, in an interesting twist, having to teach others how to do it (which obviously has as a prerequisite that the teacher must figure out how it is done).

SIMILARITY TO GENERIC EXPERIENCES

In all the examples in Figure 4-5 (and in the analyses of the other strategic thrusts as well), the kinds of experiences identified as preparing future leaders were very similar to the experiences described in Chapter 3. Figure 4-6 shows some of these similarities and demonstrates the range of experiences important for development, given this strategic goal. In analyzing the other strategic thrusts and their challenges, additional types of experience were identified. They included working for a visionary boss; staff assignments in finance, treasury, and strategy; taking courses with executives from other companies; presenting to senior management; and serving on various projects and teams. Though first appearing overwhelming (three strategies, each with thirteen or so challenges, each challenge with five to eight developmental experiences), the list ended up with a manageable number of experiences. By focusing on challenges requiring new rather than current skills, the number of potential situations considered was cut by more than half. Then, as it turned out, the experiences needed to prepare for one kind of situation often were the same as those needed for other kinds of situations, so the total experiences to be considered was reduced dramatically.

More importantly, the discussion of developmental needs focused almost exclusively on learning from experience, thereby avoiding the seductive trap of prematurely locking in on the "right stuff" traits, skills, and attributes of individuals. In thinking through the leadership challenges presented by the business strategy and the kinds of experiences that would prepare someone to meet those challenges, the tacit assumption is that these abilities can be *learned* and are not innate. Executives are quite comfortable and enjoy listing the characteristics future leaders must have, but such conversations are more likely

FIGURE 4-6

Overlap in Developmental Experiences

Experiences Identified by Executives	Experiences Identified by Research[1]
Lead a turnaround that requires changing the direction of an operation.	Turnaround
Gain general management experience early in a career (e.g., country general manager).	First supervision/ early work
Lead an expansion that requires adding something new or different.	Increased scope
Adapt a business to a new country.	Start-up/special project
Start something new.	Start-up
Participate on a team doing any of the above (early in career).	Project/task force
Work for an effective leader several layers up.	Role model
Work with a diverse, cross-functional team on an important project.	Project/task force
Design or teach a program dealing with diversity issues.	Formal program

[1]M. McCall, M. Lombardo, and A. Morrison, *The Lessons of Experience* (New York: Free Press, 1988).

to result in selection strategies (a search for the gifted) rather than development strategies aimed at growing the gifts. Personal attributes have to enter the equation (in the next chapter, in fact); at the same time, it turns out to be more useful to start by identifying *experiences* with the potential to develop people.

The result of all this analysis, which took several hours of executive committee time, was an operational matrix that directly and concretely linked specific business strategies to specific kinds of experiences that could prepare managers and executives for the new challenges the strategies would create.

Because the executives were the "experts" who provided the data and understood completely how the developmental agenda related to business need, there was no need to "sell" them on the relevance of the executive development program. It remained, however, for the staff professionals to integrate the information into a workable corporate system (boxes four and higher in Figure 4-2).

FINDING THE EXPERIENCES

The next step, which fell to the human resources staff to carry out, was to identify where the developmental experiences identified as essential to the business strategy could be found or created. If leading a turnaround is important, where in the corporation are there operations that need to be turned around? Where are the role models that developing managers need to work with? Are there country general management slots available for younger managers?

From a practical point of view, the list of experiences had to be reduced to the manageable number suggested above. Powerful experiences almost always have the potential to teach more than one important lesson, they usually appear multiple times in an exercise like this. Reducing the redundancy by finding similar experiences produces a list like the sixteen experiences described in Chapter 3. Because an analysis of the existing "schools" in the organization had already been done, many of the relevant experiences could be located quickly. Others were tracked down through interviews with knowledgeable insiders.

This process left some needed experiences that simply weren't available within the organization as it was currently structured and at this point in its business cycle. As Figure 4-2 suggests, if experiences don't exist inside, can't be created inside, and can't be found on the outside, the organization has little choice but to hire needed talent from the outside. A more permanent solution may require reengineering how the organization is structured so that needed opportunities can be provided internally.

STRATEGY AND EXECUTIVE DEVELOPMENT

This chapter began with the premise that many executive leadership skills can be learned from experience. Talented people in an organization already are exposed to powerful experiences—sometimes deliberately, sometimes not—and as a result develop many of the needed competencies in the "school of hard knocks." But as the case study demonstrated, natural processes usually can be improved upon. As suggested by Figure 4-7, a talented person, given the "right" experiences, might develop the desired executive abilities, and the business strategy is the most important factor in determining what those experiences should be.

If executive ability is the result of experience rather than a latent quality of the individual, Figure 4-7 raises a critical question. If people develop, then "talent" can't be measured by using the end states they develop to. What, then, do we mean by "talent" or "potential," and how do we determine who should get the executive development experiences that have been identified?

FIGURE 4-7

THE ROLE OF BUSINESS STRATEGY: TO SUGGEST WHICH EXPERIENCES ARE MOST IMPORTANT FOR DEVELOPMENT

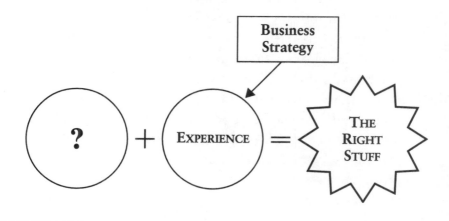

5

ASSESSING POTENTIAL: IS TALENT WHAT IS, OR WHAT COULD BE?

NO ONE SPENDS MUCH TIME DEBATING WHETHER MANAGERS, administrators, and bureaucrats are born or made. Shift the focus to leaders, however, and the issue of natural talent or special gifts (such as charisma) becomes central. The hotly debated question is whether leaders are born or made or, in slightly altered form, "Can leadership be taught?" Any discussion of leadership (or even the more grounded concept of executive leadership) will revolve around impressive achievements and the impressive natural gifts thought to have led to them. Just as the presence of the "right stuff" in fighter pilots was inferred from results achieved, the tendency is to define as a leader someone who has achieved seemingly extraordinary things and to presume that raw talent was the reason that the extraordinary things were achieved.

At the other extreme, the ideas developed in Chapters 3 and 4 could be interpreted to suggest the opposite scenario. Given the right experiences, they seem to say, "anyone" can become an effective leader. Obviously, this is not true. People who achieve unusual success in any endeavor—whether in music, athletics, physics, or in any other field—have talents that separate them from the average person. The same is true for those whose achievements are in the leadership arena. Yet there are many questions about what talent is and how much of it is the product of innate qualities and how much is determined by life's experiences.

A STORY OF TALENT

They were at a birthday party when a friend came up to Mom and asked if she had noticed, amid all the noise and hubbub, that her daughter, then three and a half years old, was sounding out "Happy Birthday" on a toy xylophone. Though she wasn't tall enough to bang on a real piano (in fact, she never did "bang" on a piano, which was yet another quality that distinguished her from other kids), she seemed to have a natural feel for music. A less musically inclined observer than her Mom or her Mom's friend might not have noticed this playful act at all or might have thought it was "cute" and left it at that. Instead, the event marked the beginning of an all-out effort to develop the talent that had been discovered.

Mom later said, "It was as if it was meant to be. We just 'happened' to have a piano teacher for small children living next door. I always intended to give her piano lessons someday, but it seemed like a good idea to start soon."

Mom and Dad bought their daughter a toy piano (which was soon followed by a real one), and she quickly taught herself to play tunes on it. Once she heard a piece of music, she could play it. By age four, it was clear she was "different," and by age five, even though she was too young for class, she was taking piano lessons from that next-door neighbor. At her first recital she was to play that kid classic, "Big Chief Indian." One day before the scheduled debut, Mom happened to be playing Liszt's *Liebestraum* while her daughter listened. When she had finished, the five year old said, "I can do that," sat down at the piano, and played it.

"Big Chief" yielded to Liszt. The first recital so frightened her that the child walked onstage in tears, and the tears kept on flowing throughout the performance. As if to defy her emotions, she played perfectly. Afterward, parents and grandparents rewarded not her talent but her courage with an omelet at the Camellia Grill.

At age five she could pick out almost anything on the piano. Having reached the consensus that the child had a natural gift, her teachers began to argue among themselves, as experts will, about whether she had perfect or relative pitch. They were concerned because people who had her talent for sounding things out quite often had trouble learning to read music. Undeterred by these prognostications, she had easily learned to read music by age six—a first example of what would become a pattern of not letting the experts' expectations prevent her from trying new things. At every turn, her teachers predicted some difficulty or another, yet she predictably proved them wrong.

The problems that come with special talent started early. Though her classmates were older than she was, she was so much ahead of them that she outgrew her music class almost as soon as she began it. In what was to become a routine pattern, Mom found herself searching for the "right" private teacher for this point in her daughter's development, then working diligently to make all of the necessary financial and logistical arrangements. The continual new challenges, endless support and encouragement, and plain hard work produced notable accomplishments. In turn, people provided even more opportunities, and the "success syndrome" began to emerge.

One such opportunity came at age nine, when one of her teachers urged her to audition for a performance with the New Orleans Symphony. Once again the youngest to compete, she won with her performance of Haydn's Concerto in D Major. Among those she defeated were several contestants from the New Orleans Center for Creative Arts (NOCCA), a prestigious school whose graduates have included Harry Connick, Jr., and Wynton Marsalis. She was considered too young to attend NOCCA, but her talent was noticed by its faculty, who were there to support their students.

She went on to win numerous competitions, establishing an

ever-stronger performance track record. Ironically, success as a performing artist led some teachers to discourage her from trying composition. Common wisdom has it that people who are outstanding piano performers are rarely as good at composition. Perhaps she should have listened to them and stayed focused on performance, but at ten her original composition "Scotch Plaid" won city and state awards.

Still much too young, she applied to the classical music program at NOCCA, hoping that her additional talent in composition would allow an exception to be made. Her earlier competition for the symphony was remembered by the faculty, and she was given an appointment to audition. She had quickly become a battle-hardened performance veteran, but the keen competition for a spot in this rigorous program, usually reserved for at least high-school-age children, presented an intimidating challenge to this ten year old. As if the pressure weren't enough, on the day of her audition, television crews were coincidentally at NOCCA to film a special segment for PBS's *MacNeil-Lehrer Report.* Seizing a public-interest opportunity, the crews chose her audition to tape for the program. She kept her cool, impressed the judges, was admitted to NOCCA despite her age, and appeared on public television.

Most organizations and systems are not designed to make easy exceptions, even for talented children, so Mom once again set to work negotiating all the necessary logistics. The elementary school had to rearrange schedules so she could attend the NOCCA program and still take her regular classes. Transportation to and from home, the two schools, and the endless performances had to be found. Funding had to be arranged. Dad had to work harder.

Finally, the first day of NOCCA arrived. What had been such an exciting opportunity only days ago now looked like a terrifying leap. All of her accomplishments to date did not change the fact that she was still a child, and she was scared to death. For the first time, Mom had to apply subtle pressure to convince her to take a risk, and she made her daughter a deal— "If you go for two weeks and don't want to continue, I'll take you out." Even so, for the first few days of NOCCA, Mom had to go with her and wait for her outside. The school didn't give the child an inch because of her age, although everyone else in the classical music program was in high school. It was a grueling schedule, and she didn't think she could do it. She did.

From then on, things happened rapidly. Her parents retained an outside music teacher and a coach to work on performance while NOCCA instructors taught her music theory and composition. And NOCCA began to promote her, helping her get into the summer program at Tanglewood—where once again she was the youngest composer they had ever accepted. Unfortunately, her family was not wealthy, and despite free music lessons and scholarships, for a while it appeared that this opportunity might be lost.

At this point, "luck" intervened again. Her brothers had both worked summers as models for a prestigious agency in New York City. Seeing potential in her, the agency agreed to sponsor her at Tanglewood in exchange for a limited modeling contract. But for a young girl to go alone to New York was out of the question—so she and her mother went together. She appeared in several issues of *Seventeen* magazine and made contacts in New York that would later open many doors. When eventually forced to choose between a career as a model and music, she chose music and took the sponsorship.

At Tanglewood she tackled composition first, then piano performance, taking master classes along the way from the likes of Leonard Bernstein. At thirteen, she was Tanglewood's youngest-ever composer, and her composition "Three Fragments of a Crystal Ball" for flute won the Music Teachers' National Association composition contest and was played in Vienna during American Music Week.

By now, she was on scholarship at Isidore Newman School, an academically demanding high school, and at the same time pursuing private music studies. She had graduated from NOCCA at age fourteen as their youngest classical musician, with the highest GPA in her class. She was offered scholarships everywhere. Still only a high school sophomore, she was recruited by Eastman School of Music at the University of Rochester, and she, Mom (for the next year and a half), and the piano moved to Rochester, New York, where she was (as usual) the youngest student and the only woman in composition. At nineteen she graduated with a Bachelor of Music in piano performance, having collected innumerable music awards along the way.

Having accomplished so much so fast, there was still one more teacher she wanted. She auditioned for the internationally renowned concert pianist Emanuel Ax, was one of two students he accepted that year, and entered Juilliard as (again as usual) the youngest in her class. Two years later, she graduated with a Master of Music degree.

The rest of the story remains to be written.

What can we learn about executive talent and development from this story of an unusually gifted musician, this child prodigy? Is her story just another case of natural gifts realized, or is there more to it than that?

Perhaps the first conclusion we have to draw is that natural talent is part of the story. Other people might have had the same or more opportunities and still never have reached this level of accomplishment. It may be true as well that a person with less natural talent but with many opportunities might accomplish more than a more talented person with few opportunities to develop.[1] Be that as it may, perhaps no one achieves true greatness at anything—whether flying jets or playing piano—without some natural gifts to help them along. Extraordinary executive leadership is no different.

The real question is not whether extraordinary people have natural talent but what happens that allows them to bring that talent to fruition. What, for example, was the innate ability the young pianist brought to her experiences? Superior hand-eye coordination? Perfect pitch? Faultless rhythm? As the story unfolds, many qualities appear. Perseverance—sticking with a tough regimen of practice over a long period—was clearly one. Courage was obviously another—taking on new challenges, facing live audiences, television cameras, music critics. What about resilience, bouncing back after the many mistakes and disappointments? Self-confidence? Risk taking? Flexibility (both in performance and composition)? Intelligence (made good grades and graduated)? Creativity? Curiosity? An even temper (staying cool under pressure)? Poise?

The list of attributes that might have helped is a long one, like a list of competencies a business leader might need. But in this case it's hard to argue that all these qualities were present when the three year old played the xylophone at the birthday party. How many were developed over time as a result of experience, as opposed to bestowed on her by the gene pool? Did her confidence precede the success or develop from it? Did her courage allow her to take on challenges, or did she learn to master her fear as she took on challenges? Was perseverance an inherited trait or something that developed because of a passion for something else? These are unanswerable questions (do answers even matter?), but it is likely that some of these characteristics were "innate," some were refined by experience, and some were developed from experience. Perhaps great musicians (and leaders?) end up having some common characteristics because achieving greatness led them through many common experiences (auditions, pressure, criticism, constantly greater challenges, competition, practice). They may have started in quite different places (had different natural gifts), which meant that different experiences had different developmental effects, depending on where each person started.

Whatever the natural gifts and whatever the developed traits, the story is filled with the willingness to make personal sacrifices in pursuit of a dream (more like an obsession). There were countless hours of practice when other kids were out having fun. She never got to go trick-or-treating on Halloween because there was always a state competition at the same time. There was no such thing as a weekend off. She wasn't able to be in school plays because of the travel. In short, she gave up a lot of other possibilities to pursue her talent, and she dedicated herself to growing it.

The roles other people play are central to the story of talent realized. The friend who noticed her playing "Happy Birthday" and called it to Mom's attention was one of the first. The music teacher next door was another. There was the teacher-coach who gave lessons gratis so money could be spent on Tanglewood, as well as a number of gifted and giving other teachers. There was the talent agent who became a sponsor. Central to it all was family support and especially a mom who bought the piano, found the teachers, provided the transportation, moved to New York, encouraged her to try new things, stayed with her in the scary parts, protected her from exploitation, and played countless parts behind the scenes. Then there was Dad, who was the chauffeur on every road trip, and the brothers, the grandparents, and on and on.

The teachers played a special part. As she outgrew each one, another teacher was found (at first) or asked to teach her. (Later on, the teachers wanted her as a student.) From a Russian piano teacher she learned to put fire in the music; another teacher taught her discipline. Bernstein, Ax, and others brought more pieces to the puzzle, all becoming part of the whole. What ability on her part allowed her to get along with all these personalities, not only putting up with their idiosyncrasies and vast differences in style but also learning from and incorporating things from all of them? What about her inspired them to give their time and knowledge (and often these teachers did not accept pay)?

Opportunities obviously played a critical part. Some of the opportunities were a matter of luck—because she was pretty and her brothers had been models, she came to the attention of the agency that would sponsor her to Tanglewood. But when luck presented an open door, she was also somehow willing and able to go through it. Her successes created additional opportunities. The more opportunities she took, the more people saw her talent and then helped create more opportunities.

Along with new opportunities came higher levels of challenge. Because she had to play a lot (to earn money as well as to build a career), she learned to play anything. Playing everywhere from concert halls to restaurants, she learned to handle mistakes with such poise that only the experts realized a mistake had been made. Facing so many difficult situations, she learned to handle almost any situation. Being attractive, talented, and successful, she learned to deal with jealousy and exploitation. Being successful in increasingly difficult challenges, she gained confidence but did not make the mistake of drifting into a kind of arrogance that would make people not want to be around her.

In many ways, of course, the arts are unique. And at some level, every person's career is unique. But what this case illustrates so clearly is that raw ability alone is not enough. Understanding talent—and potential—means considering the interaction of native gifts, what a person does, the experiences they have, other people along the way, the context in which they operate, and how things change over time. Because all of these elements are involved, there is truth in each of the various approaches to understanding and assessing talent. That this child had a gift is not in question, but native ability is not a sufficient explanation for how raw talent was transformed into accomplishments over time. In a different environment—without a parent who understood music, for example—that gift might never have been noticed. In a different environment— without people who had the time to act as chauffeur, chaperon, arrangements secretary, fashion consultant, and cheerleader— opportunities to develop the gift, had they appeared, could not have been taken. In a different environment—without access to pianos, piano teachers, or teaching programs—the gift itself might never have developed.

In retrospect, it is not clear what the original gift was (other than neural circuits and motor skills) or how abilities developed along the way made the development of that original gift possible. There is something about the person as a learner, as a taker of opportunities, as an absorber of experience, that made a big difference here. Research indicates that "musical training, in fact, alters brain anatomy," suggesting that cause and effect are far from clear. A recent article on music and the human brain put it well: "There are some rare brains that seem to be especially built to be musically engaged. Everyone knows of the precocity of Mozart's genius, which produced its first musical composition before some children learn to read. Highly gifted children seem to have an abnormal attentiveness to sounds in their environment; the young Arthur Rubinstein, for instance, could recognize people by the tunes they sang to him. While there is much dispute over the degree to which the talent of a Mozart or Rubinstein is inherited, there is little doubt that it must be encouraged early in life if it is to bear fruit. Professional pianists and violinists, for instance, almost always begin to play seriously by the age of seven or eight."[2]

This is why ways of assessing talent that begin with the "end state" (the finished product) or assume that talent is innate always come up short. Even if talent's origins are biological, bringing it to fruition requires years of hard work and conscious development.

END-STATE APPROACHES TO DEFINING TALENT

Probably the most common approach to assessing managerial ability is to study successful managers. Although there are many variations on the theme, the process usually involves identifying a large number of people who have been judged successful at doing whatever is in question (in this case, executives); studying them to discover what characteristics they have in common that seem to account for the success or that differentiate them from the less successful; constructing a model of leadership reflecting the common attributes or "competencies"; and using the model for identifying, selecting, recruiting, training, and evaluating people with executive capability. Returning to the music arena, this approach would begin by identifying the great concert pianists, studying them to find out what they have in common, and then developing ways to identify people who have those characteristics.

A variation on this theme is to start with the job or task and attempt to analyze what behaviors or attributes are necessary to do the job effectively. If applied to our music case, this approach would have us study what the job of concert pianist actually requires people to do if they are to do it well. These results would then be transformed into a set of characteristics or critical skills that would become the template for the identification and assessment of talent. Often, however, the analysis of the job is accomplished by studying successful incumbents or bosses' perceptions of incumbents which makes the process virtually identical to the person-centered approach described first.

There are some significant differences among the approaches and the ways they are implemented. Whether the focus is on traits or behaviors (or "motives," as some prefer) makes a difference. Trait advocates, after studying successful pianists, might look at our prodigy for such things as flexibility, perseverance, intuition, intelligence, risk taking, equanimity, and a host of other personal characteristics that might be associated with people who perform successfully. The implicit model is that certain traits result in the desired behaviors which, in turn, lead to success. The trait approach to leadership was actually among the first to receive scientific scrutiny; it was discredited for a time in the 1960s and 1970s, when research failed to find strong and consistent relationships between any of a vast array of personality traits and various measures of effectiveness. The past decade has seen a resurgence of interest in traits, sparked in large part by research on the "Big Five" personality traits[3] (see Figure 5-1), which seem to have some predictive power across situations. A variation of the trait approach based on personal motives (especially McClelland's needs for achievement, power, and status) also has had a resurgence, in the guise of competency models.[4]

The behaviorist is more concerned with overt behavior than with the predispositions that might underlie it. Instead of assessing the prodigy on traits, a behaviorist might look at how well she can read music, play Haydn's Concerto in D Major, recover after mistakes, or maintain poise under pressure. It matters less to the behaviorist what traits lead to behavior than what behaviors the person actually exhibits, and the underlying

FIGURE 5-1

THE "BIG FIVE" MODEL OF PERSONALITY

Surgency (**Extraversion**)	Talkativeness, assertiveness, and activity level versus Silence, passivity, and reserve
Agreeableness (**Pleasantness**)	Kindness, trust, and warmth versus Hostility, selfishness, and distrust
Conscientiousness (**Dependability**)	Organization, thoroughness, and reliability versus Carelessness, negligence, and unreliability
Emotional Stability	Emotional stability versus Nervousness, moodiness, and temperamentality
Intellect or Openness to Experience[1]	Imagination, curiosity, and creativity versus Shallowness and imperceptiveness

Source: L. Goldberg, "The Structure of Phenotypic Personality Traits," *American Psychologist* 48, 1 (January 1993): 26–34.

[1] Goldberg says that disagreement among researchers about the specific nature of the fifth factor is "somewhat of a scientific embarrassment" (27). Given the role that experience plays in the development of executive ability (or any other ability for that matter), one might argue on logical grounds that "openness to experience" would be a salient personality factor. Intellect, at least as it associated with various measures of intelligence, more logically lies in the cognitive rather than personality domain.

theory again rests on the notion that the identified behaviors cause effective job performance.

What the two approaches have in common is the outcome of the inquiry, in both cases a list (of attributes or behaviors) based on the past or current state of affairs (either job demands or successful people). In practice, the resulting list of attributes often contains a potpourri of traits, motives, values, behaviors, attitudes, skills, knowledge, and the like. I have called these "end states," because they represent what people who do a job well are (or were) like—the qualities they had when they reached "success" and, at least for the job in question, had "finished" developing. In short, these are characteristics of the end product.

Armed with a short list of end-state attributes or competencies, some organizations have redesigned all of their managerial and executive systems. In contemporary practice, one encounters assessment centers, tests, performance appraisal forms, 360° feedback instruments, recruiting interviews, ratings of potential, succession planning criteria, training programs, developmental moves, and the like that incorporate the characteristics identified. A certain comfort is to be found in consistency.

Such a systematic approach to executive effectiveness has been a marked improvement over the "good old boy" and smoke-filled-room assessment practices of the past. If an organization needs to fill a particular executive position, it can be quite valuable to base the selection on known qualities of individuals that actually relate to effective job performance. If the competency list has been developed carefully, then the selection of a qualified person can be quite accurate when the job in question is the same as it was when the list was derived; the job in question won't change significantly in the short term; the job has an identity separate from the incumbent and is not shaped by the incumbent; the requirements for effective performance in the job are the same as when the list was derived; performance is largely a result of the incumbent's actions rather than controlled by forces external to the person; there is only one way to do the job effectively, and that is the way described in the list; the characteristics actually exist in one person, as opposed to representing a generic list that represents a group but can't be found in individuals; the attributes don't interact with each other or with other attributes to change the net outcome, depending on the combinations an individual possesses; and the people don't change, therefore the assessment of them is stable, even in a new situation (like a new job).

That is a lot of "ifs," many of which don't hold for executive jobs, but they boil down to a few simple observations. This approach to the assessment of talent is most effective when the attributes relate to a specific job with specific candidates at a specific point in time. The approach becomes increasingly less effective when jobs are less easily defined, when jobs are changing, and over longer timeframes during which job demands and what constitutes effectiveness can both change. It is no surprise that practitioners using competency models are now asking how to keep the competencies from becoming outdated in the face of rapid change. Perhaps the most effective use for such models is filling an immediate vacancy in a specific job. The least effective may be to apply end-state competencies to the early identification of talent.

THE END-STATE FALLACY

Regarding the pianist, there are several ways to think about assessing talent. The end-state approach suggests looking at accomplished concert pianists or composers (the first problem in this case—should one look at performance or composition?), concocting a list of their competencies, then assessing her along those dimensions. The assumption is that these end-state qualities can be found in some miniature form in people with potential (see Figure 5-2). This approach, called the "Russian Doll" model in a critique by Christopher Bartlett and Sumantra Ghoshal,[5] posits that each of these qualities exists to a successively smaller degree and that a developing person goes through a sequence of slightly larger challenges until these qualities become full blown.

Even if the desired end state is not different in the future (in these turbulent times, odds are it will be), this approach has some serious problems. There is no reason to believe, for example, that end-state characteristics are necessarily present in diminished or latent form. Perhaps as a result of the experiences she had, our pianist *learned* many of the attributes that helped her career. Had she been assessed on those attributes prior to having the experiences, no sign would have been found. Perhaps some of the attributes are not learned in linear fashion but rather in fits and starts, or as the result of seminal events or

FIGURE 5-2

END STATES AND TALENT

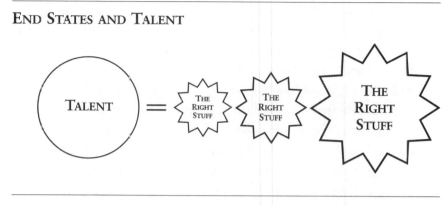

singular experiences. In other words, there may be key developmental transitions that people go through, not unlike "passages" in life development, that would make the appearance of an attribute difficult to predict. It's hard to know, but perhaps the "fire" in our pianist's performing did not ignite until after she had worked with her Russian tutor. Had the discipline training come first, any assessment might have shown her as "good technically" (which in music is damning with faint praise) rather than inspired.

Moreover, what if some attributes that appear early don't develop any further or disappear later? Early prominence may be relative or a function of environment, and early stars may get no brighter while other stars do. Or a desired attribute might be overridden by experience—humility might be replaced by the arrogance bred by success, aggressiveness might get tempered by someone's revenge or the harm it did, risk taking might be extinguished because of failure or lack of support. Yet another possibility is that undesirable characteristics may develop over time. A truly gifted person might begin to believe he or she has nothing more to learn and thus develop a closed attitude toward learning and be unable to learn from teachers.

Yet another possibility is that there is more than one way to achieve success. Certainly, the great composers and great performers have many significant differences in style, temperament, personality, and values. It may be possible to find commonalities, but to suggest that one finite list of attributes could account for success is to deny an obvious reality. Were Roosevelt, Kennedy, Lincoln, Stalin, Chiang Kai-shek, Mao Tse-tung, and Churchill more alike or different? All were eminently successful politicians. What about Montgomery, Patton, Eisenhower, Rommel, Bradley, and MacArthur? All were benchmark generals, but any military historian could point out vast differences among them in personality, values, style, career history, oratory—on almost any dimension.

The litany could be extended indefinitely, but there are many reasons to believe that the early identification of talent based on a "Russian doll" developmental model and a list of end-state attributes is far from ideal. Done carefully, it represents a vast improvement over other methods of prediction (such as bloodline, social connections, seniority, phrenology) that once were common (and still are, in some parts of the world). A reasonable understanding of what effective leaders must be able to do, which is an end-state target, is a critical link. But another approach, informed by more than a decade of accumulated research on how executives learn from experience and from recent studies of early identification that were spawned by that research, suggests a developmental alternative to what is essentially a selection approach.

EARLY IDENTIFICATION OF LEADERSHIP TALENT

If end-state competencies are the "right stuff" of executive leadership as defined by an organization, if people acquire these competencies through various experiences, and if the business strategy of an organization determines what experiences are most needed for the future, then one way to think of talent, as portrayed in Figure 5-3, is that it is the requisite ability to learn what needs to be learned from those experiences.

Consider this possibility in light of the development of the pianist. She had innumerable key experiences in her career, from the audition with the New Orleans Symphony, the challenges at NOCCA, to master classes at Tanglewood. There was

FIGURE 5-3

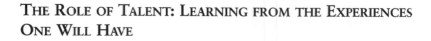

THE ROLE OF TALENT: LEARNING FROM THE EXPERIENCES ONE WILL HAVE

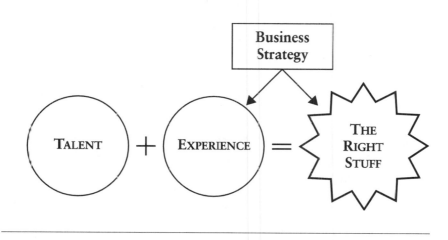

an almost endless parade of teachers, most of whom had different approaches. There were countless hardships, sacrifices, and setbacks. There were years of formal programs. Thus far, the types of shaping events she encountered bear a strong resemblance to those reported by executives. Another person of lesser raw talent, even if exposed to similar events, might never have accomplished what she did. But it might be true that a person of equal raw talent with these same opportunities might not have accomplished as much, either. In looking at her career, one sees clear indicators of an eagerness to learn, a willingness to take risks for developmental opportunities, a responsiveness to criticism and feedback, a dedication to practice and error correction, and a willingness to experiment and try new things. As success created opportunities, she took them. When teachers began to want her (rather than the other way around), she chose those who would push her into new regions rather than teachers with whom she had grown comfortable. She chose schools that would bolster her weaknesses, not just refine her strengths. She developed the interpersonal skills necessary to sustain other people's support and encouragement. Such attributes might plausibly be described as essential components of the ability to learn from experience—something distinctly different from raw musical talent—and as a key ingredient to developing that raw talent into its performance manifestations.

The possibility that learning from experience was an ability that might prove useful in identifying leadership talent, especially in international contexts, prompted a research project funded by the International Consortium for Executive Development Research.[6] Ratings by the bosses of 838 managers in six international corporations in the United States, Europe, Australia, and New Zealand identified eleven characteristics that distinguished high potentials from solid performers on a variety of criteria (see Figure 5-4). At first glance, these eleven appear similar to the dimensions one might find in typical competency models, such as those in Figure 5-5. "Brings out the best in people," for example, sounds very much like the end-state competencies "good with people" and "cooperativeness." The dimension "is insightful" certainly has similarities to "analytic thinking" and "incisiveness."

Closer inspection, however, reveals some noteworthy differences. The competency models in Figure 5-5 lack explicit learning components like "seeks opportunities to learn," "seeks and uses feedback," or "learns from mistakes." Despite similarities between the early identification dimensions in Figure 5-4 and the end-state competencies in Figure 5-5, on the whole the former are learning oriented, whereas the latter are performance oriented. This difference is consistent with the idea that end-state competencies are developed over time as a result of learning from experiences.

The dimensions reported in Figure 5-4 were derived with statistical techniques that cluster items that were rated in similar ways. There does seem to be a relationship among these variables that is related to learning—recall the relationship between derailment and an organization's errors, how experience influences the learning of executive leadership skills, and the ways learning and experience intertwined for the pianist in the case example.

PEOPLE WHO LEARN MORE FROM EXPERIENCE

Figure 5-6 reorganizes the eleven dimensions to reflect a logical process of first doing things that get the attention of the organization, then taking advantage of the opportunities generated by the visibility, creating a rich learning environment within those opportunities, and finally, taking to heart the learning and changing as a result of it.

Chapter 2 introduced what John Kotter called the "success syndrome," a pattern among successful people (general managers in his study) wherein they did well in an early assignment and were recognized by being given a more challenging assignment, with their self-esteem and self-confidence increased as a result.[7] Having challenging jobs stretched them, built skills, and built new relationships. These assets helped them continue to perform well, which led to more opportunities, and so on. This pattern holds for the piano prodigy as well; her increasingly impressive accomplishments brought visibility, learning, opportunities, and confidence. In the course of her career there was a visible shift from her family's hiring the best teachers they could find and persuading good schools to admit her, to the best teachers wanting her as a student and the best schools offering her scholarships and incentives.

THE PRICE OF ADMISSION

The first requirement for talented people, then, is to use their talent for accomplishments that draw attention to their talent, which results in more opportunities to develop it. Our study of international managers suggests that three things are particularly important in an international business context: commitment to making a difference, insightfulness, and the courage to take risks.[8] Specifically, these translate into a willingness to make personal sacrifices for the success of the organization, the ability to get to the heart of problems and bring some creativity to solving them, and the courage to take action, even when others disagree or there is some personal or business risk involved. Not surprisingly, these attributes sound much like the kinds of things that marked the careers of executives who later

FIGURE 5-4

ELEVEN DIMENSIONS OF EARLY IDENTIFICATION OF GLOBAL EXECUTIVES

1. **Seeks opportunities to learn.**
   Has demonstrated a pattern of learning over time. Seeks out experiences that may change perspective or provide an opportunity to learn new things. Takes advantage of opportunities to do new things when such opportunities come along. Has developed new skills and has changed over time.

2. **Acts with integrity.**
   Tells the truth and is described by others as honest. Is not self-promoting and consistently takes responsibility for his or her actions.

3. **Adapts to cultural differences.**
   Enjoys the challenge of working in and experiencing cultures different from his or her own. Is sensitive to cultural differences, works hard to understand them, and changes behavior in response to them.

4. **Is committed to making a difference.**
   Demonstrates a strong commitment to the success of the organization and is willing to make personal sacrifices to contribute to that success. Seeks to have a positive impact on the business. Shows passion and commitment through a strong drive for results.

5. **Seeks broad business knowledge.**
   Has an understanding of the business that goes beyond his or her own limited area. Seeks to understand both the products or services and the financial aspects of the business. Seeks to understand how the various parts of the business fit together.

6. **Brings out the best in people.**
   Has a special talent with people that is evident in his or her ability to pull people together into highly effective teams. Is able to work with a wide variety of people, drawing the best out of them and achieving consensus in the face of disagreement.

7. **Is insightful: sees things from new angles.**
   Other people admire this person's intelligence, particularly his or her ability to ask insightful questions, identify the most important part of a problem or issue, and see things from a different perspective.

8. **Has the courage to take risks.**
   Will take a stand when others disagree, go against the status quo, persevere in the face of opposition. Has the courage to act when others hesitate and will take both personal and business risks.

9. **Seeks and uses feedback.**
   Pursues, responds to, and uses feedback. Actively asks for information on his or her impact and has changed as a result of such feedback.

FIGURE 5-4

Eleven Dimensions of Early Identification
of Global Executives *(Cont.)*

10. **Learns from mistakes.**
    Is able to learn from mistakes. Changes direction when the current path isn't working, responds to data without getting defensive, and starts over after setbacks.

11. **Is open to criticism.**
    Handles criticism effectively: does not act threatened or get overly defensive when others (especially superiors) are critical.

Source: M. McCall, G. Spreitzer, and J. Mahoney, *Identifying Leadership Potential in Future International Executives: A Learning Resource Guide* (Lexington, Mass.: International Consortium for Executive Development Research, 1994).

FIGURE 5-5

Two End-State Competency Models

Specific Competency Model	Generic Competency Model
Team Player	Breadth of Awareness
Customer Focus	Incisiveness
Bias toward Action	Reasoning
Analytic Thinking	Organization
Integrity	Drive
Innovation	Self-confidence
Global Vision	Sensitivity
Good with People	Cooperativeness
	Goal Orientation

Note: The specific model on the left side is an actual corporate model that has been modified slightly to protect confidentiality. On the right side is a list of generic competencies from C. Woodruffe, "What Is Meant by a Competency," *Leadership and Organization Development Journal* 14, 1 (1993): 29–36. The Woodruffe article describes various corporate competency models.

FIGURE 5-6

How the Eleven Dimensions Relate to Learning from Experience

Pay the Price of Admission: **Get Organizational** **Attention and Investment**	Is committed to making a difference Is insightful: sees things from new angles Has the courage to take risks[1]
Have a Sense of Adventure: **Take or Make More** **Opportunities to Learn**	Seeks opportunities to learn Adapts to cultural differences Seeks broad business knowledge Has the courage to take risks[1]
Learn More: **Create an Effective Context** **for Learning**	Acts with integrity Brings out the best in people Seeks and uses feedback Is open to criticism[1]
Take It to Heart: **Change as a Result of** **Experience**	Learns from mistakes Is open to criticism[1]

[1]Dimension intentionally classified in two categories because it entails elements that fit in both places.

derailed (see Chapter 2), who were often seen as having good track records, being exceedingly bright, and willing to take action. Apparently, from a long-term career perspective and certainly from a developmental perspective, these attributes are not enough by themselves and, untempered, can cause derailment. That is why we call them the "price of admission"—in an achievement-based organization they seem to be the minimum criteria for being considered "high potential" and for having the opportunities to expand one's leadership repertoire.

These three attributes are obviously related to job performance, but less obviously, they are related to development as well. It is through commitment to making a difference that many people are willing to learn new skills. When people feel that doing something that matters depends on mastering something new, they are much more likely to invest time and energy in learning it. Success in learning new things or new approaches may depend on what was once called "being insightful," that is, asking the right questions, understanding the problem, and seeing things from a different perspective.

As Chapter 3 showed, development usually involves moving into new territory, taking on new activities, or ending up in situations in which what one knows how to do no longer works. Thus the "courage to take risks" is a crucial part of learning as well as of leadership. As my colleague Warren Bennis pointed out to me in a personal conversation, many people may never discover their talent or interest because they never take an opportunity that would allow themselves or anyone else to see it.

A SENSE OF ADVENTURE

Sometimes when one watches gifted people take on challenges, one might assume that, because of their extraordinary talent, they don't have the same fears that everyone else does. Their success at difficult undertakings makes it look as if it is easy for them to move from one achievement into the unknown territory of the next. In the career of the young pianist, overcoming fear and taking on the next unknown were almost daily fare: new schools, new teachers, new competitions, new jealousies, tougher competition, higher stakes. Whether crying through her first recital or needing her mother to take her to her first class at NOCCA, growth meant learning to cope with sheer terror. To reach the next level always meant leaving the comfort of where she was, so it was "yes" to the symphony, "yes" to NOCCA, "yes" to Eastman, "yes" to Tanglewood, "yes" to Juilliard, and on and on, as if for all intents and purposes, there were no bounds to what the child would try. And perhaps because talented people get more opportunities to move into the unknown, they seem to learn how to do it. With that learning comes a willingness to take on even more.

The data on international executives reflect this pattern.

Because they tended to take on more of the challenging opportunities they were given or made opportunities when they felt they had learned all there was to learn where they were, they seemed to have an unusually keen sense of adventure. Their bosses described them as seeking out experiences that changed their perspectives and provided them with opportunities to learn. They were seen by their bosses as perpetually seeking to understand how what they were doing fit with the larger business and how other parts of the business worked.

The thirst for knowledge seemed to go into high gear when it came to international issues, where those rated as high potential seemed to get sheer pleasure out of cultures other than their own and were willing to put a lot of energy into understanding those cultures and learning to behave effectively in them.

In sum, developmentally effective managers demonstrated a sense of adventure by getting themselves into experiences that changed their perspectives, exposed them to new things, and generally broadened their understanding of the business and their part in it. In doing so, they both showed and developed the courage to take risks, for these moves into the new always entailed some degree of risk.

CREATE A CONTEXT FOR LEARNING

But the difference doesn't stop there. Getting into challenging situations does not guarantee that a person will learn from them. It could be argued that the greater the challenge, the more likely a person is to concentrate on survival, using what he or she already knows how to do and focusing narrowly on the performance objectives of the immediate situation. For those who have achieved much, there is always the temptation to rest on one's laurels, to stop seeking new challenges and simply enjoy the practice of one's expertise. Those rated highest in leadership potential tended to avoid these learning obstacles by creating a context to increase the learning potential (especially concerning the impact of their behavior on others) of challenging opportunities. They did this in some obvious and some less than obvious ways.

When things get so hectic and demanding that there is little time to do anything but react to the immediate situation, people will comonly make such remarks as, "when you're up to your neck in alligators, it's easy to forget you came to drain the swamp." Many of the "learning opportunities" that shape executive leadership ability fall into that category. Whether the business is about to go belly-up, a new product has to get out before the competition, or some other potentially developmental situation appears, the nature of the challenge that makes situations developmental also makes them less than ideal learning venues. I may be willing to take on something outside of my comfort zone that requires using all of my accumulated abilities and experience, but it does not guarantee what or even if I will learn in the process. It is in the nature of organizations (especially at the more senior levels) that the focus is first on performance and secondarily on personal growth. High performance in a new situation almost surely requires some learning, either in a business-related content area or in using existing skills in a novel way, but it doesn't always require new skill development. Moreover, taking what seems to be a learning approach, such as "do it, try it, fix-it," does not ensure that what finally works will be understood or, if understood, retained. Significant learning about how the business works may take place, but there may be little learning about how one's actions affected other people and the role that had in producing the result. Quite often, the real learning from a challenging experience waits for a reflective time after the maelstrom, when what was done right and what was done wrong can be examined in the light of feedback and outcomes. Unfortunately, and especially where talented people are concerned, the reflective period rarely exists. The next challenge always awaits, and talent is always in demand.

People who learn more from experience, then, do things that increase the odds that they will learn what an experience offers them. Our data suggest that high-potential international executives do this in at least two different but complementary ways: They create a setting in which other people are willing, perhaps eager, to play a constructive role in their learning, and they are proactive in generating feedback on their impact and effectiveness.

If learning were always something that a person could do alone, it would not be necessary to develop relationships with other people that encourage feedback or support. But as many of the executives derailed by their insensitivity discovered too late, having other people on one's side can be critical to survival as well as to growth. Constructive relationships are built on trust, and the managers considered most likely to be effective as international executives were rated quite high on such trust-building behaviors as taking responsibility for their actions (instead of blaming mistakes on others), avoiding self-promotion, telling the truth, acting in ways that draw the best out of others, and dealing effectively with differences. When other people feel that a person is genuinely interested in them and their success, they tend to want to help that person in return. When they believe the opposite, they tend to act in the opposite way.

In short, by proving themselves trustworthy and by treating others (especially subordinates) with respect, effective managers first create a setting in which other people are inclined to help them. If, as Warren Bennis reports, seven out of ten people won't speak up when their boss is about to make an error,[9] then taking steps to create an open environment is even more crucial. Effective managers are more likely to get help when learning things they don't know before, needed information when they find themselves in trouble, candid feedback if they want it, support when they need it, and forgiveness when they make mistakes. All of these are important to learning.

Feedback is the second aspect of establishing a learning context and is traditionally acknowledged as a crucial component of learning. Years of research in a variety of disciplines have shown beyond a doubt that valid, reliable, timely, specific feedback is the lodestone of learning. Organizational settings, however, are not always healthy environments for creating such feedback, especially when criticism or mistakes can damage careers and paychecks, or when the recipient of negative feedback has sufficient power to punish the messenger. As managers grow more successful and gain more authority, the availability of feedback tends to decrease. People reporting to them have more to lose than to gain by taking the risk of giving negative feedback, and successful people have a tendency to believe they don't need much feedback from those they may perceive as less able than themselves. Those two forces together can act to create a dangerous vacuum.

Effective learners, then, are more likely than less effective ones to actively seek feedback on their impact, to respond to feedback when they get it, and to remain open when feedback is critical or is given by a threatening source. The absence of defensiveness encourages others to offer information and to be as constructive as possible when offering it.

CHANGE AS A RESULT OF EXPERIENCE

Finally, managers identified as having high potential change as a result of the experiences they have had. This change is manifested most clearly in the ratings of how effectively they learn from mistakes, respond to corrective feedback, and start over after setbacks. It is also apparent in how they deal with success, never allowing repeated successes to close them to the possibility that there might be something more to learn.

Perhaps the single most revealing question that can be asked about someone is whether or not he or she has ever changed in response to feedback or experience.

SOME CONCLUSIONS ABOUT TALENT

There are two ways to think about executive leadership talent. From a selection perspective, the traditional approach is to identify the common characteristics of effective leaders and try to identify the people who possess those characteristics. From a developmental perspective, the logical approach is to identify those best able to take advantage of developmental opportunities, if provided. Obviously, the two perspectives would converge at some point in a person's career. The successful outcome of development would be an executive leader who possesses the required competencies.

In a very practical sense, then, talent must be considered from both perspectives. The question is which perspective is foreground and which is background, in particular, which approach provides the greatest leverage in developing needed leadership talent. As I argued earlier in this chapter, what I call "end-state" approaches have several limiting characteristics, not the least of which is that they undermine a developmental approach through the assumptions they trigger about the inherent nature of attributes. Questions can also be raised about the appropriateness of any end-state model over time, about the existence of a generic set of attributes for all people, and about the relationship of generic competencies to shifting strategic imperatives. This is not to say that a developmental approach based on "ability to learn" is without flaw but rather that it leads down a different path and focuses attention on the kinds of experiences talented people should be given rather than on finding people who already demonstrate desired qualities.[10] From a competitive standpoint, it is reasonable to assume that competitive advantage lies not in finding leaders in a broad talent pool that everyone else can draw from but in creating a proprietary talent pool through judicious developmental practices.

The idea that ability to learn is central to effective leadership is not entirely new, although it has not been mainstream in the research on leaders. One of the first studies to make the idea explicit was done by Warren Bennis and Burt Nanus. Their 1985 bestseller, *Leaders,* was based on in-depth case studies of ninety leaders from a variety of disciplines. They identified four "strategies" effective leaders follow, which they labeled "attention through vision," "meaning through communication," "trust through positioning," and "the deployment of self." This last dimension reflects most closely the active learning aspect of development, and the authors observe that "nearly all leaders are highly proficient in learning from experience."[11] They noted that all the leaders they studied could cite people and experiences that had powerful effects on their subsequent beliefs and abilities, and that they were particularly attuned to learning from the events and experiences of an organizational environment. They did not let success fool them into believing that they had all the answers, and they remained vigilant for how their weaknesses might play out in changing circumstances. In that effort they constantly sought out feedback and developed specific strategies for compensating for their weaknesses. Bennis expanded his earlier observations about leaders as "self-evolvers" in a subsequent book, *On Becoming a Leader.*[12] In it he elaborated and developed the idea that leadership is a journey of personal development.

Another major contribution to understanding the development of leadership talent has come from the research of John Kotter at Harvard University, in a series of books about effective leaders.[13] Although his focus was always on what effective leaders do, he dealt extensively with how they came to be so good at what they did. He concluded that "a surprisingly large number of the items [leadership attributes he identified] are developed on the job as a part of one's posteducational career."[14] He went on to point out that the best-led firms put a lot of effort into identifying people with leadership potential and providing them with developmental experiences that challenge and stretch them.

Another piece of the puzzle comes from the derailment studies I described earlier, which identified four dynamics that caused talented people to jump the tracks. Three of these—early strengths becoming weaknesses, pre-existing flaws becoming important under changing conditions, and success leading to arrogance—can be seen as learning disorders. All reflect a failure to learn and develop as the surrounding context changes. Indeed, when compared to derailed executives, the successful differed substantially in the diversity of their background experiences, in how well they could relate to other people (especially to people different from themselves), in how effectively they handled mistakes, and in the poise with which they dealt with stress and pressure—qualities remarkably similar to the characteristics of learners described in Figure 5-4.[15]

In conclusion, a comprehensive approach to developing executive leadership will bring several perspectives to bear on the assessment of talent. Because the heart of development lies in a person's ability to learn from an accumulation of experiences, the focal point in early identification is the assessment of learning ability.[16] Notwithstanding the possibility that such an ability might be developed or enhanced, it would appear to be the fundamental building block for the acquisition of sophisticated leadership abilities. Without it, even the most substantial reservoir of raw talent would likely grow stagnant.

The derailment data pose a dilemma by demonstrating that otherwise talented people may stop growing or may change for the worse. This suggests not only that the ability to learn needs to be monitored over time (it is not safe to assume that, once demonstrated, it will remain unchanged) but that potentially derailing attributes must also be assessed and tracked. Because the "towering strengths" of talented people sometimes lead others to overlook flaws and because the derailment process reflects the deterioration of learning, there is enormous potential in assessing and tracking the "fatal flaws" of talented managers.

Finally, the assessment of end-state competencies, as flawed as it might be for identifying potential or developmental experiences, can provide a progress report on the development of talent. If one is able to learn from experience and is given the needed experiences, it is useful to assess the degree to which the learning from those experiences becomes a part of the individual's leadership repertoire. Furthermore, end-state competencies can be helpful in identifying the attributes that may be developed already. Ultimately, development is a very individualized process, and people begin at different points and progress at different rates. Assessment of end-state attributes may enhance efficiency by identifying what needs less developmental attention.

The next chapter deals with the obvious fact that getting people with talent into the experiences they need for further growth is not automatic. In fact, organizations acting rationally, as we saw earlier, can actually prevent needed development from occurring.

6

WHO GETS WHAT JOB:
THE HEART
OF DEVELOPMENT

THREE SPECIFIC ASSERTIONS ABOUT EXECUTIVE DEVELOPMENT have been identified so far: the primary vehicle for development is challenging experiences; which experiences are most important is a function of the business strategy and organizational values; and the people who should get the experiences are those who are best able to learn from them. Because such a large number of the experiences important to the development of executive leadership skills occur through work assignments, the critical question is clearly, "Who gets what job?"

Organizations have many mechanisms to move people from one assignment to another. The most common is perhaps the most informal and serendipitous—a position opens up, and the manager of that position (the "hiring manager") chooses someone to fill it. The choice is a function of who the supervisor knows about, who is available at the time, and how well the available candidates' perceived abilities match the perceived demands of the job. Pragmatic and efficient, this mechanism is also highly susceptible to bias and flawed judgment on the part of a single supervisor who makes the decisions. Nonetheless, the intent usually is to find the best qualified candidate—defined as the person who has already demonstrated the capacity to do the target job.

The effort to reduce bias and poor judgment has led to various improvements over the single-supervisor judgment. These include assessment centers, sophisticated testing programs, multiple-rater schemes, review by the "manager once removed," and review panels consisting of several managers and human resource professionals. When key jobs are identified and a systematic assessment process is installed to plan for replacements for the incumbents, the process is called "succession planning." The intent is to identify the best qualified candidates for these key jobs, who often include those who are "ready now" as well as some who, with certain experiences or more time to mature, will be qualified in the short or medium term. In some succession planning systems, people considered to have potential but are "not yet ready" are given developmental opportunities to accelerate their preparation; most succession planning systems, however, are intended for identification and selection rather than for development planning. In many cases, the succession planning system is run by different people or may be located in a different part of the organization than is the system for training and development. Ironically, decisions about who gets which assignment are at the very heart of the executive development process. Those who are "ready now," who are deemed to be fully qualified to handle a given job, by definition have the least to learn by doing it.

Recognizing that executive talent is a critical resource and that the number of people with the potential to become effective executives may be limited, some companies have created "high potential" pools to identify talent and to provide those so identified with special developmental attention. Responsibility for managing this select group usually is given to a specially designated staff group, and the people whose careers fall under this control are considered to be "corporate property." The idea is that their development may require nontraditional experiences or assignments outside of their current unit, division, business, or function, and that corporate needs take precedence over local needs.

Although the scarcity of executive resources would seem to mandate some version of a high potential pool, there is strong resistance to the practice in many foreign cultures as well as in many U.S. corporations. In some cases, succession decisions are driven by factors other than merit, such as seniority or family ties, so there is no need for a competency-based selection and development process. In other cases, the objection is rooted in a perceived violation of egalitarian principles (the creation of "crowned princes and princesses") that might alienate those not chosen or inflate the egos of the blessed.

Many issues surface in any discussion of succession planning systems, high potential pools, and the practices associated with them. What is their primary purpose? How are people assessed and on what dimensions? How does one get off a list? Who has access to the information, and how much does one tell the person rated? Who does the assessment? The list could go on and fill these pages with interesting tangents. Instead, the focus here is on the use of succession planning and high potential pools as mechanisms for getting talented people into the experiences they need to develop the skills that the business strategy requires (see Figure 6-1). The ultimate purpose, of course, is to ensure that an organization has an adequate supply of well-trained leaders for achieving its strategic aims, but achieving this objective requires the integration of different systems. This is another reason that developing a process for managing a high potential pool makes sense—the various approaches to selection, development, training, appraisal, special assignments, and the like can be integrated with a single purpose.

Several assumptions guide the following suggestions for getting talent into the "right" experiences. Not everyone is equally likely to develop into an effective executive leader; therefore it is important to identify those with the potential and motivation. Actions that are needed to develop talent may have short-term performance consequences—those who might learn the

FIGURE 6-1

The Role of Mechanisms: To Get Talented People into the Right Experiences

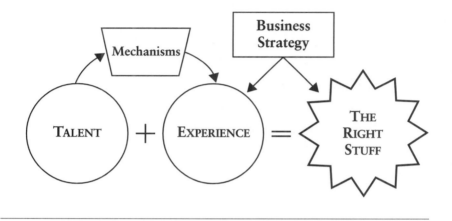

most from a particular experience are not those who have already learned its lessons. Because of the performance consequences and possible loss of the best people as they are moved for developmental reasons, there is often outright resistance to developmental moves or, at a minimum, a conflict between short-term business performance and longer-term developmental needs. Development of executive leadership ability is a career-long (if not lifelong) proposition, so any system must encompass the whole term. Development is not linear and systematic but instead takes place in fits and starts and in different ways for different people; people may develop, arrest their development, or grow worse.[1] Whereas the talent for leadership may reside in any part of an organization, by virtue of tradition or the nature of the business, the search for talent tends to focus on certain parts of the organization and overlook others. Because a rather large number of experiences are required to learn even a portion of the many executive abilities that might be helpful, developmental exposures need to start early and continue at an appropriate pace, else a person may fall seriously behind.

These assumptions translate into a set of characteristics that should describe the mechanisms an organization uses to move talent. Listed in the same order as the assumptions they address, these are the characteristics: the mechanism should be selective, concentrating efforts on people who have the most potential and who show developmental progress; it should have "teeth," so that short-term performance and parochial interests can be overcome when appropriate; it should start early in a career and encompass even the highest levels; it must be flexible enough to accommodate both organizational realities and individual differences in development; it should not become a closed system—people must be able to enter and exit a high potential pool on the basis of their demonstrated growth or lack of it, meaning that individual progress has to be monitored regularly; it must cast a wide net, to seek out talent in all parts of the organization; and it must be continuous, and not allow inertia or business cycles to impede people's continued growth.

PRAGMATIC IDEALS

At first glance, the list of desirable characteristics looks intimidating in the extreme. Visions of impenetrable bureaucracy must dance through the head of any line executive. In reality, however, the system (if such an elegant label is deserved) need not bring the business of the business to a halt. Developing executive resources requires senior management time, but the time needn't be wasted nor be accompanied by mountains of paperwork. In fact, for organizations that recognize the value of developing executive resources, taking advantage of what has been learned about how executives develop can actually save time and money that is sometimes wasted on inefficient practices. Just one example is the relatively recent emphasis in many U.S. corporations on using expatriate assignments for development. To the extent that a company is global, it is obviously a good idea that its high potential people learn about the international scene. Unfortunately, however, expatriate assignments are very expensive and can be high risk to the people taking them. All too often, talented people are sent abroad without sufficient thought having been given to what specifically they need to learn, with the result that assignments are inappropriate, structured badly, or a waste of time. According to human resource executives, the cost of a failed expatriate assignment at the executive level can easily exceed a half-million dollars, not counting the loss of a talented person and the businesses losses that mistakes can generate. What this means is that companies could realize substantial savings by more carefully considering which developmental lessons are needed for international effectiveness, which experiences might offer those lessons, and who could profit the most from having the experiences. Such are the questions a "mechanism" or process for making developmental moves needs to address.

SUCCESSION PLANNING AS A DEVELOPMENT MECHANISM

The easiest place to make development gains is by improving existing practices for filling key assignments. The traditional approach is concerned with listing "ready now," "ready later," and "never ready" replacement candidates for key jobs. People who are deemed fully qualified for those jobs might be considered "A list" candidates—they could be put in the job and be expected to perform effectively from the outset. As mentioned earlier, those who already can do a job will not learn as much from doing it as someone who would be stretched, so "A list" successions optimize short-term business performance at the expense of longer-term leadership development.

Of course, for some key positions and at certain critical times it would be a mistake to consider anyone but the most qualified candidate. The risk of doing anything else would simply be too great. Many succession possibilities leave room for calculated risk, however, and here is where having "B list" candidates—people who could *learn* the most if they had an opportunity to tackle the assignment—can improve the developmental outcomes of succession decisions significantly. Consideration of the "B list" need not entail elaborate procedures but may simply mean calling attention to the possibility of a developmental choice when a key position is to be filled.

Although simply considering alternatives may lead to significant improvement, adding a few formal procedures may further enhance the process. First, a process for identifying the "B list" candidates could be developed; perhaps simply by using an existing "high potential pool" to ensure that people from all parts of the organization, not just the particular chimney normally leading to the position, are considered. In the absence of an existing pool, the need to identify talent for succession purposes provides a valid reason for assessing the talent in an organization and is an essential precondition for making developmental job assignments.

A second addition is to consider assignments not just in terms of the performance demands they make but explicitly in terms of what the assignments might teach. Most jobs considered critical to an organization are also jobs high in developmental potential; making the learning possibilities explicit, however, is not usually part of a traditional succession process. Further, jobs that may not be so critical may also have very high learning value, a fact that may not be discovered unless the jobs are considered within a developmental perspective. Recall the suggestion in Chapter 4 that what is developmental can be interpreted relative to the business strategy and the new challenges it presents.

Finally, like almost any important objective, people are likely to be more effective if they are held accountable in some way. When rewards are connected directly to performance-based results, odds are good that succession decisions will come from the "A list" candidates. Indeed, choosing any but the most proven candidates would likely result in punishment of some sort, as would giving over integral talent to other parts of the organization for developmental reasons. Even a short-term performance decline might affect a manager's appraisal rating, achievement of objectives, and bonus. In a now-classic article, Steve Kerr pointed out "the folly of rewarding A while hoping for B."[2] Hoping for development actions when rewards are based solely on performance is a perfect example.

These three enhancements are summarized in Figure 6-2. Identifying "B list" candidates requires something resembling a high potential pool, but the definition of talent requires some careful thought (Chapter 5). Identifying assignments with development potential requires a thorough understanding of the business strategy (Chapter 4), of the nature of learning from experience (Chapter 3), and of the organization itself. Creating accountability rests on sufficient senior management commitment to revise measurement and reward systems to counter the organizational "rationality" (see Chapters 2 and 4) that contributes to the derailment of talent.

If, however, individual managers are accountable for developing talent, the odds are greater that they will increase the number of "B list" choices. As with any other business accountability, this one depends on clear objectives (what is the developmental strategy and desired outcomes?), valid measurement (how will we determine if those objectives are being met?), and rewards (what's in it for me if I meet the objectives?). The problem is not that organizations don't know what needs to be done but that they have many competing priorities. Virtually every organizational innovation—from empowerment to high-performing teams, to total quality, to customer focus, to value-based management—carries with it the admonition that success depends on top management support and on a reward system that supports the desired behavior. Few organizations exemplify serious commitment to moving people across boundaries for developmental reasons more than General Electric. When managers of key jobs have a vacancy to fill, they are given a slate of candidates that was generated by the executive resources staff. This mechanism is intended to ensure that talented people from outside the immediate chain of command, who might benefit from the experience, are considered. Few organizations are willing to go this far.

Although part of the reason organizations don't do a better job of developing talent is not knowing what needs to be done,

FIGURE 6-2

MAKING SUCCESSION PROCESSES MORE DEVELOPMENTAL

Traditional Succession Planning	Enhancements for Development
"A List" Replacement candidates for key jobs are identified primarily on the basis of previous experience, track record, and demonstrated end-state competencies. Candidates are typically classified according to "ready now," "ready later" criteria and identified from within functional or business unit chimneys.	**"B List"** People who could learn the most from having the job are considered. This approach assumes that those who are fully qualified will learn the least, so a wide range of talented people from across the organization are considered for developmental jobs.
Performance Demands of Key Assignments Jobs that are considered most critical to the business get the most attention. Job demands are analyzed in terms of what the basic job content is and what an effective performer must be able to do in order to achieve business objectives.	**Developmental Aspects of Assignments** Jobs as well as temporary assignments may be important for development even if not critical to the business. Assignments are analyzed in terms of the kinds of things a person must learn how to do in order to be successful in a job. Basic job demands may translate into developmental challenges, but the role model provided by the boss, problematic relationships, and type of challenge (e.g., turnaround, start up) are all considered as potentially important learning aspects.
Accountability for Results The primary goal is to have sufficient depth to cover vacancies in key jobs. Measures of effectiveness tend to be indirect, with contingencies based on performance. Actions that reduce performance (ineffective selection or extended vacancies, for example) result in sanctions. A results focus tends to favor selecting the most qualified candidate and hoarding talent.	**Accountability for Development** The primary goal is to develop talent to meet future strategic needs. This may or may not relate to specific positions. Measures of effectiveness need to reflect developmental goals, such as strategic cross-boundary moves, number of "B list" selections, actual skill acquisition, and growth. A development focus optimally rewards development but minimally ensures that people aren't punished for developing others.

the larger part is a lack of commitment because of competing priorities. Just how critical is the development of leadership talent to the future of an organization? There can be no objective answer to this question. Leadership is one element in a complex interaction of factors that determine the winners and the losers in the competitive arena. Some have argued that when all the other forces are taken into account, leadership has a relatively small effect.[3] There is no shortage of examples of hopeless situations, where the most courageous act of leadership was not enough to save the day because of technological change, instability in financial markets, or some other outside force. But there are also numerous examples of heroic leadership that changed the course of whole societies, not to mention corporations. A strong argument can be made that in these times of convulsive change, leadership at all levels is essential to organizational survival, and the belief that leadership makes a difference is the sine qua non of getting executive development to be taken seriously.

Even in organizations that value leadership, debate is inevitable over whether leaders are born or made (Chapter 1). Most people will concede that leadership education is noble and desirable, but not everyone believes that serious investment in development generates sufficient return. Once again, commitment depends on beliefs, and corporate culture and the attitudes of top management are clearly the fields on which the battle is fought. Which way the tide is turning can be assessed by such matters as whether the most talented managers and executives are expected to take part in developmental activities, whether senior managers take their own development seriously and actually do something to make it happen, whether development budgets are cut with every downturn, whether senior managers willingly participate in assessment and development activities, and whether the people responsible for executive resources have enough authority to assure compliance by autonomous business units.

In corporate cultures where development is not ingrained, developing mechanisms for getting talented people into developmental experiences becomes part of a larger effort at cultural change. One human resource executive, for example, collected data showing that the business strategy would require a certain number of new executives and that the current supply would fall drastically short. By framing development in strategic terms, he was able to create a sense of urgency and commitment to change, and he had a concrete proposal for what to do when the opportunity presented itself. Others have used their participation in succession planning reviews as a chance to acquaint senior executives with the leadership talent (or lack of it) at lower levels. When the talent base is outstanding, becoming familiar with it generates enthusiasm. When it is inadequate, it generates a sense of concern. Either way, involvement generates the energy for executives to be involved in other developmental activities, to gain access to the newly found talent, or to fix a serious problem before it gets worse.

A recent example of the potential such energy creates occurred at PepsiCo.[4] Former chief executive Wayne Calloway had determined that the sustained growth of the business was threatened by a shortage of aggressive leaders, but the division presidents didn't respond. Instead, according to *Fortune,* they used a substantial portion of the money intended for executive development to improve reported profits. The situation did not begin to change until vice-chairman (now chairman) Roger Enrico took a personal interest in the leadership development challenge and started a program for the highest of the high potentials. Working with small groups of nine or so at a time, Enrico spent days as executive guru, interacting with the students about how to grow the business. As the number of graduates accumulates, the payoff is multifaceted. First, the vice-chairman is developing an accurate picture of the future leaders' strengths and weaknesses—information with vital strategic implications in the hands of a senior line executive with the clout to do something with it. Second, each participant is exposed to a living PepsiCo legend who serves as a role model, not just for building a business but also for the value of developing others. Third, participants who are judged as eligible for the next generation of top executives get to see the other participants and, through working with them, draw their own conclusions about the level of talent available to the organization. Fourth, the time invested and commitment demonstrated by the company in having the program send a strong message that development really is important. Finally, because the design of the program requires each participant to carry out a significant business project, the participants stand to enhance their track records of accomplishment, thereby opening up additional opportunities.

It is important to note here that the involvement of senior management in the assessment of talent and in developmental interventions, such as the one at PepsiCo, is not without risk. Exposure to senior-level role models can be good or bad for developing leaders, depending on the attributes of the models. In an environment that disregards *how* results are achieved, for example, successful executives not only exemplify how to get results, but they also model their treatment of people and their approach to integrity.

A second concern is what senior executives may do with the information they gain through their interaction with junior managers. It is not unusual for people to draw conclusions about other people on the basis of short exposures or brief episodes, and talented people might be "written off" as the result of observations made in a developmental setting. This outcome is ironic, because such a setting is just the place where people should be able to be candid about weaknesses, receive critical feedback without threat of reprisal, and experiment with new behavior without fear of ridicule or negative judgments.

Once again, the relationship between development and the larger issues of the corporate culture and strategy is highlighted. Although years of research on how people develop and what prevents talent from being realized provides pragmatic solutions for development activities, none of it will work in a context that is hostile to the underlying assumptions. Developing talent first requires leadership—people who act to create a setting in which growth can thrive. Unfortunately, many organizations have environments that are unsupportive if not overtly hostile toward development. Unsupportive environment or not, development still requires that people with talent get the opportunities that allow them to grow. It just means that the mechanisms for moving people around may depend on heroic acts (leaders who are willing to take personal risks to give their people developmental experiences) or may have to go underground.

DEVELOPMENT AS GUERRILLA WAR

Even in organizations operating under rationalities that undermine development, some significant victories are possible. Carrying out the guerrilla war often falls to people in human resources, but individual executives should carry responsibility as well. Tactics that can make a difference include making deals with other managers, influencing individual executives, counseling talented people to take control of their development, and leveraging motherhood and apple pie.

Because development comes down to getting people with talent into experiences from which they can grow, it is also about bargaining with the people who control the talent and those experiences. Where no formal system for movement exists, managers can still agree to exchange talented people or to take on a person for developmental reasons. Such was the case in the research and development (R&D) division of a large chemical company. The company was not opposed to development but did little to abet it. The people in human resources spent most of their time as personnel generalists and as organizational consultants to management. Within R&D, the quality of leadership had become a problem. As is the case in many technical professions, the route to management was through technical achievement, and here the piper was finally being paid, as a large number of technically sophisticated but interpersonally Neanderthal and managerially naïve people were filling managerial posts. In consequence, the unit was not functioning well. The most senior management was savvy enough to recognize a problem and decided that it had to do something to change the caliber of leadership, or there would be no future for the group. With the help of a senior human resource adviser and an outside consultant, the company's ten top managers met to identify the developmental needs of the most talented managerial personnel. They then discussed where in the division various of those needed attributes could be acquired. There was no precedent for moving people out of narrow technical pathways and no system for doing so, but they began to make arrangements with each other to swap people: "I'll take Charlie and put him on the new product team so he can learn to work with the marketing and financial folks if you'll take Susan and put her under Charlene so she can learn how to effectively manage male bosses." Or, "I've got someone who is a genius at creating novel technical changes but has absolutely no sense of what the customer wants. Does anyone have any ideas on what experiences we could give him to help him grow more sensitive to the customer's perspective?" After one afternoon of wheeling and dealing, developmental actions had been determined and agreed to for the top twenty-five managers. In addition, agreements were reached on the kinds of things that would be done to assist the learning, ranging from support and coaching to setting formal objectives and holding people accountable. In addition, the senior management team had learned something valuable, not only about each other but also about the broad issues concerning talent that were facing the division. Though it would have been helpful to have had access to a larger portion of the organization (many of the developmental needs actually required cross-boundary experiences), significant progress was made using only the resources within the division.

Cutting deals can go a long way toward moving talent into developmental opportunities, and the payoff often exceeds expectations. Many times, a person coming in for development brings with him or her a new perspective that actually contributes more to the business than does someone more familiar with the job.

The second guerrilla tactic—influencing individual executives—may be a subset of the first but deserves separate emphasis. All organizations have at least some executives who believe in the importance of development. When the system neither supports nor encourages developmental activities, these potential allies may not act on their beliefs. Or some may be willing to act but don't really understand how development works or what they need to do to help others grow. In such cases, counseling these individuals can result in some significant developmental actions. One division executive in a large power systems organization, for example, believed in development and was always experimenting with people and challenges. But his background was in engineering, and some of his efforts at coaching were welcomed by his subordinates like the Romans welcomed Attila the Hun. He later remarked that one had to understand the laws of physics to be an engineer, but one needed to understand psychology to be a leader. With guidance from a human resources consultant, he learned to channel his commitment to development and experimentation into his managerial actions, soon creating a virtual garden of growth. He set up expectations that people would try new things and treat mistakes as learning, filled many key positions with nontraditional people, encouraged people to disagree with him and modeled constructive conflict resolution, moved people around so that they got to know the business, gave people challenging assignments, and set up a context that reduced the risk that they would be destroyed if they failed. Executives who developed under his supervision went on to lead other parts of the business and even other companies, and they took with them what they had learned from this boss. In a sense, he did more to influence development within that company than a dozen training programs ever could have achieved and without ever budgeting anything in a column called "development."

A third tactic begins at the other end, by influencing the people who want to be developed. Just as bosses sometimes have no idea how to help people develop, talented people sometimes don't know how to develop themselves. A striking example is the pianist in Chapter 5—she would have had a very difficult time knowing what or how to teach herself. Especially in an achievement-driven context, people are inclined to focus on performance rather than on growth. Although the need to learn new things in order to sustain top performance is a powerful developmental incentive, there are at least two serious limitations to the natural process. A focus on the present may mask what a person really needs to be learning for future challenges, and being expert in some functional or business specialty does not equate to being skilled in how to learn from experience. Indeed, maximizing performance can mean doing what one has always done, over and over, until one is the best at it. Maximizing growth may mean doing things one has never done and learning how to do them better. A critical role for someone with more experience or broader perspective is to help talented people see what they need to do for themselves if they want to develop. In organizations that are passive about development, an aggressive individual can create many opportunities simply by asking for them. In any organization, a talented person will have opportunities, and developmental wisdom is essential to choosing the most useful ones. (Organizational rationality often means asking talented people to do more of what they already know how to do.) In other words, if the organization won't help a person manage his or her career, he or she has to take charge of it, anyway. One individual found himself trapped by his own accomplishments in a sequence of jobs within the same technical specialty. His progress was rapid and the financial rewards were great, but he foresaw being trapped forever within the narrow chimney, when what he really needed was an opportunity to do things in other parts of the business. When he asked for opportunities to broaden by transferring to another function, he was told that he was too critical where he was. Eventually, he resigned and went to work somewhere else where he could broaden his experience.

Finally, guerrilla war can be waged by taking advantage of the "motherhood and apple pie" quality of development. Very few people are against developing leadership, even if they believe in the "right stuff," are fixated on immediate performance, and question the value of training. To declare publicly that effective leadership is not important or that talent does not need to be cultivated is to risk being seen as irrational. Because of that, it can be relatively easy to get senior management endorsement for developmental activities, if not their actual support. Sometimes agreement in principle can lead to at least modest financial investment (more so in fat times or if the investment is a useful deduction), willingness to support at least some developmental moves, modest investments of personal time in specific development activities, and other actual contributions. In some cases, motivation through guilt is better than no motivation at all, although the degree of support that can be counted on may be modest.

SHORTCUTS

Creating mechanisms for moving talent into needed experiences assumes that the needed experiences are to be found somewhere other than where people already are, and that the natural progression of things would not get them where they need to be. This is not—or need not—always be true. Because it can be disruptive, expensive, risky, and politically difficult to move people to different experiences, it is important to consider mechanisms for moving experiences to people who need them.

If people can't be moved across boundaries, perhaps the boundaries can be moved. Reengineering and corporate restructuring present numerous opportunities to redesign jobs and relationships without necessarily reassigning people. Just as succession planning can be more effective by considering the developmental possibilities, redesign can be enhanced by considering what experiences are being created and the developmental opportunities they might present. Design changes present opportunities to add to or change the responsibilities in a job, to shift the central working relationships, and otherwise to generate new and possibly developmental challenges within an existing framework.

Special projects, temporary assignments, and task forces also provide numerous opportunities to create growth. These are especially useful interventions because they can be used in either way. When they are created directly out of a business need, the developmental intervention is to influence who gets the opportunity and to engineer it so that whoever does it can learn from it. When someone needs an experience but can't move to it, these same kinds of experiences can be "created" as an addition to or as a temporary release from existing jobs. As long as the reason for them is real and important, project-like experiences offer efficient ways to frame new challenges and relationships.

Training and other formal programs also can be used as opportunities to bring experiences to people who need them. As discussed in Chapter 3, the key is how these experiences are structured and the nature of the challenges they create for the participant.

IN CONCLUSION

The principle is simple: people learn most by doing things they haven't done before. In an organization where using people's existing skills is a rational way to optimize performance, getting people into the challenges they need for further development often requires mechanisms that can override short-term decisions.

It's not that mechanisms don't already exist for moving people around. Vacancies are filled as a matter of course by various means, including succession or replacement planning systems, on-the-spot decisions by the manager of the job, executive review panels, and other mechanisms that usually emphasize finding the most qualified available candidate. The developmental value of existing mechanisms can be enhanced significantly by paying attention to who will develop most as well as to who has proven they can do the job.

Some organizations accept that valuable development results from moving talented people around the organization.

Many old-line Japanese corporations, for example, routinely rotate their managers through various parts of the business, a practice enhanced by a lifetime employment philosophy and seniority-based promotion. Movement for its own sake is better than no movement at all, but it's very inefficient. It is costly to move people, in terms of the expenses associated with relocation and salary adjustment, the disruption caused by having to establish new relationships, and the learning curve's effect on performance. And the greater the distance between what a person has done before and the new demands, the greater the possibility of a derailment. In short, rotation needs to be handled well if it is to be an effective mechanism for development.

Part of the problem with rotation strategies is that they are often rooted in assumptions about the value of exposure as a developmental process. Again, it is probably better to have broad exposure than limited exposure, but the key to development lies in what you have to do—not just in what you are exposed to. Being around customers is not the same as having to deal with an angry customer. Hearing a lecture from an effective boss is not the same as working for one. The bottom line for a developmental mechanism is its utility in getting people who need them into the experiences that will help them grow most effectively.

The options for getting the right person to the right place at the right time depend, ultimately, on the willingness of senior management to take responsibility for the nurturing of talent. If leadership is viewed as a critical resource, people will get serious about corporate "property," accountability, and measurement. The specific mechanisms for getting people and experiences together may be informal or formal, but the commitment to making it happen makes it happen. When it comes to a developmental opportunity, some talented people may not want to take it, some may want it but can't get it, and some don't know that they need it. Organizations may not recognize where the real developmental opportunities are, who needs them, or the long-term value of making developmental choices. For these reasons, having effective mechanisms for forcing the match of talent and experience is crucial. Without them, even organizations loaded with talent and rife with challenges can end up with a shortage of leadership talent.

7

CATALYSTS FOR DEVELOPMENT

IF CHANGE WERE EASY, NO ONE WOULD BE OVERWEIGHT AND no one would smoke. Never has the mandate for change been stated so clearly as it has been in the last decade. Not without irony did John Akers, derailed CEO of IBM, bluntly lay out the challenge when he said, "Our people have to be competitive, and if they can't change fast enough, as fast as our industry . . . Good Bye."[1] More recently, McDonnell Douglas' chief executive, Harry Stonecipher, whose career took him from top positions at General Electric and Sundstrand to his current post, could serve as spokesperson for corporate America for saying, "If you see change as a threat, you won't be happy and you won't survive."[2] Against this backdrop of corporate upheaval playing out from Samsung to IBM, the mandate is clear: People must change at least as quickly as their environment is changing or risk being left behind. (In another ironic twist, Mikhail Gorbachev, former president of Russia, is said to have admonished that "those who do not learn to change in life are left behind.") No one is immune from his or her particular tapestry of strengths and weaknesses falling out of alignment with the context, as happened to so many of the derailment cases discussed earlier. But it is one thing to talk about change and to endorse it, and quite another to actually make fundamental changes in oneself.

Corporate practice in executive development tends to leave the creation of change up to the individual. Perhaps because of embedded right stuff assumptions described earlier, even organizations that do a good job of putting talented people into challenging assignments tend to step back and wait to see how they do. If they do well—if they demonstrate the right stuff—then they get another opportunity that stretches them more, and so on until they either reach the top or fail in one of the assignments. As I have shown, it is difficult enough to identify talented people and potentially developmental assignments, and to make a connection between the two. But having done that much, is it really the wisest strategy to step back and see how everything turns out? That amounts to treating challenge as a test—assuming that a passing grade is evidence that something was learned.

This attitude of "you've got your chance, now sink or swim" might make sense if the goal were selection rather than development, and if all the people taking the test weren't talented. But if the people are talented, a better goal might be to see them learn and develop rather than to push them until they fail. Contrast the testing approach organizations take toward development with the attitude a parent takes with a child who needs to learn to cross the street alone. I've dubbed this corporate mindset the "Harbor Freeway" model of development because it sees the street as a test. The Harbor Freeway in Los Angeles is one of the notorious, multilaned (probably a dozen or so at some points) major arteries for which the city has become famous. Traffic is usually congested, and driving on it is not for the fainthearted. Corporate logic would be to find children who looked promising, take them to the Harbor Freeway, and then stand back and see if they make it across. If they do, obviously they have the right stuff, and the next challenge must be found—perhaps the San Diego Freeway. A parent, however, is less interested in testing a child's resourcefulness than in seeing him or her survive while learning to cross streets. The primary motivation is to see the child succeed. By taking responsibility for creating a context in which a child can learn, a parent considers whether the Harbor Freeway is the right place to start, what safety precautions need to be taken, and what instructions or practice might come first. All the while a parent realizes that he or she cannot always hold the child's hand and that, in the final analysis, the child must do it alone.

If an organization is interested in developing its talented people, it follows that its goal should be for talented people to *succeed in learning* from challenging experiences. This kind of success may be achieved even when performance goals are not met. And the organization must share responsibility for the outcome if a talented person derails, for it plays a decisive part in creating the environment in which the learning must take place.

Recognizing that an organization cannot force someone to develop, an effective executive development process must take into account the reasons that intelligent people, aware of the need to change, may not try to change or, trying, may not succeed. Historian Barbara Tuchman noted that fiascos tended to repeat across time. She set out to understand such things as why the Trojan horse was let in (a phenomenon of more than passing interest at the University of Southern California!), how the British managed to lose the American colonies, and how the United States got ensnared in Vietnam. One of her conclusions was that "learning from experience is a faculty almost never practiced," reflecting the dismaying tendency for people with power to lose their capacity to benefit from experience. She attributed much of the problem to "wooden-headedness" which, she argues, is "assessing a situation in terms of preconceived fixed notions while ignoring or rejecting any contrary signs. It is acting according to wish while not allowing oneself to be deflected by the facts."[3] Although she was referring largely to political figures facing grand world events, the applicability of the observation to individuals seeking personal change should not be lost on us. In a more contemporary and personal context, resistance to change is described in drug treatment as "doing the same thing over and over again, expecting it to come out differently."

Overcoming this nasty little human tendency is an important challenge for executive development. Warren Bennis, in his study of how people become leaders, observed that "each of these individuals has continued to grow and develop throughout life,"[4] but achieving success and power often encourages a misplaced belief that there is nothing left to learn—a sure ticket to derailment. It is in a corporation's self-interest to do all that it can to keep its talented people open to learning. To derail talented people by putting them in a challenging situation they cannot rise to is but a Pyrrhic victory.

Figure 7-1 captures schematically the catalytic role an executive development system can play in helping people convert experience into learning. "Catalyst" is a term from chemistry for a substance that precipitates or speeds up a reaction. In the development context, it refers to actions that can be taken to facilitate a person's learning what an experience might teach.

WHY PEOPLE DON'T CHANGE

Understanding what might be done to assist learning first requires understanding what gets in the way. There is no shortage of discourse on why people don't change, especially in contemporary writing on leadership. Indeed, leadership has been *defined* as creating change,[5] or, more dramatically, as transforming organizations or whole societies.[6] Because change requires exceptional leaders to create it, it is very difficult to change systems and people, even when change is obviously necessary.

Apparently, the same is true of individuals who attempt to change, and success may be more difficult to achieve depending on what the person is trying to change. Some aspects of personality, for example, are extremely stable over time. Moreover, things that appear more amenable to change often remain rock solid, despite the good intentions of their possessor. Surprisingly, talented people are frequently aware of what needs to be changed and of the reasons they haven't changed, yet they

FIGURE 7-1

THE ROLE OF CATALYSTS: TO HELP TRANSLATE EXPERIENCES INTO LESSONS LEARNED

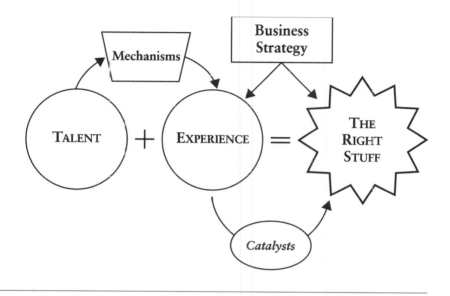

---

continue on paths that will make them candidates for the derailment chapter of this book.

When asked why they haven't changed something they
believe they should have, people generate lush lists of reasons
(see Figure 7-2).[7]

The specifics of the list are interesting (and the list is by no
means all inclusive), but the sheer quantity of excuses is pro-
hibitive. Figuring out what actions might reduce the barriers to
learning created by these obstacles (or, more positively stated,
increase the probability that learning will take place) requires
reducing the list to a manageable number of central themes.
Although different people will see different things in the same
list, it seems safe to say that both the individual and the organization play a part in creating obstacles to change. From the
point of view of a development system, an organization needs
to do what it can to create a context conducive to learning.

FIGURE 7-2

Some Reasons People Don't Change

- Garbled feedback
- Mixed messages
- No feedback
- Don't understand the message
- Don't believe the message
- Don't listen
- Don't accept it
- Have to admit mistakes or flaws
- Doesn't fit self-image
- Don't hear it all
- Take it personally
- Tend to overreact
- Don't react well to criticism
- Suspicious of others' motives
- Source not credible
- Others don't know the real me
- Fear that ugly facts might be true
- Don't trust feedback giver
- Hurts to hear bad things
- Negative feedback makes me mad
- Feel it's incorrect
- Makes me feel like a child being scolded
- No incentive to change

- Rewarded for staying the same
- Costs in time and energy
- Cost outweighs benefit
- Benefit unclear
- Imposed from outside
- No personal commitment to change
- Don't see the real importance of it
- Not clear what needs to change
- Not sure what change will create
- Can't tell what's really important
- Requires giving up something valued
- Don't know how to change
- No opportunity to practice
- No role models
- I've been successful as I am
- Comfortable like I am
- Don't want to change
- Can't change it
- Look stupid
- Feel incompetent
- No support

- Context not changed
- Too busy
- Focused on other things
- Other people aren't changed
- People don't see the change
- People won't allow the change
- Painful, humiliating
- Fear of manipulation
- Fear of the unknown
- Arrogance
- Afraid to make mistakes
- Vulnerable while trying to change
- Fear of failure
- Afraid I won't be good enough
- Have tried to change before and failed
- Too lazy
- Fear of being exposed
- Convinced I'm right
- Need to be liked
- Undermines self-confidence
- Threatens self-image
- Distorts self-image
- Too much pride
- Intimidated by others

Source: Condensed from managers' and executives' responses to the question "Why haven't you changed something you believe you should have" in numerous personal development workshops run by the author.

Three ways to facilitate learning are to improve the nature of the feedback people receive to help them identify a need for change, to provide the incentives and resources needed for change, and to support the change effort.

CATALYST 1: IMPROVING INFORMATION

The importance of feedback for improving performance and its critical relationship to learning have been well documented by many years of research.[8] As if to prove the point, "not getting the message" is one of the most common reasons people give for not changing. Figure 7-3 highlights some of the specific comments people have made. This list is by no means comprehensive, but it suggests a variety of ways that poor information flow blocks learning. Many of the blocks reside within the person who may not want to hear, is too well defended, or otherwise refuses to accept potentially useful feedback that is available. At the same time, blocks within a person are irrelevant if there is little or no feedback or if the feedback that does exist is obscure or ambiguous to begin with. Figure 7-3 suggests that feedback can baffle a recipient if it is unclear, arouse suspicions when it comes from an untrustworthy source, and not be heard when the way it is delivered triggers strong emotional reactions or when it otherwise comes in forms that reduce individual receptivity. An organization may be limited in its ability to affect human nature, but it can work to improve the quality of the information it provides.

When feedback is unclear, it is often because the message is vague or not grounded in specific examples. One of the most common complaints about performance appraisals is their broad generalizations about performance ("not a team player," "poor judgment," "not a risk taker," "not aggressive enough") that are not supported by specific examples. Without something concrete to relate to, a person can't understand exactly what he or she did wrong, much less what he or she needs to do differently. The vagueness may be a result of poor observation or recordkeeping on the supervisor's part, but unfortunately it is

FIGURE 7-3

LACK OF CLEAR INFORMATION

- Garbled feedback
- Mixed messages
- No feedback
- Don't understand the message
- Don't believe the message
- Suspicious of others' motives
- Source not credible
- Others don't know the real me
- Don't trust feedback giver
- Feel it's incorrect
- Makes me feel like a child being scolded
- Benefit unclear
- Don't see the real importance of it
- Not clear what needs to change
- Can't tell what's really important

---

sometimes the result of a lack of courage—a supervisor may not confront performance issues for fear that someone who has performed well will be angry or quit if candid feedback is delivered.

Sometimes feedback is tangential or peripheral to what is really important about the person's development. This happens when there is no agreement about what behaviors and skills lead to effective performance or about what are the criteria for performance. (One of the best reasons to have a competency model is to ensure that the same criteria are applied in assessments of leadership ability—at least then it is possible to argue about the criteria.) Peripheral or vague feedback is common when the person giving the feedback has no firsthand information on which to base an evaluation (which is often the case in matrix structures), when the person being assessed has a lot of autonomy, when the boss has a large span of control, and when there is substantial geographic separation between boss and subordinate.

A dangerous situation arises when feedback is about superficial manifestations of a deeper issue. One way to hint at a problem without really telling the person what the problem is, for example, might be to criticize a person for having a messy desk or coming late to meetings, when the real issue is perceived as rebellion against the system—a belief by the supervisor that the person in question is "acting out" by actively refusing to accept the culture and is trying to make that refusal obvious to other people. Rather than put the serious issue on the table, however, the feedback is on trivial manifestations that the receiver can easily dismiss as trivial or become angry about.

Yet another source of distortion occurs when a person gets feedback from different sources who see similar things differently. A previous boss, for example, might have admired risk-taking and the flouting of tradition, whereas the current boss sees the same behavior as bravado and arrogance. (Worse yet is in a matrix structure, where two current bosses may see things very differently.) Sometimes the same person will praise an action at one time and criticize similar behavior at another. In some cases, judgment of the merit of an action is based solely on the outcome, so that the ends are seen to justify the means. The frequency of this type of judgment was observed by Abraham Lincoln, who once said, "If the end brings me out all right, what is said against me won't amount to anything. If the end brings me out wrong, ten angels swearing I was right would make no difference."[9] Whatever the reason for mixed messages, they at best leave recipients confused and at worst enable self-serving interpretations of ambiguous information.

Feedback can be delivered in language or in terms that a recipient doesn't understand. It can be delivered in hostile, insulting, or provocative ways that elicit strong emotional responses rather than openness. It can be hidden in vague language and cryptic references. The list goes on and on. But the bottom line is that individuals have many psychological blocks that can distort feedback, so the first catalytic function for development is to do everything possible to ensure that talented people receive clear, timely, and candid feedback on the significant aspects of their behavior and performance. That means building a system or a culture that minimizes the organizational mistakes that contribute to derailment (described in Chapter 2), especially tendencies to forgive the sins of those who get results and to keep people in situations that play to their strengths. Specifically, it means giving honest feedback on serious flaws to everyone—including star performers who might take offense— not allowing self-confidence to blossom into arrogance that shuts off listening and learning, and anticipating how new situations might change the impact of a person's strengths and weaknesses.

Of course, preaching that feedback is necessary for continued learning is dangerously close to spewing a human resources homily that is easy to endorse but less frequently incorporated into action. The most pragmatic way to look at enhancing this kind of catalyst for development is that for people to change, they must have accurate information. "Feedback" in its original electronics sense is the return of part of an output to the input. The most effective feedback is that which comes directly from one's actions, unmediated by bosses or by any other filter. With modern information technology, it is often possible to provide people with such information.[10] But development requires more than just assessing the impact of one's actions— it also depends on information about what the organization's expectations are, how the environment it operates in is changing, and other aspects of context that make it possible for someone with the desire to adapt to actually do so.

CATALYST 2: PROVIDING INCENTIVES AND RESOURCES

Just as the importance of feedback has been well researched, so has the impact of both incentives and resources. B. F. Skinner, perhaps the most influential researcher in a long tradition, demonstrated beyond question that behavior can be shaped by the systematic application of rewards and punishments.[11] In the corporate context, research linking goal setting and rewards to performance has a long history. Again, there is no question that under the proper conditions (which include, incidentally, access to the resources needed to achieve the goals), specific goals and contingent incentives do affect behavior.[12] Although this enormous literature will not be reviewed here, its validity is reflected in the reasons people give for not changing. Figure 7-4 highlights statements that reflect blockages to change resulting from inadequate goals, incentives, and resources. To reduce such barriers, an organization can provide catalysts by setting clear developmental goals, making sure that rewards and sanctions are consistent with developmental agendas, and providing the resources necessary for achieving developmental plans.

Most organizations have discovered that managerial behavior can be shaped if people are held accountable for specific objectives. The systems developed to make accountability explicit, such as management by objectives, are far from perfect, but it is an unusual corporation that does not use some formal procedure to set targets, goals, or objectives. When it comes to development, however, the importance of accountability is usually overlooked. In practice, personal developmental objectives—if any are made explicit—are usually included (almost as an afterthought) at the end of an appraisal form and often consist only of training programs a person might attend or vague behavioral changes a person might attempt, in stark contrast to performance-based objectives, which are often specific and measurable. Consequently, developmental objectives are not always taken seriously, especially by talented people who are challenged by the work at hand. It is unfortunate but true that unless and until people believe that they will be held accountable for specific developmental objectives, they are likely to find other priorities more compelling. In that vein, it is difficult to hold someone accountable for something that is too general to be measured, so the first step in putting teeth in development is to make explicit the developmental objectives and how progress

FIGURE 7-4

LACK OF INCENTIVES AND RESOURCES

- No incentive to change
- Rewarded for staying the same
- Costs in time and energy
- Cost outweighs benefit
- Benefit unclear
- Imposed from outside
- No personal commitment to change
- Don't see the real importance of it
- Requires giving up something valued
- Don't know how to change
- No opportunity to practice
- No role models
- I've been successful as I am
- Comfortable like I am
- Context not changed
- Afraid to make mistakes
- Vulnerable while trying to change
- Convinced I'm right

towards them will be assessed. At the same time, these objectives have to be developed in a way that engenders commitment to them from the person being asked to change. The comments in Figure 7-4 suggest that people want to see why the change is important because they have other priorities—busy people don't always have slack time to take on new things without giving up something else. They also react negatively to demands for change that are imposed from the outside, which suggests that individuals should be involved in the setting of developmental goals. Of course, research over many years has demonstrated that commitment is enhanced when people are involved in making decisions about things that affect them and when they see what they are doing as important. The problem with many talented people is that the demands of the current assignment are sufficiently challenging and engaging that "development" is easily deferred and, given their success to date, perhaps unnecessary.

An example of this deferral surfaced by accident in some research some colleagues and I did on the "ability to learn" that contrasted high potential managers (those likely to rise to higher levels) with those considered to be solid performers (valued highly in their current position but unlikely to go much higher).[13] In one major international corporation, a sample of high potential managers was selected from those who had attended an elegant leadership and personal development course designed especially for them. Fearing that the high potentials who chose to attend the course might have a predilection toward education and learning, we compared high potentials who attended the course with a sample of high potentials who did not. It turned out that the people rated highest by their bosses were disproportionately represented in the group that did *not* attend the program, even though the program was intended as a special developmental opportunity for them. The explanation offered was that they were too indispensable to be released for the program! The message sent, of course, is that the truly valued don't have time to go to programs. When it comes to the most talented people, development often boils down to a matter of priorities.

Because a day has only so many hours—even for managers who work long hours, and because organizations and people have compelling priorities other than personal growth, having explicit developmental goals and good intentions is rarely enough. There is the issue of incentives: Most telling in Figure 7-2 is the statement "[I am] rewarded for staying the same," which simply reflects a reality of organizational life for talented people.

Rewards (and punishments) take many forms, from tangible extrinsic rewards like merit pay and bonuses to more subtle rewards like recognition or personal satisfaction. In considering how an existing reward system supports or inhibits learning, it is crucial to take the overall picture into account. Do bosses encourage or discourage developmental risk? Do only "ready now" candidates get promoted into key jobs, or are people put into important jobs for developmental reasons as well? Do the people who get promoted personify the developmental ideal in the sense that others see them as people who have taken developmental risks and have grown over time? Is merit-based pay contingent solely on outcomes, or does it reflect growth as well?

Because organizations rarely make "developing people" their first priority, reward systems are usually structured around specific job demands and outcomes. This is not to say that gearing rewards to growth is impossible, and in fact some organizations have installed sophisticated pay systems based on increasing one's repertoire of skills. Called "skill-based pay," this approach bases salary increases on the mastery of specific new skills and abilities rather than on seniority or output.[14] Although most current applications are limited to nonexempt and occasionally to technical workers, there is no obvious reason that some variation of this approach couldn't be tailored to managerial levels. When it isn't practical to base salary on learning, some part of merit or bonus pay might still be made contingent on the acceptance of developmental opportunities or on measurable growth. At a minimum, pay policies should not reward short-term performance at any cost, in so doing creating the precise conditions for derailment discussed in Chapter 2.

Initiating pay-for-development may be a long shot in most places, and tinkering with executive pay plans can be akin to using a flaming torch to read the label on a powderkeg. An easier victory may be had by adjusting promotion and selection practices (see Chapter 5). To use changes in succession practices as a catalyst for growth, however, requires going beyond making "B list" choices and holding business units accountable for cross-boundary moves. When a "B list" choice is made, for example, a catalytic element can be added by insisting that the new boss and the new subordinate mutually set clear and accountable developmental agendas before the subordinate begins the new job. Or if review panels are created as a mechanism for moving people into developmental assignments, the panels might also make explicit developmental objectives and plans for the people being reviewed and later review progress against those goals. In these ways, accountability and measurement are introduced for both the person being developed and for that person's boss. Such accountabilities may be seen as imposed from the outside, but they are not as arbitrary as the idiosyncratic actions of a single boss who is not accountable.

In the realm of intangible rewards, potentially catalytic actions cover the same broad spectrum of possibilities that are used in efforts to shape behavior. These possibilities include various kinds of recognition (such as visibility to senior management), special privileges or access, relief from some obligations, and perhaps a simple "thank you."

The overall goal is to make engaging in developmental activities as rewarding to people as what they have to give up to do them. But achievement of that goal may be limited by practical concerns, which force an organization to ensure that the existing system doesn't work against development rather than actually provide tangible rewards for development. For instance, no one should have to take a salary cut to take a developmental job, whether that job is evaluated at a lower pay level or not. A boss who allows one of his or her best people to transfer out for developmental reasons should not be "punished" for performance losses that occur as a result. A person who takes on a challenging assignment for developmental reasons should not have to put his or her career at risk. As a general rule, if people are not actively learning and growing, organizations should examine the reward system and how it is perceived.

When a reward system does support development, change may require additional help in the form of resources. The comments in Figure 7-4 suggest some of the directions this help could take, including role models, opportunities to practice, and insight into how to acquire a new skill. These specific comments reflect more generic issues in learning. Feedback may tell people what they're doing that's ineffective but doesn't always tell people what would be more effective. There is an implicit assumption that doing the opposite of what doesn't work will provide a cure, but that breaks down quickly once we get specific. For example, feedback that someone is "too distant" provides very little information on how "close" that person should become or how to learn to be "close." Or—a favorite example—if the feedback says someone is an insensitive S.O.B., what is the opposite? A sensitive S.O.B.? One of the most effective sources of learning, as has long been known, is "modeling" after someone who does well whatever it is a person wants to learn.[15] One of the most important catalysts for growth, especially in developing the elusive skills of leadership, is the availability of role models. Want to learn how to be a good team player? Watch carefully what a good team player does.

Unfortunately, there can be a large gap between watching someone who is good at something and learning to do it ourselves. If one thinks about it, learning from a role model is not all that easy—it involves perceptive observation, figuring out which behaviors are the most central, determining which approach fits with one's style, and then practicing the new way of acting. It is disconcerting to see "no opportunity to practice" on the list of obstacles to change, because learning any new behavioral skill requires a "practice field" of some sort. Whether caused by the demands of other priorities or by a fear of the consequences of a mistake, to eliminate practice is to eliminate change. Because of that, both time and safety are catalytic resources for growth.

Finally, but perhaps most significantly, an enormous obstacle to change is not knowing how to learn to do something differently or, before getting that far, assuming that the desired change is not possible ("I cannot learn to be charismatic"). Everyone lives in a land of best intentions, ritualized by the January 1 charade of self-improvement projects. Guided by right stuff assumptions, people tend to believe that change is a matter of willpower and that failing to change reflects some personality flaw. Better not to try than to prove oneself not up to the challenge.

If one lesson is to be drawn from the research reported in *The Lessons of Experience,* it is that significant change is not a matter of new year's resolutions.[16] It comes from putting oneself in situations like those described in Chapter 3 and creating an environment in which learning is a prerequisite for achieving something important. A critical resource, then, is having help in understanding what must be done to learn the new "something." Catalysts in this domain could include coaching or training in how to learn.

CATALYST 3: SUPPORTING THE CHANGE EFFORT

The comments highlighted in Figure 7-5 reflect how a nonsupportive context can block personal change. Two kinds of obstacles are identified: the emotional costs of trying to change and the ways in which the actions of others can undermine the effort to change. The message of both is that change is difficult to achieve all alone.

Personal change is an emotional undertaking. Uncertainty, fear, inadequacy, loss, damage to self-esteem, intimidation, and humiliation (see Figure 7-5), are significant and potentially debilitating emotions. Despite the common proclivity to approach development and change as a macho endeavor carried out by a lone warrior, change requires emotional as well as more objective sources of support. As with any weighty challenge, knowing that people care about and will offer support can help someone hold on, try again, get back up, and otherwise persevere. Perhaps the only place to find the kind of support these emotions require is through friends and family, but anything an organization can do to create a supportive environment when people undertake difficult challenges will serve as a catalyst for development. Whether that support takes the form of encouragement from a boss or an acknowledgment from a human resources coach, it is helpful to know that someone else knows what one is going through and cares.

FIGURE 7-5

LACK OF SUPPORT

- Not sure what change will create
- Requires giving up something valued
- Look stupid
- Feel incompetent
- No support
- Context not changed
- Too busy
- Focused on other things
- Other people aren't changed
- People don't see the change
- People won't allow the change
- Painful, humiliating
- Fear of manipulation
- Fear of the unknown
- Afraid to make mistakes
- Vulnerable while trying to change
- Fear of failure
- Afraid I won't be good enough
- Have tried to change before and failed
- Fear of being exposed
- Undermines self-confidence
- Threatens self-image
- Distorts self-image
- Intimidated by others

Other people can make or break a change effort through their expectations, attitudes, and behavior. An organization is a system, and one piece of that system cannot change without affecting the other parts. If the system changes, people in it either adapt or get left behind. Conversely, if a person tries to change, yet the system in which he or she is embedded remains the same, then the person faces a dilemma. Sometimes people have worked with someone for so long that they have come to expect certain behaviors. When that person tries to change, others still see what they expect to see and act accordingly. A boss who doesn't support development, for example, can certainly keep a person focused on other things.

The power of others was described poignantly by one manager who discovered, as he tried to change his style, that his peers and subordinates wanted him to stay the way he was—warts and all. It turned out that they had learned to anticipate his style and to manage it, so the idea that he would change something threatened to disrupt a status quo they had come to enjoy. Better the devil you know . . .

Many of the fears—of making mistakes, of being manipulated, of being humiliated—all reflect the tangled interdependencies of organizational life. Other people can make change a terrifying experience, or they can provide the support that encourages it. In a sense, a major catalyst for growth is an environment with people who themselves are growing and support others who try to.

THE CATALYSTS

Change is not easy. When a talented person ends up in a potentially developmental experience, he or she has few guarantees that what is there to be learned will be learned. Whether the goal is broadening by adding new skills or improving by fixing identified flaws, the context in which the development effort occurs can make all the difference. Although individuals are responsible for their own development (see Appendix), many of the potential obstacles to constructive change are within an organization's purview. What is important is that a context is created in which learning is maximized, so that talented people don't have one year of experience twenty times, but have twenty years of experience instead. The challenge is not unlike that described by Lewis Thomas, in ruminating on what it takes to inspire bees to make honey: "What it needs is for the air to be made right. If you want a bee to make honey, you do not issue protocols on solar navigation or carbohydrate chemistry, you put him together with other bees . . . and do what you can to arrange the general environment around the hive. If the air is right, the science will come in its own season, like pure honey."[17]

In this case, the "general environment around the hive" consists of clear, timely, and accurate information from credible sources; specific developmental goals for which people are held accountable; an incentive system consonant with or at least not antagonistic to development; adequate resources for a person to have both the opportunity and the capability to enact the desired change; and lots of emotional and systemic support. Figure 7-6 lists examples of interventions that might help, though the list is by no means exhaustive.

The potential for improving the context to support development is enormous, but the variety of possible actions are not within the reach of any one person or group. Some interventions traditionally fall to human resources professionals, who design appraisal systems, provide training, recommend incentive packages, and manage the succession process. But the larger part of the environment is in the hands of senior line managers who, through their actions and the models they provide, create a climate that either supports or inhibits development. Their control of priorities, opportunities, rewards, and values is much more direct and potent than anything human resources staff can do. Senior management makes it "safe" to take developmental risks and moves people for developmental purposes, even when those moves have short-term costs. Senior management allows talented people to believe that, because they have been successful, there is nothing left to learn. And if senior managers don't model growth—if they refuse to take advantage of developmental opportunities and demonstrate that learning, growth, and change are fundamental values, if they don't have time to tend to their own development, if they

FIGURE 7-6

Possible Catalysts for Learning

Improving Information	Providing Incentives and Resources	Supporting Change
Provide specific feedback.	Set specific and measurable developmental goals.	Provide emotional support.
Provide lots of examples.	Put development in context of the business strategy.	View change in a systems context— consider how the desired change will affect other people, the nature of the work, etc.
Provide feedback on important criteria, possibly on identified competencies.	Find ways to assess progress on developmental goals.	
Provide feedback on development as well as on performance and outcomes.	Hold people accountable for achieving developmental objectives.	Change the context as necessary.
Expect supervisors to confront problems.	Involve the person in setting the goals and measures.	Create an environment in which change is supported and encouraged.
Use credible (to the recipient) sources.	Make development a real priority.	
Don't dance around the issues: Give needed feedback even if the person is performing well.	Make part of pay contingent on development as well as performance.	
When messages are mixed, provide perspective.	Promote/move people for developmental reasons.	
Interpret feedback in terms of the future as well as the present.	Promote people who model desired developmental behavior.	
Provide a context for feedback that reflects the organization's future strategy.	Provide as many rewards and as much recognition as possible for growth.	
Give feedback in a form acceptable to the recipient.	Involve multiple sources in setting developmental agendas.	
When possible, enrich feedback from the job, customers, and other "natural" sources.	Above all, be sure the existing reward system is not contradictory to development.	
	Provide access to role models.	
	Make it safe to practice, try new things.	
	Coach/train people on how to acquire new skills.	

don't take the time to help in others' development—then even the most elegant development "system" will be little more than an exercise.

If we're after honey and we've done all we can to make the air right, we still have to depend on the bee.

8

MAKING EXECUTIVE DEVELOPMENT A STRATEGIC ADVANTAGE

EVEN THE HARDIEST OF SEEDS STANDS A BETTER CHANCE IF IT lands in fertile soil, has sufficient water, and enjoys generally favorable conditions. So too, it seems, with the managers in a twenty-year longitudinal study at AT&T, where regardless of how much ability was assessed early on, job opportunities that provided "stimulation, challenge, and enough freedom to develop their own resourcefulness" had a significant effect on later success.[1] No matter how gifted a person might be, and even though personal responsibility is paramount in successful development, a developmentally effective context can, without question, have a significant effect on whether talented people reach their full potential. But to say that talent can be nurtured does not prove that nurturing it is either cost effective or astute strategically. Like trying to prove that love enriches one's life, proving that investing in development has bottom-line benefits requires an act of faith. It is not enough to observe that several out of the ten "most admired" companies in America—Coca-Cola, Hewlett-Packard, Motorola, and Johnson & Johnson, for example[2]—are also considered by many to be benchmark companies for developing talent, while few in the bottom of the rankings enjoy such stature. Organizational performance has many determinants, and the contribution of leadership, much less leadership development, can be hard to isolate. That said, there are at least seven compelling reasons to take seriously, to invest in, and to put priority on strategic executive development (see Figure 8-1).

THE CASE FOR STRATEGIC EXECUTIVE DEVELOPMENT

Leadership makes a difference.[3] The more change that lies ahead, the more important effective leadership will be. In a major study of the relationship between culture and performance in two hundred companies, John Kotter and co-author James Heskett concluded that "the single most visible factor that distinguishes major cultural changes that succeed from those that fail is competent leadership at the top."[4] Not only does the *quality* of leadership need to be improved, but flatter, more responsive organizations require a greater *quantity* of leaders at all levels. In organizations that are skeptical of developing leadership abilities, the need for a coherent strategy for finding sufficient talent is even more compelling. A cursory look at the state of the art in executive selection and development or a brief survey of the practices of benchmark companies quickly reveals that both selection and development strategies are deployed in any serious effort to improve the supply of executive leadership. Developmental activities are often highly visible in "programs" (such as those at General Electric's renowned training facility in Crotonville, New York, or Samsung's Human Resources Development Center), but some of the most powerful developmental activities lie in on-the-job challenges. Sometimes these latter activities aren't even thought of as development!

The traditional solution to a leadership shortage is to raid the leadership larder of the competition or of one of the most admired companies. The market in "previously owned" executives is brisk, and the almost mythical quality associated with certain companies is something to see.[5] The prevalence and

FIGURE 8-1

THE CASE FOR STRATEGIC EXECUTIVE DEVELOPMENT

1. Leadership makes a difference. The more change that lies ahead, the more important effective leadership will be. The quality of leadership can be improved through development.

2. Companies can't always find outside or buy the leadership they need. If they do, it is expensive and does not come with a money-back guarantee.

3. Derailments are expensive. The higher the level, the more expensive they are. There are many false positives.

4. Survival of the fittest is not the same thing as survival of the best. Leaving leadership development up to chance is foolish.

5. Most of the cost of development is already sunk. Not to reap a return on the investment is bad business.

6. Creating a learning environment is consistent with business strategies that involve having employees take on more responsibility, assume more risk, and solve problems.

7. It's good business practice. Investors consider the quality of a corporation's management. Talented people prefer to work for companies that invest in their development. Customers prefer to work with corporations that can solve their problems. Companies like that have strong cultures that place high value on leadership.

---

apparent success of headhunting firms belies the fact that *companies can't always find or buy on the outside the leadership they need.* Like the world of professional sports, buying top-level executive talent has grown quite expensive. But unlike professional sports, the transferability of executive skills is not entirely obvious. So much of a leader's effectiveness depends on relationships and on organizational and industry knowledge, that outsiders can be at a distinct disadvantage.[6] And where transfers do work (turnaround specialists can be brought in from the outside to stop the bleeding), a single executive hire is seldom enough to cure a leadership shortage, for once the immediate problems are solved, the outsider may turn out to be a cultural misfit. In short, frequent trips to the outside turn out to be costly and don't come with a money-back guarantee.

Derailments are expensive. Whether the mistake is made internally, resulting in high-level promotions of people who later derail, or by bringing in an outside hire who fails, the costs are not limited to wasted salary, relocation expenses, finding and installing a replacement, buy-out packages, and other out-of-pocket expenses, but also must be calculated to include damage to morale, lost productivity and opportunities, and a host of intangibles. The costs can be dramatically higher when derailments occur at higher executive levels, involve international assignments, or entail the additional expenses of outside recruiting. Of course, some errors cannot be avoided, and one can argue about what a reasonable cost of bad choices should be as a matter of doing business. The data indicate, however, that there are many "false positives"—people who are promoted who later derail.[7] The forces described in Chapters 1 and 2 of this book suggest that organizations can do a great deal to reduce their role in these affairs.

Survival of the fittest, even when it works, is not the same thing as survival of the best. Our misplaced belief in the quality of the ultimate outcome of evolution has been attributed by Stephen J. Gould to a misunderstanding of Darwin's revolution. Far from following a predictable ascending path, from the most primitive of creatures at the bottom to human beings at the pinnacle, evolution has been messy and chaotic. Gould observes:

> Humans are not the end result of predictable evolutionary progress, but rather a fortuitous cosmic afterthought, a tiny little twig on the enormously arborescent bush of life, which, if replanted from seed, would almost surely not grow this twig again, or perhaps any twig with any property we would care to call consciousness. . . .
>
> We may then view life's history as an unpredictable set of largely fortuitous, and eminently interruptible, excursions down highly contingent pathways. And we will understand successful species as islands of temporary stability, not as striving entities in a flux of constant improvement.[8]

In other words, left to its own devices, nature follows

unpredictable pathways.[9] To believe that natural forces operating within organizations will defy cosmic rules and, left to their own devices, produce effective executive leaders, is a triumph of hope over experience. Trial by fire is as likely to produce people in asbestos suits as it is to yield a next generation of leaders uniquely equipped to handle the new challenges of the future. In short, leaving leadership development up to chance is foolish.

Most of the cost of development is already sunk.[10] Research has demonstrated beyond question what has long been evident: executive ability is learned primarily on the job. Challenging assignments, remarkable bosses, living with mistakes, and the other experiences so powerful in development already exist within any organization. Not to take advantage of them and thereby reap a return on the investment is, quite simply, bad business.

Creating a learning environment is consistent with—indeed required for—business strategies that involve having employees take on more responsibility, assume more risk, and solve problems.[11] Perhaps the most influential work on "the learning organization" in the last decade of the twentieth century was Peter Senge's book *The Fifth Discipline.* In it, he defines a learning organization as "an organization that is continually expanding its capacity to create its future." He goes on to describe a new role for leaders in such organizations: "In a learning organization, leaders are designers, stewards, and teachers. They are responsible for *building organizations* where people continually expand their capabilities to understand complexity, clarify vision, and improve shared mental models—that is, they are responsible for learning."[12]

It's good business, and it's the right thing to do. Rarely is it possible to maximize organizational performance while simultaneously occupying the moral high ground, but developing talent presents one such opportunity.[13] Investors consider the quality of a corporation's management when they evaluate risk and potential. Talented people prefer to work for companies that will invest in their development and provide them with

challenging opportunities.[14] Customers prefer to work with corporations that are responsive to their needs and can help them
solve their problems. The data suggest that companies with
strong corporate cultures that emphasize stockholders, employees, and customers, and place high value on leadership outper-
form those with weak cultures or imbalanced emphasis.[15]

A GENERAL MODEL FOR DEVELOPING EXECUTIVE TALENT

Building on the agricultural metaphor, Figure 8-2 depicts the
model for nurturing talent created thus far. In essence the
approach is simple: people with the ability to learn from experience, when given key experiences as determined by the business strategy, will learn the needed skills if given the right kind
of support.

However simple the general model, putting it into practice
is no small accomplishment. Each of its components is complex, and often the actions that best promote development vio-
late the organization's short-term performance mandate. How
to think about talent poses the first of the dilemmas. It would
be much easier if the competencies needed for the future could
be found in some primitive form in the managers of today. One
could then simply identify talent and wait for it to mature (or
as organizations facing some urgency are prone to do, try to
find a magic elixir that will speed up the maturation process).
Development would be relatively simple because the prerequisite skills already exist, and "experience" consists of exposure
to various functional and organization-specific content. In
chapters 1, 2, and 5, I made the case that it isn't so simple, that
in fact, learning is never finished. Like snowflakes, executives
may look alike from a distance but are all different up close.
There is an important lesson to be learned from physicists
struggling to understand underlying order in unpredictable
events. Snowflakes, for example, obey mathematical laws, but
it is impossible to predict how any particular one will turn out:
James Gleick noted that "it was impossible to predict precisely

FIGURE 8-2

A GENERAL MODEL FOR DEVELOPING EXECUTIVE TALENT

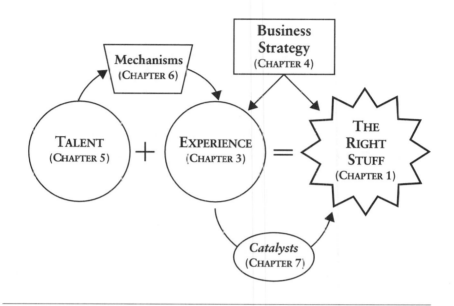

how fast a tip would grow, how narrow it would be, or how often it would branch."[16]

Paleontologist Gould points out that people like to think of progress in terms of "movement from small to large, simple to complex, primitive to advanced—an ideal of perpetual growth and expansion." He goes on to describe a theme, particularly prevalent in Western cultures, of "misconstruing the less complex as the primitive precursor," and notes that "small and short are often just different from big and long, not little brothers gliding toward a more intricate manhood."[17]

So it is with talent: whatever the gifts that start the journey, the events and experiences that unfold along the way will shape where a person eventually ends up. Life—and executive development—is a creative tension between stability and change, and talent is best viewed as a promise that, if conditions are right, may eventually be realized.[18] From an executive development perspective, as I have argued, that promise is best assessed by looking for evidence of ability to learn.

A second dilemma is posed by the mechanisms for getting talented people into the opportunities they need to grow. The bottom line is that whatever process controls who gets what experiences is actually controlling—to the extent that it can be controlled—development. The dilemma is created by the co-incidence between important developmental opportunities and key managerial assignments. Because challenging assignments also tend to be the critical ones in terms of organizational performance, there is a tension between choosing someone who has already proven the ability to handle the assignment versus the person who would learn the most from having it. It boils down to how much risk the hiring manager or the organization is willing to take. All too often, development is a heroic act by isolated managers or parts of the organization, who do it even though they are not rewarded—indeed, are usually punished—for it (by losing good people, being held responsible for mistakes and performance targets that don't leave room for learning, and having time taken away from bottom-line action).

A third set of dilemmas revolves around the possibility that experience is ubiquitous, but the lessons it teaches may be many or few, good or bad, intended or accidental. On the one hand, development is spurred by challenge and risk, whereas organizations prefer predictability and security. Pursuit of the latter can lead to jobs being simplified, bottom-line responsibility being saved for only the most senior levels, or close controls and approvals being built in—all of which serve to reduce jobs' developmental potential. On the other hand, organizations prefer to play it safe and promote people within chimneys or silos, in a progression of increased responsibility but within the same function or business. "A little bit more of the same" may make sense in one light, but it is contrary to what is known about development, which often requires breaking out of a straight-line progression.[19] Perhaps conservative experiences teach people to be conservative.

The fourth dilemma arises because learning from experience is not automatic. Once a manager has gone to all the trouble of finding talented people and getting them into the "right" experiences, it might seem possible to step back. Unfortunately, setting the stage does not guarantee a performance. The dilemma arises because the same actions that can be used to improve short-term performance—setting goals, making people accountable, contingent rewards—are also the ones that might be used to encourage development. But which gets a manager's priority: getting the job done or promoting development? Furthermore, constructive feedback, support, tolerance of mistakes, and other actions that encourage development may be seen as contradicting command and control assumptions (or demands).

Finally, an organization can face a strategic dilemma in that the business strategy must address multiple possibilities. Is development of leadership talent more or less important than technology, customer focus, global alliances, value creation, or any of a number of potentially potent sources of competitive advantage?

These dilemmas and others (for example, reliance on an annual performance appraisal cycle versus a career-long developmental cycle) are not resolved easily. What is clear, however, is that all the components in the model are related, so if someone chooses to walk the development path, all the pieces must align, or time, talent, and money will be wasted. Rather than do the job halfway, an organization should make a conscious choice, then commit to it. There are three alternatives: doing nothing, relying on selection, or pursuing development.

"If you keep on doing what you've always done, you'll keep on getting what you always got." An organization that is doing nothing about development and is happy with the results need not catch a case of program envy. If the unmanaged process is working well enough, barring a major change in the internal or external environment, "good enough" may very well be that. Better a conscious hands-off approach than a hypocritical token effort. If the choice is to do nothing active about development, it is still wise to run the business so that challenging assignments abound, good people are moved around enough to develop perspective, and subsystems are built to measure and reward performance. By being consistent in worshiping only performance, an organization will attract people who thrive on "kill or be killed."[20] I have already shown that survival of the fittest is not an optimal strategy, but if it is the strategy of choice, then at the least, the organization should make the most of the suboptimal.

An alternative to doing nothing is to adopt a deliberate and systematic selection strategy. Selection is not optimal for many reasons, but if it is the only choice, then doing the best possible job of selecting is the preferred option. This means developing a performance-based template of executive leadership competencies, measuring those competencies thoroughly and effectively (that is, using multiple raters, focusing on behavior, dealing decisively with performance problems), and using assignments and other on-the-job challenges as "tests" of individual mettle. Many of the principles of development can be adapted to a selection strategy, but the underlying assumptions are drastically different. Selection erroneously assumes that end-state competencies exist in embryonic or hidden form within people who have potential. The challenge is to get such people into the assignments (experiences) that will allow those inherent abilities to be demonstrated. As with developmental experiences, the business strategy should determine which assignments are germane and, like the winnowing out of the fighter pilots described in Chapter 1, set progressively more demanding tests to determine who moves up the pyramid. Unfortunately, this strategy also preserves all the dysfunctions described in Chapter 1 and is terribly wasteful of talent. It may, however, be the only choice in very macho environments where Vince Lombardi posters line the executive office walls.

This discussion brings us to the third choice, which I believe is the optimal one. Conscious and systematic development of executive leadership talent is, in the long run, the most effective strategy and the one most likely to ensure competitive advantage over time. Selection strategies do little to develop new skills once the "right" people have been selected, therefore constant turnover is required to fulfill new leadership demands as the business environment changes. Especially when the selection process is based on generic competencies, it is easy to copy, and it is also tempting to steal the executives the process identifies. In contrast, an effective development process is tailored to the leadership challenges of a specific business strategy and to the kinds of experiences available within a particular company, both of which make the process harder to copy. The executives identified may still be desirable to pirates, but they may be less inclined to go somewhere else when where they are holds more developmental opportunities.

A Prescriptive Model

It is always dangerous to make specific recommendations when issues are complex and data are sparse. Yet the compelling logic of the developmental model has direct implications for practice, and the various components of the prescriptive model (Figure 8-3) are commonly found in many benchmark companies (though they are rarely found all together in one place). As should be clear by now, executive development is not an isolated human resource program that operates independently of the business goals or the organization. To make development a viable proposition is an act of leadership that encompasses strategic concerns.

Strategy

As I have emphasized throughout this book, the reason to develop executive leadership is that it is needed to achieve a business' strategic aims. Any prescriptive model, then, must begin with those strategic concerns, and the first order of business is for senior leadership to define leadership development as a strategic imperative. Only if it is a priority will it be given the time, the attention, the resources, and above all, the accountability that is necessary to sustain the system. There is no magic formula for making believers out of senior management, since

FIGURE 8-3

A Prescriptive Model for Developing Executive Talent

Business Strategy
Establish executive leadership development as a strategic priority.

Create a development-oriented context from the top down.

Translate the business strategy into specific leadership challenges.

Assess existing leadership strengths and weaknesses vis-à-vis the challenges.

Experience
Make extensive use of existing assignments, both permanent and temporary, that will prepare people to meet strategic challenges.

Identify effective coaches and role models, and make extensive use of temporary and permanent assignments to access them.

Identify and develop courses and programs that provide or substitute for needed experiences.

Create target experiences.

Establish and use "corporate schools" as appropriate.

Talent
Base the recruiting and early identification process on the ability to learn from experience.

Annually assess demonstrated competencies.

Annually assess derailment potential (fatal flaws).

On an ongoing basis, assess what was learned from each assignment.

Establish a performance management system with development accountability.

Mechanisms for Movement
Establish a formal succession planning process that identifies both a high potential pool and a "B list" pool of candidates.

Formally identify key developmental assignments and "schools."

Ensure that the executive resource function is strong and centralized, and has the authority to manage "corporate assets."

Track developmental experiences and progress over the long term.

Ensure that the performance management system emphasizes development.

FIGURE 8-3

A PRESCRIPTIVE MODEL *(Cont.)*

Catalysts   Line accountability: set specific developmental goals and accountability; provide development opportunities and resources; offer development-contingent rewards.

Human Resources accountability: provide developmental feedback and interpretation (e.g., 360° surveys); provide training and coaching; coach line managers in the use of experience; provide a safety net.

Individual responsibility: expect to take personal responsibility for development; take the initiative in seeking out developmental opportunities.

---

commitment to developing talent, like commitment to any other strategic aim, is either an act of faith or an expression of deeply held values.

Once development is a strategic priority, however, the rest flows from it. Leadership is required to create a development-oriented organizational environment, and that may require a cultural change. Key elements of context are the measurement and reward systems, the attitudes toward mistakes and risk, the design of work and organizational boundaries, and other such factors, discussed previously, that either make development difficult or ease its path. As with most other strategic priorities, it helps if this one is modeled at the top—especially if there are glaring developmental needs among senior officers. Their willingness to subject themselves to the rigors of development can inspire others to do the same. Clearer yet is the message they send if they will not.

On a more immediate level, for a development system to work, the business strategy must be translated into leadership challenges—current and future—that developing leaders need to prepare to tackle. (Chapter 4 discussed how this translation can be achieved.) Analysis of what an organization is already good at developing versus what needs more support is important to any effective development system. Updating the leadership challenges and perceived readiness probably should be a part of an annual senior-level meeting in which strategic priorities are reviewed, succession and development plans for key executive resources are examined, and operation of the system as a whole is assessed.

EXPERIENCE

The primary vehicle for development is experience, so there is a critical linkage between the strategic leadership challenges and the experiences that would prepare talented people to meet those challenges. The key to the system lies in identifying and accessing developmental experiences, wherever they might be in an organization, with the same intensity that traditional systems generate for assessing people. Where experiences do not exist or cannot be made available for development, new experiences need to be created or substitutes found. (This may be a central role for training programs and a very good reason for developing a strong training organization.) An audit of valuable opportunities should include task forces, projects, and potent staff assignments, as well as courses and programs that might be used for specific developmental needs. Often neglected but just as important is the identification of role models throughout the organization—people who demonstrate the desired qualities and could be used to help develop others.

The details of developmental experiences were discussed in Chapter 3, but the bottom line is that the system has to identify key experiences (or, at the broadest level, the corporate "schools") and what they might teach. The method of choice for doing so is to select executives who are considered successful and who approximate the desired future state and interview them about experiences that were important to them and about what they learned. The choice of experiences will at some level always be a judgment call, so the premium is on finding the best judgments available. The recommendation here is that something resembling a succession plan used to chart people for specific job assignments be created to link job assignments to specific strategic challenges.

TALENT

Chapters 1 and 2 described the nasty things that can happen to talented people as they succeed their way through an organization, and Chapter 5 went into some detail on ways to look at talent from a developmental perspective. Whereas end-state competencies are a necessary part of the overall picture, a development strategy makes other assumptions. The practical systems created must take into account that the ability to acquire needed competencies is of paramount importance until and unless the competencies themselves have been demonstrated. By focusing on ability to learn, it is possible to avoid the trap of assuming that the finite list of competencies important for today will be the same in the future.

Translated into recommendations, the assessment of talent as it relates to the development of executive ability has at least three aspects. First, recruiting and early identification procedures need to include some version of "ability to learn from experience" in addition to any technical and cognitive requirements. It has long been known that recruiting based on technical skills alone can later hamper both team play and leadership, but until recently, knowing what else to look for has been problematic.

Second, the effective integration of development objectives into the annual assessment of performance is essential. The performance management system that is connected with primary organizational rewards like pay, bonuses, and promotion must be connected in a meaningful way to the achievement of development objectives. In an objectives-based system, for example, one or more of the stated objectives for which a person is accountable should reflect a developmental target, and the annual review (more often is desirable) should include feedback and assessment of progress against that target. It is not sufficient to relegate developmental needs to a box at the bottom of the appraisal form, an act that makes the activity seem an afterthought. Integrating development into the performance management system serves several important functions. It keeps development "on the screen," along with performance-based objectives; it connects developmental success with organizational rewards; it provides a forum for dialogue between boss and subordinate about developmental issues; and it makes the symbolic point that personal growth is an expectation. In addition, putting development in the same paragraph with bottom-line performance gets rid of the "soft" image that often accompanies the false dichotomy between development and performance.

Third, because development of talent accumulates over a career rather than in discrete annual increments, there needs to be a separate system tailored to this longer-term perspective. A review board consisting of higher-level managers that meets at least once a year to review the progress of key corporate assets is one approach. In some companies, these review boards cascade throughout the business, using managers from two levels above the target level as reviewers. Among the activities of these boards should be the assessment of demonstrated competencies, identification of potentially derailing flaws, and documentation of "what was learned" from each significant assignment. It should be the responsibility of these boards or of the executive development group that supports these boards to keep track of each individual's growth over time. Using multiple assessors and considering longer periods of time sharply distinguish review board activities from annual performance reviews, and giving these boards significant power to control career moves can put teeth in the process.

MECHANISMS FOR MOVEMENT

Because "who gets what assignment" is so important in development, the mechanisms provided by the organization to make such decisions for the people in the talent pool is the critical link in the process. The characteristics that the mechanisms must have follow directly from the previous discussion of experience and talent. At a minimum, the process must provide for identifying people with the potential to develop executive leadership skills, assess their developmental needs against the business strategy, identify the experiences across the organization that could meet those needs, exercise the authority to get talented people into the experiences identified, and track their progress over time. That means that the development system will have to include some version of a high potential pool, of succession planning, and of an empowered executive development staff. The review board system described above has special advantages over a system run only by an executive development staff, but the primary advantage is that it puts line managers in charge of the assessment and decision-making process. The role of the staff is properly to guide the process, collect the necessary data, and follow up on the decisions. This staff also can be charged with assessing how well the system is working by coming up with performance measures and criteria that reflect broad developmental goals. Although there are no precise measures, helpful indicators include the number of development plans actually implemented, the number of cross-boundary moves achieved, improvement against diversity goals, learning success rate, perceptions of the developmental climate of the organization, depth of leadership talent, and number of derailments.

Whatever the mechanisms designed to ensure the movement of talent into developmental experiences, the system should be monitored closely by the top executives. It is their responsibility to ensure that the system is working properly, that the leadership needs of the corporation are being given priority, and that the talent pool is adequate given the strategic direction of the firm. There is no substitute for leadership if development of talent is to be realized.

CATALYSTS

Even when the ability to provide talented people with strategically desirable experiences is constrained, experience happens every day. Providing catalysts to help people extract the available learning from any assignment, new or old, large or small, can result in significant development gains for the organization. Many of the traditional development practices, particularly those in the bailiwick of human resources staffs, serve this function. Providing feedback through surveys, sending people to training, coaching, and mentoring programs, and many other organizational development interventions essentially make learning more accessible. Unfortunately, these kinds of activities are often unconnected to the other critical pieces of the model and therefore act in isolation from the overall development process. To further dissipate the impact of human resource interventions, line management's performance goals and accountabilities, which are all too often devoid of meaningful developmental targets, set priorities that can be antithetical to the growth of new skills and that undermine personal responsibility for growth. The real challenge in creating catalysts lies in influencing line management to take a more active role in their own and others' development, not in devising new human resources practices and procedures. As with so many other aspects of leadership, getting the desired results is often a matter of attention and focus.

THE BOTTOM LINE IN DEVELOPMENT

Taking development seriously is a great deal of trouble. The visible indicators so often equated with development—sending lots of people to seminars and training programs; 360° feedback and development plans; mentoring, coaching, and diversity programs; elaborate succession plans—can be important features of a development system but, by themselves, are severely limited. Whether an organization will realize the full potential of its leadership talent is itself a leadership issue. It begins with a commitment to the strategic priority of executive leadership and clarity of purpose on how to achieve it. If the choice is development, the organization will need to take a long, hard look at how the business strategy translates into development needs, at the structural implications (possible reengineering to expand the developmental opportunities), at policies about the identification and control of human assets, at what is measured and rewarded, and at a host of fundamental questions that involve the purpose, structure, and culture of the organization.

People can't *make* other people develop, but organizations can create an environment in which development is supported, design a context in which it is expected and rewarded, model it, and ultimately see to it that those who choose not to grow join companies where that stance is appreciated.

Jan Carlzon, former CEO of Scandinavian Airlines System, observed that "it is up to the top executive to become a true leader, devoted to creating an environment in which employees can accept and execute their responsibilities with confidence and finesse. . . . To succeed he can no longer be an isolated and autocratic decision-maker. Instead, he must be a visionary, a strategist, an informer, a teacher, and an inspirer."[21] To this, I would add that a true leader creates an environment in which people continually learn and grow. And not just those who appear to have the basic skills necessary to climb to the top of an organization. Development of talent is appropriate for everyone who can make a contribution to their organization or to society. Warren Bennis put it well: "Since the release and full use of the individual's full potential is the organization's true task, all organizations must provide for the growth and development of their members and find ways of offering them opportunities for such growth and development. This is the one true mission of all organizations and the principal challenge to today's organizations."[22]

And it's not just CEOs who, from their lofty perches, create a learning context for others. Everyone—managers, coaches, parents, friends—has a part to play in the development of those around them. For, you see, this book is not just about how executives develop, it is about how *people* develop. People grow through challenging experiences that stretch them, that force them to explore new things, that call on them to cultivate yet another fantastical quality. Most people lead lives in which they find themselves in such experiences while on their way to somewhere else—as a result of accident, fate, or some force outside themselves. It often takes an act of real courage to deliberately put ourselves in situations that force us to change, to learn something new. Yet that is where our potential lies: one step beyond where we thought we could go.

APPENDIX

TAKING CHARGE OF YOUR DEVELOPMENT

IN AN IDEAL WORLD, ORGANIZATIONS WOULD CHERISH THE potential of individual employees, understand completely how to help develop that potential, provide developmental opportunities based on that understanding, and take responsibility for ensuring that each person lived up to his or her full potential. It is not an ideal world. To trust that an organization will do what is in the best interest of even its most talented people is like hoping the IRS will find errors in your favor if it audits you. There is a poster that says, "Pray to God, But Row Toward Shore," and it could serve as a guidepost to self-development. An organization may have the best of intentions, but you still have to do what you can to get yourself where you want to go.

This is excellent advice, for at least seven reasons (see Figure A-1). These reasons boil down to the obvious: change is inevitable; people who do not grow to meet the challenges presented by change will not continue to be successful; and the person with the greatest vested interest in your success is you.

FIGURE A-1

SEVEN REASONS YOU HAVE TO TAKE CHARGE OF YOUR DEVELOPMENT

1. There is no standing still for organizations or for the people in them. Change is a constant for the foreseeable future.

2. When situations change, strengths can become weaknesses; weaknesses that didn't matter before can become central; and arrogance based on past success can become dangerous.

3. Your organization probably does a lousy job of developing people.

4. As long as the organization has or can get enough of the talent it thinks it needs, it doesn't care if it's you in particular.

5. The implied lifetime employment contract no longer exists. Even satisfactory performance is not enough to guarantee a job for life.

6. Organizations may make change difficult, but the real obstacles to change are within you.

7. It's the right thing to do.

IT'S THE RIGHT THING TO DO

> Those quiet men who always stand on piers asked where we were going and when we said, "To the Gulf of California," their eyes melted with longing, they wanted to go so badly. . . . [T]hey do not know that they would carry their globes of boredom with them wherever they went.[1]
>
> —John Steinbeck

> It's you who makes the world what it is. Reality is *you*.[2]
>
> —Saul Bellow

> There is nothing you can do about your early life now, except to understand it. You can, however, do everything about the rest of your life.[3]
>
> —Warren Bennis

John Steinbeck might have been describing what happens when we stop learning: Ignorance, death, and stasis versus learning, growth, and change: a choice each of us has to make. With everyone telling us that today is the first day of the rest of our lives, have we learned anything useful about how to take charge of it? The answer is, "yes, but . . . ." Yes, by looking at how successful people have developed we can see what some of the key ingredients are. But there is no pat formula that will work for everyone, and there are no guarantees. Perhaps the excitement is that no one can know how it will turn out, but for sure the journey won't be dull.

Figure A-2 outlines the key ingredients in taking charge of your development. Not surprisingly, there is a parallel relationship between what an organization can do to enhance development and what individuals can do on their behalf. Briefly stated, taking charge of your development means knowing yourself, knowing what you want to achieve, identifying opportunities for growth in that direction, being proactive in getting those opportunities, and creating an environment that promotes learning from them.

SELF-AWARENESS

To those who want to become leaders, Warren Bennis has laid out a clear challenge: "'Know thyself,' was the inscription over the Oracle at Delphi. And it is still the most difficult task any of us faces. But until you truly know yourself, strengths and weaknesses, know what you want to do and why you want to do it, you cannot succeed in any but the most superficial sense of the word. The leader never lies to himself, especially about himself, knows his flaws as well as his assets, and deals with them directly."[4]

Effective leaders are self-aware, reflecting the ultimate form of self-confidence that makes it possible to welcome negative feedback and criticism. Knowing one's weaknesses is power, because then something can be done about them; the real danger lies in what one doesn't know. Seeking out feedback, openness to criticism, and learning from mistakes all distinguish managers considered high potential from those considered solid performers.[5] Lack of awareness, whether through neglect or arrogance, is a major contributor to derailment.

FIGURE A-2

TAKING CHARGE OF YOUR DEVELOPMENT

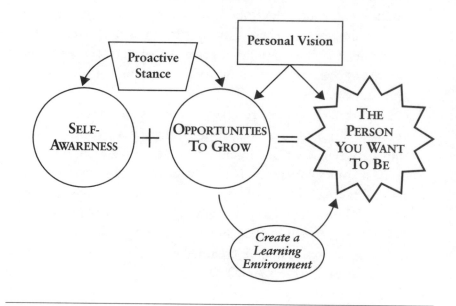

Awareness begins with three basic components: knowing your strengths, knowing your weaknesses, and recognizing undeveloped areas that need bolstering if you are to achieve future goals. "Knowing" is not just a general awareness but rather implies a deep level of understanding. Two simple tests of such knowledge are whether you can predict how you will react in specific situations and what impact your reaction will produce, and whether you can accurately predict what other people would say if asked to describe your strengths and weaknesses. The recent popularity of 360° feedback, in which people compare self-assessments with data from boss, peers, and subordinates, is a result of the potency of such comparisons. You cannot always be an unbiased observer of yourself, so finding more objective sources of feedback is a crucial component of development.

Figure A-3 provides you with an opportunity to assess your strengths and weaknesses. Based on findings from the derailment studies described in Chapter 2, Figure A-3 incorporates the complication that there is no such thing as an unqualified strength. As an indicator of the depth of your self-awareness, Part 1 asks you to identify the strengths that have made you successful so far and then to describe the potential dark side of those strengths. Your ability to do this is important, because talented people can overplay their strengths and organizations like to use people in areas of strength, thus inadvertently encouraging both the overuse of existing strengths and the neglect of developing of new strengths. As people enter new situations, strengths that served them well can turn on them, becoming weaknesses that do them harm. This is particularly true of expertise, which can blind an expert to issues outside of a narrow field. Everyone has heard the jokes about medical specialists—if you have a headache and go to a migraine specialist, you have migraine. If you go to a stress specialist, you have stress headaches. The same may be true of an engineer, or a financial analyst, or a marketer—problems that have no disciplinary boundaries can be defined from an overly narrow perspective and thus remain unsolved.

Part 2 of Figure A-3 asks you to describe your flaws and then to identify those flaws on which you have received repeated feedback. After picking the weakness you think has the most serious implications for you, identify a situation or type of situation in which that flaw could become fatal. If that kind of situation is at all likely as you consider the changes that the future may bring (Part 3 in Figure A-3), then it may be a good idea to do something about it.

Some people continue to live with their flaws because they assume that the only way to deal with a flaw is to correct it—and for some flaws, that can seem like a difficult (perhaps impossible) task that is hardly worth the effort. A serious introvert, for example, can have a difficult time imagining transformation into an extrovert, even if he or she knows that extroversion can be helpful in a leadership role. A pessimist may not believe it is possible to become an optimist and therefore may not try to change, even if he or she knows that optimism

FIGURE A-3

SELF-ASSESSMENT OF STRENGTHS AND WEAKNESSES

General Instructions: The following questions ask you to reflect on your strengths, your potential weaknesses, and the changes that lie ahead for you. This exercise might prove valuable to you as you think through your developmental needs and aspirations.

Part 1: Strengths

1. List as many as five strengths that you believe have led to your success thus far. Try to list them in order, starting with your greatest strength.

    A. _____

    B. _____

    C. _____

    D. _____

    E. _____

2. It has been suggested that every strength can also be a weakness. Can you see how each of your strengths can be or could become a weakness? If so, note how each strength listed above could get you into trouble.

    A. _____

    B. _____

    C. _____

    D. _____

    E. _____

3. Given that strengths are not always unqualified assets, can you identify a strength that you would like to manage better?

    _____

    _____

FIGURE A-3

SELF-ASSESSMENT OF STRENGTHS AND WEAKNESSES *(Cont.)*

Part 2: Potential Weaknesses

4. Everyone—even the most successful executive—has weaknesses. What do you think are your most significant weaknesses?

A. _____

B. _____

C. _____

5. Looking back over the weaknesses you listed above, are there any that you have heard about from someone associated with you? Put an "*" by the weaknesses you've heard about from someone else. Now put "**" by any weaknesses that you've heard about from multiple sources or that you've known about for a long time.

6. Pick the one weakness that you think is most likely to get you in trouble later in your career. Can you briefly describe a situation that would play to that weakness—a situation in which this particular flaw is a serious handicap?

_____

_____

_____

7. Just as every strength can be seen as a potential weakness, it can be argued that every weakness was at one time a strength, or at least at one time served a useful purpose. Can you describe how your most serious flaw may serve you well or might have served you well at one time in your life?

_____

_____

_____

_____

FIGURE A-3

SELF-ASSESSMENT OF STRENGTHS AND WEAKNESSES *(Cont.)*

Part 3: Changes That Lie Ahead

8. What is the most significant change that lies ahead for you in terms of your work or your career?

_____

_____

_____

9. Will any of the following things change for you in the foreseeable future? (Check as many as apply.)

____ Change in your employer

____ Change of boss

____ Change in the country you work in

____ Change in the possibility that things will go wrong

____ Change in your job

____ Transfer to another part of the organization

____ Change in the type of work you do

____ Change in expectations for your performance

is useful to leaders (and is valued by their followers, especially in times of stress). Indeed, changing one's personality significantly—especially when the attribute is important enough to warrant it—can require extensive therapy, and even that has no guarantee. But other options besides changing one's personality can have a substantial impact on effectiveness. An obvious strategy is to avoid situations in which the flaw is particularly dangerous. Another common strategy is to be sure that other people on one's staff have strengths where one is weak, and to use them in situations that call for those strengths.

A third possibility is not to worry about underlying personality but to focus instead on changing outward behavior. If an introvert does the same things that an extrovert does, or a pessimist does the same things an optimist does, then an observer will respond to the behavior, regardless of the unseen internal state. As long as the changed behavior is driven by a sincere desire to be more effective (manipulation is quickly transparent), followers will experience the behavior, not the underlying causes of the behavior. For example, some people are by training or predilection inclined to see the flaws in new ideas before they see the potential in them. Recognizing that immediate criticism of new ideas is likely to discourage people from offering ideas, naysayers might learn not to let critical analysis be the first thing they talk about. Instead, they might learn to hold their breath, let the second wave come in with the positive side, and begin the conversation there. This approach is not insincere as long as the positive and the negative are both valued; it is rather a change in the order of presentation in an effort to achieve a better outcome for all.

Changing overt behavior is not an easy task, especially when habits are deeply ingrained. It first requires carefully observing people who behave in more effective ways to see what they do and how they react in specific situations. Second, it takes practice to learn to respond in a different way. The real advantage of this third strategy, unlike the first two, is that it neither requires you to avoid situations that may be important to engage, nor others to cover your weaknesses when they should be pursuing more important things. Furthermore, psychologists have long known that if you change your behavior, attitudes may eventually fall in line with it.

Sometimes the needed change in behavior can be so inconsistent with internal states that it feels fraudulent. The aforementioned pessimist might feel that acting optimistic is phony or deceitful, which it will be unless it's driven by a sincere desire to change. In the case of the pessimist, however, acting like an optimist may not be as important as *not* acting like a pessimist. In other words, another strategy for dealing with a flaw is simply *not to express it* in behavior in situations where it is counterproductive.

Part 3 of Figure A-3 elicits the kinds of changes that may lie ahead in the same terms that derailment was discussed earlier. This part of self-assessment is crucial, because changing situations can cause both strengths to become weaknesses and weaknesses to become more pronounced. They also can cause dormant strengths to become important and weaknesses to become less important, so a thorough analysis will consider all the possibilities. If any major aspect of your situation is going to change, and especially if multiple changes are occurring at once, reflective self-assessment is critical.

After completing the exercise in Figure A-3, you should be able to identify some areas you could profitably work on as part of your development. These may be strengths that are out of hand, flaws that are becoming dangerous, or new strengths you need to develop to meet future demands.

Knowing where you stand now and what are some of the changes that lie ahead is essential information for creating a personal development plan, but this knowledge is singularly reactive and, in that sense, not sufficient. It's like pushing off from a port knowing only that you don't want to be where you were, maybe knowing the first stop but not really knowing where you want to end up. Just as leaders must provide their constituents with a tangible vision of what can be, it's helpful for individuals to think through what they want to achieve before they put together a developmental plan to achieve it.

A Personal Vision

I will put some perspective around this idea of "vision" as applied to personal development. It would be odd, after all the emphasis placed in this book on change, to suggest that an individual should have a fixed target. Surely, there are times in everyone's lives when just stumbling forward is a victory. There is little doubt that people change over the course of their lives and that what seems a noble aspiration at thirteen looks a little different at fifty. So it probably isn't useful to seek a "personal vision" consisting of a single specific goal carved in stone for all time. What you are seeking, then, is the best possible description of where you want to go, given where you've been and what is important to you at this point in time.

In coming up with a vision, there are at least two levels of analysis: the larger picture of yourself as a human being—your relationships with a family, community, society, and destiny—and your relation to your work organization and career. For some people, these two domains are synchronous, but for many people the two are separate spheres or are conflicting domains. The three parts of Figure A-4 allow you to examine both aspects and, having considered both, work out a tolerable compromise to guide your development planning.

In Part 1 you are asked to look at the larger purpose in your life and are given three different ways to think about it. Question 1 is the traditional "what do you want out of your life?" query. Can you formulate a guiding vision or sense of purpose for yourself, much as a leader might articulate a vision for his or her organization? State as briefly and clearly as you can just what it is you would like to achieve within a reasonable span of time.

In Chapter 3, I mentioned the hero's journey as described by Joseph Campbell in his research on myths and legends. A crucial aspect of the great challenges these mythical heroes faced was their decision about what values they were willing to sacrifice to achieve their quest. Question 2 is a variation on that theme. What do you stand for? Particularly as a leader, but even if your ambition is limited to individual achievement, your values will be tested. What are your fundamental beliefs about how you will treat people? About honesty? How far will you go to achieve the vision you set out in Question 1 (and will analyze further, in Part 2)?

Question 3 will push you to your deepest level, if you choose to answer it. Although it is certainly not an original way to define one's life purpose, it is perhaps the most powerful. If you were to die tomorrow, how would you want to be remembered by the people whose lives you touched? What would you want the people who worked for you to say about you? As a prod to such thoughts, consider the legacy of Mike Walsh. He

FIGURE A-4

Developing a Personal Vision: Part 1, Personal Vision

1. What are you about? At the broadest level, what do you want to achieve with your life?

2. What do you stand for? What are you willing to sacrifice to reach your goals? What values do you hold sacred?

3. If you were to die tomorrow, what would you want your legacy to be? What would you want people to say that you had meant to them?

first came to public attention as chairman of Union Pacific Railroad, which he guided through deregulation and restored to preeminence in the transportation industry. In 1992 he left to take on a turnaround at Tenneco, then in deep financial trouble. As a leader, he had to take tough action, and his actions affected many lives. Unexpectedly, at age fifty-one, Mike Walsh was felled by brain cancer. Here is a literal answer to Question 3:

> When I learned of Mike Walsh's death on May 6, I felt a strange mix of sorrow and betrayal. Sadness at the loss of a man I had come to know and like through hours of interviews about the kinds of things that touch the soul, not the balance sheet—family, brain cancer, and death. And betrayal, strangely, because Walsh had inadvertently deceived me. My reporter's skepticism had yielded to his powerful optimism; I had let myself believe, despite the odds, that Walsh, 51, could beat cancer. . . . [I]nfectious determination was Mike Walsh's real power. He made those close to him believe that they, too, were capable of untold strength and courage.[6]

What do you think will be written about you?

Part 2 of Figure A-4 is more pragmatic. Chapter 4 described in detail the relationship between business strategy and executive development: The strategic direction of a company should determine the kinds of experiences its future leaders receive. This approach has very practical implications for those who aspire to leadership roles, because an organization will seek out people it believes can carry out those strategies. Your challenge, if you would like to be one of those found, is to seek out the experiences that would prepare you to meet the future challenges of the strategy and thereby be positioned for leadership. To do this, you have to be able to answer Questions 1 and 2 in Part 2 of Figure A-4. Together, they should guide you in translating strategic intent into specific challenges you would need to learn how to meet. Preparing to meet them is the challenge of Question 3.

As a brief example, consider a company whose strategy is to be a major player in the emerging markets of India, China,

Developing a Personal Vision: Part 2, Organizational Strategy

1. Where is the organization going? What are the most important strategic thrusts?

2. What are the leadership challenges presented by these strategic thrusts? What will leaders of the future need to be able to do if the strategy is to succeed?

3. What experiences do you need to have if you are to be one of the people the organization will turn to?

and South America. Your task in Question 2 is to figure out what are the challenges in achieving that objective—what do leaders have to be able to do if the company is to achieve that strategy? With that having been answered, Question 3 asks what experiences could prepare a person for leading through those challenges.

If you cannot answer Question 1, one of your developmental objectives has to be to better understand your organization, its strategies, and the challenges its strategies will present. If you can answer the first question but not the second, your plan may need to include finding out who knows the implications of the strategy and perhaps has fought some of the battles suggested by it. If you can answer the first two questions in Part 2 of Figure A-4, Question 3 raises the pragmatic issue of what kinds of experiences you need to have to learn how to lead in situations of central importance to your organization.

As competitive pressures and the fast-changing global marketplace have forced organizations to abandon any implied promises of lifetime employment and to increase their speed of response by significantly reducing the layers of management, the nature of managerial careers has also changed.[7] Traditional career progression through successive management layers and predictable career paths is no longer possible in many organizations. Although this change has been the stimulus for innumerable conferences, books, and formulas about "careers in flat organizations," it is actually consistent with the careers of the successful executives discussed earlier. Almost none of them had followed anything resembling a career path, and their growth was usually the result of a variety of experiences (not a gradual progression within a functional or technical chimney), unexpected twists (not programmed steps), and dramatic changes (their careers were punctuated with jump shifts rather than with gradual increases in responsibility). Predictability and career paths are useful developmental strategies, but they are rarely the route traveled by talented executives. In a sense, competitive readjustment has meant that more people will now have careers that are more like what the successful executives had all along—careers characterized by variety, different kinds of challenges, movement across boundaries, and unexpected (often opportunistic) leaps into new areas.[8] What this suggests developmentally is that people who aspire to leadership careers in fast-changing organizations need to acquire the skills that their organization will need as future challenges unfold. You must understand the strategy, then get into experiences that prepare you for the challenges that strategy will create. When your organization looks around for the leaders who can make it successful, you want it to spot you.

Part 3 of Figure A-4 is the most difficult and the least defined part of coming up with a personal vision. Providing your own magic, you must somehow review your self-assessment (Figure A-3) and Parts 1 and 2 of Figure A-4 to determine what your developmental agenda should be. It may be as "simple" as correcting a flaw or learning a specific new skill or as complex as learning how to empower people in a turnaround situation. It may be as difficult as learning how to lead a joint venture in an emerging market or as straightforward as improving public-speaking skills. It may be related to the strategic direction of the organization, or it may be an extremely personal goal, related more to your values and the legacy you want to leave. It could be positioning yourself to stay with your organization, or it may involve a shift in your career aspirations that would take you to a very different place.

IDENTIFYING OPPORTUNITIES FOR GROWTH

Sometimes it is easier to know what one needs to do than it is to know how to do it. Most people don't have a good understanding of what it takes to create lasting change and so base their development hopes on good intentions. I'll listen more, I'll be more thoughtful, I won't be so disorganized, I'll consider the long-term consequences before I make a decision, I'm not going to procrastinate, I'm going to take more risks—all are promises that will be hard to keep. If all it took was wishing it were so or if resolve were enough, serious personal shortcomings would have been eliminated long ago. The best of intentions

FIGURE A-4

Developing a Personal Vision: Part 3, Reconciling Parts 1 and 2 and Your Self-Assessment

1. Given your personal vision, the strategic direction of the organization, your personal goals and values, and the self-assessment you did in Parts 1 and 2 of Figure A-4, can you create a developmental agenda for yourself?

2. Looking back over your agenda, can you put the list in order of priority, beginning with the most pressing need?

and dogged determination are more likely to create frustration or, after repeated failure, to cause people to give up than they are to create change.

The reason, as was described at length in Chapter 3, is that people are almost always changed by powerful experiences, not by powerful intentions. But many of the experiences that created change happened by accident or fate, and one might not have gotten into many situations if one had known what lay ahead. Perhaps because of their unprogrammed nature, rich experiences aren't always where development thinking begins.

People know intuitively that experience is the teacher they must hire if they want to change. It is easy enough to demonstrate. Put yourself in the role of a coach to someone who wants to learn a foreign language. Many options exist, from buying cassettes that promise fluency in a few weeks to going to school for several years. Typically, however, you would recommend that somebody who really wanted to learn a foreign language would learn faster by being immersed in the culture, being forced to speak it all the time.

A similar strategy would likely emerge for learning to speak in public. Bizarre though it sounds, people are said to be more afraid of public speaking than they are of snakes. Still, the usual recommendation for someone who wants to conquer that fear is a total immersion program. In other words, if you want to learn to speak in public, the first thing you have to do is speak in public—a lot.

What these simple examples demonstrate is that the first step in developing a new skill is to put oneself into a situation requiring the use of that skill. Just how uncomfortable that can be is also obvious—if I can't speak the language, am I really going to allow myself to be sent to a place where only that language is spoken? If I'm terrified of public speaking, will I really put myself in a situation where I have to speak in public? In designing a personal development plan, it is sometimes easier to pretend that you are designing it for someone else precisely because of that basic principle—you have to put yourself in a situation that requires you to do whatever it is you are not good at if you want to get better at it.

Though one can readily see this principle at work with language and speaking, it is not so evident that the same is true for other skills. It appears that adults learn best when they have to learn something new in order to achieve something that matters to them. That means finding experiences in which mastering a deficiency is a necessary precondition for success. If you want to learn to operate more effectively in teams, the first requirement is to get into an experience that forces you to work on teams. The same would be true for learning strategy, negotiation, listening, or just about any other developmental target.

Figure A-5 gives you a chance to test this approach. The first question asks you to take your developmental target one step further by thinking of it in terms of specific situations you need to be good at handling. You will then be a step closer to thinking in experience terms—what kinds of experiences could prepare you to handle a particular situation or challenge?

Question 2 gets to the heart of the matter. Brainstorm as many experiences as you can think of that might teach what you need to learn. It is very useful to ask other people for ideas, to put yourself in the position of someone coaching someone else, and to refer to various source materials.[9] Be sure to consider a change in job assignments, enlarging or recasting your current job, participating in projects and task forces, having exposure to other people, being involved in community activities, and taking courses. (Be careful not to overemphasize formal programs.)

After you have generated as many ideas as you can, answer Question 3, which asks how powerful each of these experiences might be in forcing you to learn the new skill. A good development plan will contain multiple experiences and obviously will include the most powerful ones. For now, don't worry about the possibility that an experience you have listed might end in failure or put too much at risk, personally or professionally. A little later, you'll look at whether a context for learning can be created that is safe enough for undertaking a given experience.

FIGURE A-5

IDENTIFYING DEVELOPMENTAL OPPORTUNITIES

1. State your developmental priority in terms of a situation or situations that you would like to be able to handle well (e.g., "When I have a good idea and need to get senior management to support it, I'd like to learn how to develop a strategy to get them on my side").

2. How many different experiences (such as assignments, projects, working with certain people, community activities) can you think of that would force you to learn that ability? (See Chapter 3 for more ideas.)

3. Which experiences would be the most powerful teachers? Use "***" to indicate very powerful, "**" to indicate moderately powerful, and "*" to indicate not very powerful.

Transfer the viable experiences to the appropriate boxes in Figure A-6.

A PROACTIVE STANCE

The research on high-potential international executives showed that they differ from other people in their sense of adventure. They seek out opportunities to learn new things, especially those that broaden or change their perspectives.[10] Your organization and fate may sometimes determine your path, but it is up to you to make and take opportunities to grow in ways you choose. Take the previous two simple examples: the person who wants to learn a foreign language can volunteer for a foreign assignment rather than wait passively to be selected for one; and the person who is weak in public speaking can attend a presentation skills workshop and look for opportunities to give talks rather than avoid speeches or wait until the deficiency results in a performance problem.

It may seem odd to suggest that people have to put themselves in strange, uncomfortable, and unfamiliar places in order to grow, but development requires a proactive stance. There are just too many forces that encourage inertia, even in changing times. Look again at the experiences you listed in Figure A-5 and transferred to A-6. How can you take the initiative to make them happen?

Sometimes, the most straightforward strategy is the best: just ask for the opportunity. It may seem unlikely that your boss or the organization will give you the opportunity you want, but you might be surprised. Sometimes developmental opportunities aren't offered for fear that talented people will think their organization is proposing the move because it is not happy with them, or will go elsewhere rather than accept a move, or will see the proposed change as a lateral or downward move. ("Next" developmental steps often involve nonsequential assignments.)

Other tactics to consider include volunteering (you can almost always find something interesting going on that would welcome a talented volunteer, or find an important problem

FIGURE A-6

How You Can Get There

Think of ways you can get the powerful experiences you identified in Figure A-5. List as many paths as you can think of. (Be sure to consider such things as making changes within your current job, making a deal with your boss, joining a task force, volunteering, and asking for a new assignment.)

Experience: Paths:	Experience: Paths:
Experience: Paths:	Experience: Paths:
Experience: Paths:	Experience: Paths:

lying around that no one is working on), joining (various clubs, groups, and associations sometimes offer opportunities), trading and bargaining (you may be able to promise your first born in exchange for a valued opportunity), and buying (if the organization won't fund it, maybe you can pay for it yourself or find another source of funds).

Sometimes you can't get a different assignment or get on a special project because of the perception that you can't be spared. Having a replacement can be a prerequisite for convincing the organization to allow you to move on.

When all efforts to get a new opportunity fail, there are still ways to change the existing situation. It is almost always possible to delegate some activities to free up time for other activities, to take on additional challenges, to convince your boss to give you some new opportunities, or to change your priorities to gain exposure to something new.

Chapter 5 showed that learners "make and take" opportunities to do interesting things. It is difficult for people to continue to learn and grow if they stay in the same place past the point of mastering its challenges. The basic rule seems to be to find experiences that will allow growth. Some jobs change in content so rapidly that new experiences come whether you want them or not. Some jobs are mastered, and then the only way to grow is to go somewhere else, but even when people are trapped by circumstance in seemingly routine places, it may be possible to change the circumstances enough to grow. Don't write "it can't be done" in any of the boxes in Figure A-6 until you are sure you've explored every avenue.

CREATING A LEARNING ENVIRONMENT

Chapter 7 showed how organizations could enhance the learning context around important experiences by improving information, incentives, available resources, and support—all of which could serve as catalyts for growth (see Figures 7-1 and 7-6). If your organization provides any of these opportunities, by all means take advantage of them, but there is still much you can do to create a better learning environment. Figure A-7 is intended as a prod for exactly that. Think about the kinds of information you will need if you are to learn as much as you can from an experience. First on the list is usually feedback, so that you have some way of tracking your progress toward your developmental target. What feedback do you need, how can you get it, and whom do you need to involve? What other information might be helpful—can you find role models? A coach? People to talk to who can be of help? The high-potential managers mentioned in Chapter 5 made it a point to seek out feedback, remain open to criticism, learn from mistakes, and broaden their business knowledge.

From a business point of view, it is recognized that to shape desired behavior in subordinates, managers need to set specific goals, to measure those goals, and to hold subordinates accountable for reaching them. Though you may feel that such actions apply to fostering change in others but not yourself, busy people rarely change unless they can make development a real priority. Doing so means setting specific and measurable developmental goals for yourself, just as you would for any other performance objective. The most effective way to put a priority on development is to make it one of the concrete objectives for which your boss will hold you accountable.

If your boss is not the kind of person you trust with developmental accountability or won't go along with your ideas, you will need to find ways to hold yourself accountable for achieving your developmental objectives. Since, however, the primary vehicle for development is a challenging experience, it is likely that developmental objectives can be put in the context of business objectives. For example, if the business plan calls for starting up a new product line, you may choose to make leading it one of your performance objectives because the developmental potential of a start-up fits your growth objective.[11]

It can help steel your resolve if other people are involved in the change attempt. The more people you have rooting for you (best case) or checking up on you (sometimes more effective), the more reminders there will be of what you've promised to do. Involvement can take a variety of forms, ranging from

FIGURE A-7

CREATING A LEARNING ENVIRONMENT

Consider how you will get the support you need to make this a valuable learning experience for you.

Information	Incentives
Resources	Support and Encouragement

simple awareness of your intentions, to participation in defining the goals and measures, to providing coaching and feedback. (List these people in the "support" box in Figure A-7.)

In the "incentives" box in Figure A-7 you may also want to consider how you can reward yourself for making progress. Although not everyone can, some people motivate themselves through planning self-administered rewards, like a trip to a favorite place, a special dinner, or buying a long-wanted item, as a way of keeping focused on the change plan. A sense of progress can also be a reward, and one of the most important parts of a development plan is entering specific developmental events and milestone dates in your daily calendar.

Resources are another crucial piece in any growth plan. Significant change often is not possible without some additional resources, which may be as concrete as money and time or as nebulous as good advice. It's easiest when the organization will give you whatever you think you need, but most often you'll be thrown back on your own resourcefulness.

One of the most important resources in development is finding ideas and models that can show you how to do whatever it is you want to do. It's one thing to know you aren't doing something effectively or to have a general noble goal, but it's quite another to get specific about alternative behavior. Books, courses, and conversations with gurus can be helpful, but perhaps the most powerful resource is access to an effective role model whom you can observe in action.

Another crucial aspect of learning something new is having a safe place to practice, to try out new approaches. The high pressure and low tolerance of a workplace under duress may not be the right environment for an autocrat to try out a new participatory style. If the workplace is not suitable for experimentation, many volunteer, community, religious, sports, and cultural organizations might provide a "safer" place to practice change. One of the great advantages of behaviorally oriented "public" training programs is that they can offer a chance to try out new behavior with people who aren't part of the normal work environment.[12]

The last box in Figure A-7 is about the kind of support, over and above incentives and resources, you will need to achieve your developmental goal. It is easy to underestimate just how taxing change can be, especially by getting caught up in the "heroes don't need help" syndrome. Change means giving up something, usually something quite important. At one extreme, it can mean giving up security, because it means leaving what was comfortable and safe (perhaps a job or a current employer) to risk something new. At another, it can mean giving up strengths that have worked in the past (sometimes strengths that have led to success) or one's self-image or self-definition. Physicians who must give up clinical practice to pursue a managerial career, for example, report serious emotional struggles in reconciling the new career and the old one.[13] The physician-managers experienced several difficult psychological adjustments as well as a host of difficulties in acquiring new skills, and their families also went through varying degrees of trauma as the social implications played out. But these physicians are just an extreme example of what anyone goes through in making a significant change, and support from significant others can make the difference between successful change and failure. Having a friendly ear, having someone who cares about you and will encourage you during the tough times, and enlisting the help of kind, patient people contribute heavily to successful developmental efforts.

And of course, you have to support yourself when you are trying to learn something new, which means taking time to reflect on what you are doing, getting away from it when it becomes too much, and celebrating when you succeed.

Perhaps the most crucial skill of all when it comes to personal growth is learning how to create a learning environment wherever you are. There is no pat formula, but there are some common-sense actions that might help. Treat people in ways that make them want to coach you, support you, give you feedback, and allow you to make mistakes.[14] Seek out feedback on your impact and information on what you might do differently. Experiment. Take time to reflect, absorb, and incorporate.

THE DEVELOPMENT PLAN

It dignifies the exercise to call the product a "development plan," as if growth could be programmed and controlled. But as my colleague David Campbell has observed, "If you don't know where you are going, you'll probably end up somewhere else."[15] A reasonable approach is somewhere between the logic and order presented in Figures A-3 through A-7 and the chaos of life as it is lived. In that vein, I close this appendix with some general guidelines for thinking about your growth and development.

YOUR DEVELOPMENT IS YOUR RESPONSIBILITY

Your development is not someone else's responsibility, but it certainly helps if your organization and other people take an interest in it. Whether or not they do doesn't change where the ultimate control must lie, and you must make the choices that will determine your growth. The context in which you find yourself will make it harder or easier, but you choose whether to remain aware of your impact on others by seeking out feedback and creating an environment in which others will provide it. You choose whether to make or take the opportunities that will promote your development. You choose whether to turn your experiences into a chance to learn or to let your focus be driven solely by performance goals (when the job is exciting and challenging), or to let yourself drift aimlessly (when the job is exasperating or dull). You choose whether to build a support base from which you can take the personal risks of growth.

BE SURE YOU BELIEVE IN WHAT YOU ARE TRYING TO DO

Significant change is an arduous task. One thing that is known about getting people to undertake the difficult and persist through setbacks is that they must be committed. True commitment comes from within—not from an organization's mandate, a boss's performance appraisal, an inspirational guru's recipe, or a spouse's threats. All of these might cause a person tc initiate change, or want to change, but the single most important motivation is a deep, internal desire for change. The danger of externally induced or halfhearted efforts at change is not only that they will fail but that the failure will also make it that much harder to try again. So don't try to change for someone else, no matter how much you fear them or love them. Do it because you think it's right.

A PLAN IS NOT THE DESTINATION

Writing a development plan can in itself feel like a satisfying victory. The danger in elaborate schemes is that one might justify all one's effort by making the "plan" immutable. John Steinbeck conjectured that "in the development of navigation . . . how often must the questing mind have wished for a constant and unvarying point on the horizon to steer by."[16] It is essential to have a destination in mind, something specific to steer toward and to guide decisions about which opportunities to take and which to avoid. But the destination may change, a new route to it may emerge, or you may even arrive there and need to head for someplace new, so it is important to remain open and revisit the development plan frequently in light of new developments.

A DEVELOPMENTAL OPPORTUNITY IS NOT ALWAYS A PROMOTION

The ziggurat of *The Right Stuff* aside, ascending the pyramid is not the only or always the best route to personal development. Higher levels usually carry with them greater responsibility, but as I have explained repeatedly, responsibility is not the only challenge needed to develop executive skills. All too often, a promotion means staying in the same function or division and, in reality, means doing more of the same. If this is true, then a promotion may even retard development. Opportunities for development may be anywhere—even in assignments that appear lower in the hierarchy, for example. It is what the experience challenges you to do that counts, not the points assigned for compensation or job analytic purposes. Because careers are usually erratic and often serendipitous, you may have to go backward to get a needed experience that was missed along the way.

DEVELOPMENT IS NOT AUTOMATIC (BUT IT CAN BE)

It is often assumed that if a task is challenging, then meeting the challenge automatically ensures learning and growth. As I have shown, that assumption can be valid when what one hopes to learn must be learned in order to meet the challenge successfully. The rub is that success at a particular task does not always require learning significant new skills, nor does it always require learning the skills that a person really needs to learn. It may be true that one can learn something from everyone and everything, but at some point, development has to be directed for skills to accumulate in a particular direction. It is therefore very important, especially in a valuable assignment, to be conscious both of the learning you want and the learning you are getting. This may require "coming up for air" to look around—have you created a learning context, or are you so busy with the alligators that learning is by happenstance?

HUNKER DOWN FOR THE LONG HAUL

Perhaps one of the most difficult things for a talented, successful person to do is to have the patience to achieve real change. Used to quick and tangible results, the painful fits and starts, two-steps-forward-one-step-back nature of change can be frustrating. The awkwardness and self-consciousness of trying something new, especially around people who may already be good at whatever it is, can quickly lead to abandoning the effort. If what you want to do is really a stretch, it will take a long time and a lot of effort to achieve it. People who are used to you acting one way may not even notice your first attempts or worse, may make light of them. Just try to remember what it was like when you learned to ride a bike (or, to choose a more modern example, to in-line skate) or to drive a stick shift. Awkward at first, gradually better, and finally automatic.

FIGURES

NOTES

PREFACE

[1] M. McCall, M. Lombardo, and A. Morrison, *The Lessons of Experience* (Lexington, Mass.: Lexington Books, 1988).

[2] L. Stammer, "Evolution Is More Than a Theory, Pope Tells Scientists," *Los Angeles Times,* October 25, 1996, A14.

[3] D. Fossey, *Gorillas in the Mist* (Boston: Houghton Mifflin, 1983), 1.

[4] R. James, *Churchill: A Study in Failure, 1900–1939* (London: Weidenfield, 1970).

CHAPTER 1

[1] Ken Stevens, former president of Taco Bell, in an address to the University of Southern California MBA core program on November 22, 1993.

[2] R. Vartabedian, "The Remaking of Douglas by McDonnell," *Los Angeles Times,* October 15, 1989, D-1ff.

[3] J. Carlzon, *Moments of Truth* (Cambridge, Mass: Ballinger, 1987).

[4] I first encountered this idea of "earning one's pay" in G. Patton, *War as I Knew It* (Boston: Houghton Mifflin, 1947).

[5] R. Heifetz, *Leadership without Easy Answers* (Cambridge, Mass: Harvard University Press, 1994), 20.

[6] T. Wolfe, *The Right Stuff* (New York: Bantam, 1980).

[7] Ibid., 18–19.

[8] Ibid., 19.

[9] Ibid., 31.

[10] Ibid.

[11] For full development of this idea, see R. Kaplan, *Beyond Ambition* (San Francisco: Jossey-Bass, 1991).

[12] Wolfe, *The Right Stuff,* 24.

[13] Ibid., 29.

[14] Ibid., 27.

[15] E. Hollander, "Conformity, Status, and Idiosyncrasy Credit," *Psychological Review* 65 (1958): 117–127.

[16] W. Mischel, *Personality and Assessment* (New York: Wiley, 1968); L. Goldberg, "The Structure of Phenotypic Personality Traits," *American Psychologist* 48, 1 (January 1993): 26–34.

[17] For a review of the various "contingency" approaches that revolutionized leadership research beginning in the 1960s, see G. Yukl, *Leadership in Organizations,* 3rd ed. (Englewood Cliffs, N.J.: Prentice Hall, 1994), especially Chapter 10, 285–312.

[18] B. Morris, "Roberto Goizueta and Jack Welch: The Wealth Builders," *Fortune,* December 11, 1995, 80–94; M. Carver, ed., *The War Lords: Military Commanders of the Twentieth Century* (Boston: Little, Brown, 1976).

[19] C. Yeager and L. Janos, *Yeager: An Autobiography* (New York: Bantam, 1985), 318.

[20] For example, see M. McCall and M. Lombardo, *Off the Track: Why and How Successful Executives Get Derailed,* Technical Report 21 (Greensboro, N.C.: Center for Creative Leadership, 1983).

CHAPTER 2

[1] R. Gibson, "Personal 'Chemistry' Abruptly Ended Rise of Kellogg President," *Wall Street Journal,* November 28, 1989, A1, A8.

[2] George Will was speaking about the perils of New York City (*Newsweek,* July 25, 1977, 80).Through the years, the overwhelming interest in our work on derailed managers and executives would seem to support his observation in a different context.

[3] McCall and Lombardo, *Off the Track.* A version of this article was published as M. McCall, Jr., and M. Lombardo, "What Makes a Top Executive?" *Psychology Today* 17, 2 (February 1983): 26–31.

[4] See, for example, J. Leslie and E. Van Velsor, *A Look at Derailment Today: North America and Europe,* CCL No. 169 (Greensboro, N.C.: Center for Creative Leadership, 1996); M. Lombardo and C. McCauley, *The Dynamics of Management Derailment,* Technical Report 34, (Greensboro, N.C.: Center for Creative Leadership, 1988); and M. McCall and J. Clair, "Why Physician Managers Fail," *Physician Executive* pt. 1, 16, 3 (May-June 1990): 6–9, and pt. 2, 16, 4 (July-August 1990): 8–12.

[5] These cases have been selected for illustrative purposes only. All information reported here about these people and events came from previously published sources. To the best of my knowledge, none of the "front pagers" participated in any of the derailment studies.

[6] Gibson, "Personal 'Chemistry'," A1.

[7] From the poem "If—'Brother Square-Toes'—Rewards and Fairies," in Rudyard Kipling, *Complete Verse* (New York: Anchor Books, 1989), 578.

[8] M. Cox and J. Roberts, "How the Despotic Boss of Simon & Schuster Found Himself Jobless," *Wall Street Journal,* July 6, 1994, 1ff.

[9] R. Rose, "After Turning Around Giddings & Lewis, Fife Is Turned Out Himself," *Wall Street Journal,* June 22, 1993, 1ff.

[10] R. Suskind and S. Alexander, "Fired Sunbeam Chief Harangued and Hazed Employees, They Say," *Wall Street Journal,* January 14, 1993, 1ff.; G. Smith, "How to Lose Friends and Influence No One," *Business Week,* January 25, 1993, 42–43.

[11] T. Dodds, "Kings' Success Doesn't Save Ftorek's Job," *Los Angeles Times,* May 3, 1989, C-1.

[12] John Kotter, *The General Managers* (New York: Free Press, 1982), 47.

[13] Suskind and Alexander, "Fired Sunbeam Chief," 1ff; Rose, "Fife Is Turned Out Himself," 1ff.

[14] Rose, "Fife Is Turned Out Himself," 1ff.

[15] Cox and Roberts, "Despotic Boss of Simon & Schuster," 1ff.

[16] P. Ingrassia and J. White, "Stempel Quits as Head of General Motors; Workers Fear Cost Cutting Will Quicken," *Wall Street Journal,* October 27, 1992, A-3.

[17] See McCall and Lombardo, "What Makes a Top Executive?", 26–31, and McCall et al., *Lessons of Experience.* McCall and Clair, "Why Physician Managers Fail," (May-June 1990): 6–10, and (July-August 1990): 8–12. Leslie and Van Velsor, *A Look at Derailment Today.*

[18] J. Conger, "The Dark Side of Leadership," *Organizational Dynamics,* 19, 2 (Fall 1990): 44–55.

[19] J. Martin, "Ignore Your Customer," *Fortune,* May 1, 1995, 121–126.

20 J. Wilke, "At Digital Equipment, A Resignation Reveals Key Problem: Selling," *Wall Street Journal*, April 26, 1994, 1ff; E. Jensen, "NBC News President, Burned by Staged Fire and GM, Will Resign," *Wall Street Journal*, March 2, 1993, 1ff.

21 R. Rose, "Fife Is Turned Out," 1ff.

22 McCall and Lombardo, *Off the Track*.

23 Gibson, "Personal 'Chemistry'," A1, A8.

24 Cox and Roberts, "Despotic Boss of Simon & Schuster," 1ff.

25 J. Steinbeck, *The Log from the Sea of Cortez* (New York: Viking, 1962), 158.

26 Quoted in W. Safire & L. Safir, *Words of Wisdom* (New York: Simon and Schuster, 1989), 32.

27 A. Taylor III, "The Odd Eclipse of a Star CEO," *Fortune*, February 11, 1991, 88.

28 B. Saporito, "The Eclipse of Mars," *Fortune*, November 28, 1994, 92.

29 J. Byrne, W. Symonds, and J. Siler, "CEO Disease," *Business Week*, April 1, 1991, 52–60.

30 Byrne et al., "CEO Disease."

31 Jensen, "NBC News President," 1ff.

32 W. Manchester, *American Caesar* (New York: Dell, 1979), 751–769.

33 Manchester, *American Caesar*, quoting Gunther, 566–567.

34 McCall and Clair, "Why Physician Managers Fail."

35 Manchester, *American Caesar*, 567.

36 Suskind and Alexander, "Fired Sunbeam Chief, " A-8.

37 Quoted in Byrne et al., "CEO Disease," 55.

38 Ingrassia and White, "Stempel Quits," A-3, A-5.

39 McCall et al., *Lessons of Experience*.

40 Cox and Roberts, "Despotic Boss of Simon & Schuster," 1ff.

41 P. De Llosa, "Famous Failures: Where They Are Now," *Fortune*, May 1, 1995, 53.

42 Cox and Roberts, "Despotic Boss of Simon & Schuster," 1ff.

43 D. Campbell, *If I'm in Charge Here Why Is Everybody Laughing?* (Niles, Ill: Argus Communications, 1980), 62.

44 W. Bennis, *Why Leaders Can't Lead: The Unconscious Conspiracy* (San Francisco: Jossey-Bass, 1990).

45 J. Kotter, *The General Managers*.

CHAPTER 3

1 The research leading to this conclusion is fully reported in McCall et al., *Lessons of Experience*, and in E. Lindsey (now Hutchison), V. Homes, and M. McCall, *Key Events in Executives' Lives*, Technical Report 32 (Greensboro, N.C.: Center for Creative Leadership, 1987).

2 One version of the story, attributed by Dr. Sample to Abraham Lincoln, was published in *USC Trojan Family* (Winter 1993): 41.

3 McCall et al., *Lessons of Experience*; Lindsey (now Hutchison) et al., *Key Events*; C. McCauley, *Developmental Experiences in Managerial Work: A Literature Review*, Technical Report 26 (Greensboro, N.C.: Center for Creative Leadership, 1986); J. Kotter, *The Leadership Factor* (New York: Free Press, 1988), Chapter 7; Kotter, *General Managers*, Chapter 3; W. Bennis, *On Becoming a Leader* (Reading, Mass.: Addison-Wesley, 1989).

4 M. Lombardo and R. Eichinger, *Eighty-eight Assignments for Development in*

Place: Enhancing the Developmental Challenge of Existing Jobs, Report No. 136 (Greensboro, N.C.: Center for Creative Leadership, 1989); R. Eichinger and M. Lombardo, *Twenty-two Ways to Develop Leadership in Staff Managers,* Report No. 144 (Greensboro, N.C.: Center for Creative Leadership, 1990).

[5] These descriptions are adapted primarily from Lindsey (now Hutchison) et al., *Key Events.*

[6] L. Hill, *Becoming a Manager* (Boston: Harvard Business School Press, 1992).

[7] J. Gabarro, *The Dynamics of Taking Charge* (Boston: Harvard Business School Press, 1987).

[8] V. Jon Bentz, *Explorations of Scope and Scale: The Critical Determinant of High-Level Executive Effectiveness,* Technical Report 31 (Greensboro, N.C.: Center for Creative Leadership, 1987).

[9] Lindsey (now Hutchison) et al., *Key Events,* 87.

[10] Kotter, *Leadership Factor.*

[11] Lindsey (now Hutchison) et al., *Key Events,* 177–189.

[12] Ibid., 221.

[13] A. Howard and D. Bray, *Managerial Lives in Transition* (New York: Guilford Press, 1988), 174.

[14] McCall et al., *Lessons of Experience.*

[15] J. Campbell, *The Hero with a Thousand Faces,* 2nd ed. (1968; rpr. New York: Princeton/Bollingen Foundation, 1973).

[16] I had the privilege of hearing David Oldfield describe the hero's journey in a leadership development workshop sponsored by the University of Southern California, in conjunction with Esther Hutchison of Executive Education and Development, held in Newport Beach, California, in June 1995.

CHAPTER 4

[1] The appropriate unit of analysis will depend on the way an organization is structured and on the projected use of results.

[2] "Graduates" are defined as managers whose successes had earned them promotions through the unit or function to senior level and who were still considered high potential.

[3] Bennis, *On Becoming a Leader,* 199.

[4] This approach was initially described in M. McCall, "Executive Development as a Business Strategy," *Journal of Business Strategy* (January-February 1992) 25–31.

[5] See, for example, R. Spekman, L. Isabella, T. MacAvoy, and T. Forbes III, *Alliance and Partnership Strategies: Managing for the 21st Century* (Lexington, Mass: The International Consortium for Executive Development Research, 1995).

[6] To protect the confidentiality of the information and the anonymity of the corporation, some details have been altered and a substantial amount of detail has been left out. The changes do not affect the general description of the process.

[7] The other strategic thrusts received the same scrutiny, and a similar number of specific situations were identified. For the sake of brevity and to preserve confidentiality, the results will not be discussed here.

[8] This assumption needs to be verified. Any major change in a system—in the culture, in the way work is done or structured, in how people are chosen for jobs—may cause changes in the proficiencies and deficiencies of the executives the system produces.

CHAPTER 5

1 Howard and Bray, *Managerial Lives in Transition,* 174.

2 J. Shreeve, "Music of the Hemispheres," *Discover* 17, 10 (October 1996) 96.

3 Goldberg, "Phenotypic Personality Traits," 26–34.

4 D. McClelland and D. Winter, *Motivating Economic Achievement* (New York: Free Press, 1969). R. Boyatzis, *The Competent Manager: A Model for Effective Performance* (New York: Wiley, 1982).

5 C. Bartlett and S. Ghoshal, "The Myth of the Generic Manager: New Personal Competencies for New Management Roles," *Harvard Business Review* (under revision, 1996).

6 M. McCall, "Identifying Leadership Potential in Future International Executives: Developing a Concept," *Consulting Psychology Journal* 46 (1994) 49–63; G. Spreitzer, M. McCall, and J. Mahoney, "Early Identification of International Executives," *Journal of Applied Psychology* (in press, 1997).

7 Kotter, *The General Managers* 46–48.

8 Although the study focused on international executives, the findings do not appear restricted to the international context. It does appear that an international context magnifies the effects of these factors, which apply broadly to leadership. G. Spreitzer, M. W. McCall, Jr., and J. Mahoney, "The Early Identification of International Leadership Potential: Dimensions, Measurement and Validation," paper presented to the Careers Division, annual meeting of the Academy of Management, Vancouver, British Columbia, August 1995.

9 Warren Bennis as quoted in M. Loeb, "Where Leaders Come From," *Fortune,* September 19, 1994, 241.

10 One danger in the developmental approach, for example, is assuming that everyone is equally able or equally willing to develop necessary skills.

11 Warren Bennis and Bert Nanus, *Leaders: The Strategies for Taking Charge* (New York: Harper & Row, 1985), 188.

12 Bennis, *On Becoming a Leader.*

13 Kotter, *The General Managers;* J. Kotter, *The Leadership Factor* (New York: Free Press, 1992); J. Kotter, *A Force for Change* (New York: Free Press, 1990).

14 Kotter, *The Leadership Factor,* 34.

15 McCall and Lombardo, "What Makes a Top Executive?" 30–31.

16 One such measure, "Prospector," was generated from Spreitzer, McCall, and Mahoney, "Early Identification of International Leadership" and M. McCall, G. Spreitzer, and J. Mahoney, *Identifying Leadership Potential in Future International Executives: A Learning Resource Guide* (Lexington, Mass.: International Consortium for Executive Development Research, 1994). It is available from the Center for Creative Leadership, Greensboro, N.C.

CHAPTER 6

1 Howard and Bray, for example, found that interpersonal skills actually declined over the twenty-year period they followed the managers (Howard and Bray, *Managerial Lives in Transition*).

2 S. Kerr, "On the Folly of Rewarding A, While Hoping for B," *Academy of Management Journal* 18 (1975): 769–783.

3 For example, see J. Pfeffer, "The Ambiguity of Leadership," in *Leadership: Where Else Can We Go?* ed. M. McCall and M. Lombardo (Durham, N.C.: Duke University Press, 1978), 13–34.

4 N. Tichy and C. DeRose, "Roger Enrico's Master Class," *Fortune,* November 27, 1995, 105–06.

CHAPTER 7

[1] Paul Carroll, "Akers to IBM Employees: Wake Up!" *Wall Street Journal,* May 29, 1991, B1.

[2] Speech by Harry Stonecipher to McDonnell Douglas executives in Huntington Beach, May 1995.

[3] Barbara Tuchman, *The March of Folly* (New York: Ballantine, 1984), 7.

[4] Bennis, *On Becoming a Leader,* 5.

[5] Kotter, *A Force for Change.*

[6] James MacGregor Burns, *Leadership* (New York: Harper Colophon Books, 1978).

[7] This list was condensed from managers' and executives' responses to that question in numerous personal development workshops run by the author.

[8] One excellent example in an organizational setting is D. Ilgen, C. Fisher, and M. Taylor, "Consequences of Individual Feedback on Behavior in Organizations," *Journal of Applied Psychology* 64 (1979): 349–371.

[9] Conversation at the White House, reported by Francis B. Carpenter in *Six Months at the White House with Abraham Lincoln* (1866).

[10] One example of such a use of technology was developed by Taco Bell in 1988: Total Automation of Company Operations (TACO) put networked computers in every restaurant and provided reams of data on everything from customer satisfaction to food cost (L. Schlesinger and R. Hallowell, "Taco Bell Corp.: Part One: 1982–1988," Case #9-692-058 (Boston: Harvard Business School, 1991). At the organizational level, Union Pacific Railroad put a computer in every locomotive to provide all engineers with access to centralized data.

[11] See, for example, B. Skinner, *Science and Human Behavior* (New York: Macmillan, 1953).

[12] E. Locke and G. Latham, *A Theory of Goal Setting and Task Performance* (Englewood Cliffs, N.J.: Prentice Hall, 1990).

[13] McCall, Spreitzer, and Mahoney, "Identifying Leadership Potential."

[14] G. Ledford, Jr., "Paying for the Skills, Knowledge, and Competencies of Knowledge Workers," *Compensation and Benefits Review* 27, 4 (1995): 55–62.

[15] A. Bandura, *Principles of Behavior Modification* (New York: Holt, Rinehart and Winston, 1969).

[16] McCall et al., *Lessons of Experience.*

[17] L. Thomas, *The Lives of a Cell* (New York: Viking Press, 1994; Bantam Books, 1975), 120.

CHAPTER 8

[1] Howard and Bray, *Managerial Lives in Transition,* 175.

[2] A. Fisher, "Corporate Reputations," *Fortune,* March 6, 1996, 90–98.

[3] Kotter, *The Leadership Factor.*

[4] J. Kotter and J. Heskett, *Corporate Culture and Performance* (New York: Free Press, 1992), 84.

[5] General Electric has developed a reputation as the supplier of choice for chief executives. As long ago as 1991, fourteen GE alumni were holding such positions in other companies (*Fortune,* April 8, 1991, 12).

[6] J. Gabarro, *The Dynamics of Taking Charge* (Boston: Harvard Business School Press, 1987).

[7] Howard and Bray, *Managerial Lives in Transition,* 420, report that 40 percent

predicted to reach fourth level did not (false positives), while only 21 percent predicted to reach less than third level attained fourth (false negatives).

8 S. Gould, *Dinosaurs in a Haystack* (New York: Harmony, 1995), 327, 333.

9 J. Gleick, *Chaos* (New York: Penguin, 1987).

10 McCall, "Executive Development," 25–31.

11 E. Lawler III, "Substitutes for Hierarchy," *Organizational Dynamics* (1988), 5–15.

12 P. Senge, *The Fifth Discipline* (New York: Doubleday Currency, 1990), 14, 340.

13 It is of course, possible to justify almost any action if one accepts Nestlé Chairman and CEO Helmut Maucher's premise:"Since the free market economic system is 'ethical' in the broad sense that it does good things for mankind, one might say that businesspeople who do their best within the system are, from an objective point of view, acting morally and ethically. Everything harmful to our economic system would then be wrong and immoral because it would reduce the beneficial effect of the economic system on society" (H. Maucher, *Leadership in Action* [New York: McGraw Hill, 1992], 105).

14 M. Csikszentmihalyi, *Beyond Boredom and Anxiety* (San Francisco: Jossey-Bass, 1975), 181.

15 Kotter and Heskett, *Corporate Culture and Performance.*

16 Gleick, *Chaos,* 309.

17 Gould, *Dinosaurs in a Haystack,* 345, 346.

18 Although some aspects of personality are relatively stable, that managers can and do change over time is not in doubt. See Howard and Bray, *Managerial Lives in Transition.*

19 Ibid.; McCall et al., *The Lessons of Experience.*

20 Ironically, that phrase was the chant recited by my high school football team in the team huddle just prior to the start of each game. There is something primitively motivating about it, especially in Western cultures. Whether "Ming the Merciless" leadership will prove the most effective way to manage in the global environment of the twenty-first century remains to be seen.

21 J. Carlzon, *Moments of Truth* (Cambridge, Mass: Ballinger, 1987), 5.

22 Bennis, *On Becoming a Leader,* 187.

APPENDIX

1 J. Steinbeck, *Log from the Sea of Cortez,* 41–42.

2 S. Bellow, *Henderson the Rain King* (New York: Fawcett Crest, 1969), 105.

3 Bennis, *On Becoming a Leader,* 80.

4 Ibid.

5 See Chapter 5, Figure 5-4, for a complete list of the characteristics.

6 Wendy Zellner, "Requiem for a Heavyweight," *Business Week,* May 23, 1994, 36.

7 Even in Japan, where lifetime employment has been a tradition in big firms, things are starting to change.

8 For a telling example, see the paths to the top followed by Roberto Goizueta of Coca-Cola and Jack Welch of General Electric (Morris, "Roberto Goizueta and Jack Welch," 80–94). Not only did neither one follow a "traditional" career path, but their experiences were also dramatically different.

9 Among the materials that might be useful are McCall et al., *Lessons of Experience;* B. Davis et al., *Successful Manager's Handbook: Development Suggestions for Today's Managers* (Minneapolis: Personnel Decisions International, 1996);

M. Lombardo and R. Eichinger, *Eighty-eight Assignments for Development in Place;* Eichinger and Lombardo, *Twenty-two Ways to Develop Leadership in Staff;* Lindsey et al., *Key Events.*

[10] G. Spreitzer, M. McCall, and J. Mahoney, "Early Identification of International Executives," *Journal of Applied Psychology* (in press, 1997).

[11] See information on startups in McCall et al., *Lessons of Experience,* in Lindsey (now Hutchison) et al., *Key Events,* and C. McCauley, *Developmental Experiences in Managerial Work: A Literature Review,* Technical Report 26 (Greensboro, N.C.: Center for Creative Leadership, 1986).

[12] J. Conger, *Learning to Lead* (San Francisco: Jossey-Bass, 1992).

[13] M. McCall and J. Clair, "In Transition from Physician to Manager," Pt. I, *Physician Executive* 18, 2 (March-April 1992): 3–9; and M. McCall and J. Clair, "In Transit from Physician to Manager," Pt. II, *Physician Executive* 18, 3 (May-June 1992) 15–19.

[14] As the case example in Chapter 5 demonstrated, talented people attract coaches and mentors who want to work with them because of their potential. Sustaining this natural advantage over time, however, requires the person who wants coaching to remain open to learning even as he or she improves and to develop the skills necessary for dealing with a variety of personality and coaching style differences.

[15] D. Campbell, *If You Don't Know Where You Are Going, You'll Probably End Up Somewhere Else* (Niles, Ill.: Argus Communications, 1980).

[16] Steinbeck, *Log from the Sea of Cortez,* 37.

BIBLIOGRAPHY

Bandura, Albert. *Principles of Behavior Modification.* New York: Holt, Rinehart and Winston, 1969.

Bartlett, Christopher, and Sumantra Ghoshal. "The Myth of the Generic Manager: New Personal Competencies for New Management Roles." *Harvard Business Review,* under revision, 1997.

Bellow, Saul. *Henderson, the Rain King.* New York: Fawcett Crest, 1969.

Bennis, Warren. *On Becoming a Leader.* Reading, Mass.: Addison-Wesley, 1989.

———. *Why Leaders Can't Lead: The Unconscious Conspiracy.* San Francisco: Jossey-Bass, 1990.

Bentz, V. Jon. *Explorations of Scope and Scale: The Critical Determinant of High-Level Executive Effectiveness.* Technical Report 31. Greensboro, N. C.: Center for Creative Leadership, 1987.

Boyatzis, R. *The Competent Manager: A Model for Effective Performance.* New York: Wiley, 1982.

Byrne, John A., William C. Symonds, and Julia Flynn Siler. "CEO Disease." *Business Week,* 1 April 1991, 52–60.

Campbell, David P. *If I'm in Charge Here Why Is Everybody Laughing?* Niles, Ill.: Argus Communications, 1980.

———. *If You Don't Know Where You Are Going, You'll Probably End Up Somewhere Else.* Niles, Ill.: Argus Communications, 1974.

Campbell, Joseph. *The Hero with a Thousand Faces.* New York: Pantheon Books, 1949; 2d ed. Princeton, N.J.: Princeton/Bollingen Foundation, 1968, 1973.

Carlzon, Jan. *Moments of Truth.* Cambridge, Mass.: Ballinger, 1987.

Carrol, Paul. "Akers to IBM Employees: Wake Up!" *Wall Street Journal,* 29 May 1991.

Conger, Jay. "The Dark Side of Leadership." *Organizational Dynamics* 19, no. 2 (Fall 1990): 44–55.

———. *Learning to Lead.* San Francisco: Jossey-Bass, 1992.

Cox, Meg, and Johnnie L. Roberts. "How the Despotic Boss of Simon & Schuster Found Himself Jobless." *Wall Street Journal,* 6 July 1994.

Csikszentmihalyi, Mihaly. *Beyond Boredom and Anxiety.* San Francisco: Jossey-Bass, 1975.

Davis, Brian L., Carol J. Skube, Lowell W. Hellervik, Susan H. Gebelein, and James L. Sheard. *Successful Manager's Handbook: Development Suggestions for Today's Managers.* Minneapolis: Personnel Decisions International, 1996.

DeLlosa, Patty. "Famous Failures: Where They Are Now." Pages 53–54 in "So You Fail. Now Bounce Back!" by Patricia Sellers. *Fortune,* 1 May 1995, 48–66.

Dodds, T. "Kings' Success Doesn't Save Ftorek's Job." *Los Angeles Times,* 3 May 1989.

Eichinger Robert W., and Michael M. Lombardo, *Twenty-two Ways to Develop Leadership in Staff Managers.* Report No. 144. Greensboro, N. C.: Center for Creative Leadership, 1990.

Fisher, A. "Corporate Reputations." *Fortune,* 6 March 1996, 90–98.

Gabarro, John J. *The Dynamics of Taking Charge.* Boston: Harvard Business School Press, 1987.

Gibson, Richard. "Personal 'Chemistry' Abruptly Ended Rise of Kellogg President." *Wall Street Journal,* 28 November 1989.

Gleick, James. *Chaos: Making a New Science.* New York: Penguin, 1987.

Goldberg, L. "The Structure of Phenotypic Personality Traits." *American Psychologist* 58, no. 1 (January 1993): 26–34.

Gould, Stephen Jay. *Dinosaur in a Haystack.* New York: Harmony, 1995.

Heifetz, Ronald A. *Leadership without Easy Answers.* Cambridge, Mass.: Harvard University Press, 1994.

Heinlein, Robert A. *Farnham's Freehold.* New York: Signet, 1965.

———. *Tunnel in the Sky.* New York: Balantine, 1955.

Hesse, Hermann. *Steppenwolf.* New York: Bantam, 1969.

Hill, Linda A. *Becoming a Manager: Mastery of a New Identity.* Boston: Harvard Business School Press, 1992.

Hollander, E. "Conformity, Status, and Idiosyncrasy Credit." *Psychological Review* 65 (1958): 117–127.

Howard, Ann, and Douglas W. Bray. *Managerial Lives in Transition: Advancing Age and Changing Times.* New York: Guilford Press, 1988.

Ilgen, Dan, Cynthia Fisher, and M. Taylor. "Consequences of Individual Feedback on Behavior in Organizations." *Journal of Applied Psychology* 64 (1979): 349–371.

Ingrassia, Paul, and Joseph B. White. "Stempel Quits as Head of General Motors; Workers Fear Cost Cutting Will Quicken." *Wall Street Journal,* 27 October 1992.

Jensen, Elizabeth. "NBC News President, Burned by Staged Fire and GM, Will Resign." *Wall Street Journal,* 2 March 1993.

Kerr, Steve. "On the Folly of Rewarding A, While Hoping for B." *Academy of Management Journal* 18 (1975): 769–783.

Kotter, John P. *The General Managers.* New York: Free Press, 1982.

———. *The Leadership Factor.* New York: Free Press, 1988, chapter 7.

Kotter, John P., and James L. Heskett. *Corporate Culture and Performance.* New York: Free Press, 1992.

Lawler, Edward III. "Substitutes for Hierarchy." *Organizational Dynamics* (1988): 5–15.

Ledford, Gerald. E., Jr. "Paying for the Skills, Knowledge, and Competencies of Knowledge Workers." *Compensation and Benefits Review* 27, no. 4 (1995): 55–62.

Leslie, Jean, and Ellen Van Velsor. *A Look at Derailment Today: North American and Europe.* CCL No. 169. Greensboro, N. C.: Center for Creative Leadership, 1996.

Lindsey, Esther, Virginia Homes, and Morgan W. McCall, Jr. *Key Events in Executives' Lives.* Technical Report 32. Greensboro, N. C.: Center for Creative Leadership, 1987.

Locke, Edwin, and Gary Latham. *A Theory of Goal Setting and Task Performance.* Englewood Cliffs, N. J.: Prentice-Hall, 1990.

Loeb, Marshall. "Where Leaders Come From." *Fortune,* 19 September 1994, 241–242.

Lombardo, Michael M., and Robert W. Eichinger. *Eighty-eight Assignments for Development in Place: Enhancing the Developmental Challenge of Existing Jobs.* Report No. 136. Greensboro, N. C.: Center for Creative Leadership, 1989.

Lombardo, Michael M., and Cynthia D. McCauley. *The Dynamics of Management Derailment.* Technical Report 34. Greensboro, N. C.: Center for Creative Leadership, 1988.

Manchester, William Raymond. *American Caesar: Douglas MacArthur, 1880–1964.* New York: Dell, 1979.

Martin, J. "Ignore Your Customer." *Fortune,* 1 May 1995, 121–126.

Maucher, Helmut. *Leadership in Action: Tough-Minded Strategies from the Global Giant.* New York: McGraw-Hill, 1992.

McCall, Morgan W., Jr., "Executive Development as a Business Strategy." *Journal of Business Strategy* (January/February 1992): 25–31.

———. "Identifying Leadership Potential in Future International Executives: Developing a Concept." *Consulting Psychology Journal* 46 (1994): 49–63.

McCall, M., Jr., and J. Clair. "In Transition from Physician to Manager." Parts 1 and 2. *Physician Executive* 18, no. 2 (March–April 1992): 3–9; no. 3 (May–June 1992): 15–19.

———. "Why Physician Managers Fail." Parts 1 and 2. *Physician Executive* 16, no. 3 (May–June 1990): 6–9; no. 4 (July–August 1990): 8–12.

McCall, Morgan W., Jr., and Michael M. Lombardo. *Off the Track: Why and How Successful Executives Get Derailed.* Technical Report 21. Greensboro, N. C.: Center for Creative Leadership, 1983.

———. "What Makes a Top Executive?" *Psychology Today* 17, no. 2 (February 1983): 26–31.

McCall, Morgan W., Jr., Michael M. Lombardo, and Ann M. Morrison. *The Lessons of Experience: How Successful Executives Develop on the Job.* New York: Free Press, 1988.

McCauley, Cynthia D. *Developmental Experiences in Managerial Work: A Literature Review.* Technical Report 26. Greensboro, N. C.: Center for Creative Leadership, 1986.

McClelland, David C., and David G. Winter. *Motivating Economic Achievement.* New York: Free Press, 1969.

Mischel, Walter. *Personality and Assessment.* New York: Wiley, 1968.

Morris, Betsy. "Roberto Goizueta and Jack Welch: The Wealth Builders." *Fortune,* 11 December 1995, 80–94.

Pfeffer, Jeffrey. "The Ambiguity of Leadership." In *Leadership: Where Else Can We Go?* edited by Morgan W. McCall, Jr., and Michael M. Lombardo, 13–34. Durham, N. C.: Duke University Press, 1978.

Rose, Robert L. "After Turning Around Giddings & Lewis, Fife Is Turned Out Himself." *Wall Street Journal,* 22 June 1993.

Saporito, B. "The Eclipse of Mars," *Fortune,* 28 November 1994, 92.

Senge, Peter M. *The Fifth Discipline: The Art and Practice of the Learning Organization.* New York: Doubleday Currency, 1990.

Shreeve, J. "Music of the Hemispheres." *Discover* 17, no. 10 (October 1996): 90–100.

Sloan, Allan. "The Hit Men." *Newsweek,* 26 February 1996, 44–48.

Smith, Geoffrey. "How to Lose Friends and Influence No One." *Business Week,* 25 January 1993, 42–43.

Spekman, Robert, Lynn Isabella, Thoms MacAvoy, and T. Forbes III. *Alliance and Partnership Strategies: Managing for the 21ˢᵗ Century.* Lexington, Mass.: The International Consortium for Executive Development Research, 1995.

Spreitzer, Gretchen, Morgan McCall, Jr., and Jay Mahoney. "Early Identification of International Executives." *Journal of Applied Psychology* 82, no. 1 (1997): 6–29.

Steinbeck, John. *The Log from the Sea of Cortez.* New York: Viking, 1962.

Suskind, Ron, and Suzanne Alexander. "Fired Sunbeam Chief Harangued and Hazed Employees, They Say." *Wall Street Journal,* 14 January 1993.

Taylor, Alex III. "The Odd Eclipse of a Star CEO." *Fortune,* 11 February 1991, 87–96.

Tichy, Noel, and C. DeRose. "Roger Enrico's Master Class." *Fortune,* 27 November 1995, 105–106.

Tuchman, Barbara W. *The March of Folly: From Troy to Vietnam.* New York: Ballantine, 1984.

Vaill, Peter B. *Learning as a Way of Being: Strategies for Survival in a World of Permanent White Water.* San Francisco: Jossey-Bass, 1996.

Vartabedian, Ralph. "The Remaking of Douglas by McDonnell." *Los Angeles Times,* 15 October 1989.

Wilke, John R. "At Digital Equipment, a Resignation Reveals Key Problem: Selling." *Wall Street Journal,* 26 April 1994.

Wolfe, Tom. *The Right Stuff.* New York: Farrar, Straus, and Giroux, 1979.

Yeager, Chuck, and Leo Janos. *Yeager: An Autobiography.* New York: Bantam, 1985.

Zellner, Wendy. "Requiem for a Heavyweight." *Business Week,* 23 May 1994, 36.

INDEX

ABOUT THE AUTHOR

Morgan McCall is a professor of management and organization in the Marshall School of Business at the University of Southern California. He also works with the Office of Executive Education in the design and delivery of executive programs, is involved in the development of the USC Leadership Institute, and teaches in the International Business Education and Research program. Prior to joining the University of Southern California, he was director of research and a senior behavioral scientist at the Center for Creative Leadership in Greensboro, North Carolina.

Executive leadership—especially the early identification, assessment, development, and derailment of executives—is the primary focus of McCall's work. In addition to conducting workshops and seminars on executive leadership for a variety of organizations, he works with senior executives to develop corporate strategies and systems for executive succession and development. He recently completed an international research project, sponsored by the International Consortium for Executive Development Research, on the early identification of global executives.

He is a fellow of the American Psychological Association, the American Psychological Society, and the Society for Industrial and Organizational Psychology. He has served on numerous editorial boards, including *Academy of Management Review, Academy of Management Exercise, Human Resource Development Quarterly,* and *Executive Development Journal.* McCall is co-author of *The Lessons of Experience, Whatever It Takes: Decision Makers at Work, Leadership: Where Else Can We Go?* and *Key Events in Executives' Lives;* author of articles in a number of scholarly books and journals as well as in *Psychology Today, Across the Board, The Physician Executive,* and the *New York Times;* and leader of the team that created *Looking Glass, Inc.,* a simulation of managerial work widely used in corporate management development and in university programs.